M. T. NEWBY

HELLENISTIC RELIGIONS

The Age of Syncretism

The Library of Religion

A Series of Readings in the Sacred Scriptures and Basic Writings of the World's Religions, past and present

Editorial Board: Herbert W. Schneider, Chairman; Herbert G. May; Henry G. Russell; Francis R. Walton

Vol. I: *Buddhism. A Religion of Infinite Compassion.* Ed. by Clarence H. Hamilton

Vol. II: *Hellenistic Religions. The Age of Syncretism.* Ed. by Frederick C. Grant

Vol. III: *Judaism. Postbiblical and Talmudic Period.* Ed. by Salo W. Baron and Joseph L. Blau

OTHER VOLUMES IN PREPARATION:

The Religions of the Ancient Near East. Ed. by Isaac Mendelsohn

Ancient Greek Religions. Ed. by Francis R. Walton

Eastern Orthodox Christianity. Ed. by G. Florovsky and C. A. Manning

Islam, Muhammad and His Faith. Ed. by Arthur Jeffery

Ancient Roman Religion. Ed. by Frederick C. Grant

Hellenistic Religions
The Age of Syncretism

Edited, with an Introduction, by
FREDERICK C. GRANT
Edward Robinson Professor of Biblical Theology
UNION THEOLOGICAL SEMINARY

THE LIBERAL ARTS PRESS
NEW YORK

Published at 153 West 72nd Street, New York 23, N. Y.

———————————————

Printed in the United States of America

PREFACE

It is a pleasure to record my indebtedness to the following persons for their counsel, suggestions, and criticism in the course of preparing this volume: Professor Horace L. Friess of Columbia University, Professor Robert M. Grant of the University of Chicago, Dean Sherman E. Johnson of the Church Divinity School of the Pacific, Professor Arthur D. Nock of Harvard University, Professor Herbert W. Schneider of Columbia University, and Professor Francis R. Walton of the University of Chicago. Professor Nock has greatly increased my obligation to him by permitting me to incorporate in its entirety his translation of Sallustius, *Concerning the Gods and the Universe,* and also his translation of the briefer aretalogy of Karpokrates. To my son, Professor Robert M. Grant, I am deeply grateful for his translation of the passage from Alexander, son of Numenius. I am also indebted to the Cambridge University Press for their kindly consenting to my reproduction of Dr. Nock's translation of Sallustius; to Professor Walter Marg of the University of Kiel, editor of *Gnomon,* for generous permission to use the translation of the Karpokrates; and to the Oxford University Press for their permission to use the passages from the *Oxyrhynchus Papyri.*

Other aspects of Hellenistic religions—Judaism, Christianity, Hermeticism, Gnosticism, Neoplatonism—will be illustrated by other volumes in this series.

I have given references to both the second and third editions of Dittenberger's *Sylloge Inscriptionum Graecarum,* except where inscriptions appear in only one of these editions. I have also added references to other publications of the text of the inscriptions here translated. In all cases where credit is not given some other translator, the translations are my own.

F. C. G.

PUBLICATIONS OF INSCRIPTIONS
USED IN THIS VOLUME

Bulletin de Correspondance Hellénique (1877–).

Cauer, P., *Delectus Inscriptionum Graecarum,* second edition (1883).

Corpus Inscriptionum Graecarum (1828–1877).

Dittenberger, W., *Orientis Graeci Inscriptiones Selectae* (1903–1905).

——————*Sylloge Inscriptionum Graecarum,* second edition (1898–1901); third edition (1915–1924).

Inscriptiones Graecae (1873–).

Michel, C., *Recueil d'Inscriptions Grecques* (1900); *Supplément* (1912–1927).

For the usual abbreviations, see *Oxford Classical Dictionary* (1949), pp. ix-xix. See also the article entitled, "Epigraphy, Greek," pp. 327–330.

CONTENTS

INTRODUCTION

The Hellenistic age was that period in Mediterranean and Near Eastern history which was inaugurated by the conquests of Alexander of Macedon, who died in 323 B.C. The conquered area included Greece, Asia Minor, Syria, Egypt, Mesopotamia, Persia —in short, from the Aegean eastward the whole territory of the old Persian Empire, extending as far east as the Indus River. This vast area was steadily Hellenized during the centuries after Alexander. A common language, a vast world trade, Greek settlements throughout the whole "habitable earth," with Greek scholars, musicians, artists, philosophers, poets traveling ubiquitously— these were important factors in the development of a more or less uniform civilization which embraced the whole Mediterranean basin and the Near East, and whose far-flung outposts extended, eventually, from the Strait of Gibraltar to the River Indus, and from the forests of Germany and the steppes of Russia to the Sahara Desert and the Indian Ocean. Its influence traveled even farther; works of Greek art, or reflections of its influence, have been found in India and China, in Britain and on the borders of Ethiopia. It was inevitable that the pooling of civilization's resources should include the religions of this far-flung *oikoumene*. It was also inevitable that among all the cults of the various peoples embraced within this area the most influential should be the old Greek religion, its cultus, its deities, its conceptions and beliefs.

It is important to realize that only very rarely, if ever, did an ancient cult really come to an end, supplanted by the dominant cult of the conquerors. Instead, the old cults lived on, some of them extremely primitive, others more advanced. On the borders of civilization, as among the Celts, Germans, Getae, and Scythians, wholly barbarous rites still survived, including (as among the Druids) human sacrifice. And even within close range of the

xi

centers of civilization, indeed even within Greece itself and in Egypt, some extremely primitive cults and beliefs lived on. At the same time there was a genuine advance in religious ideas during this period, an advance to which philosophy made a considerable contribution and in which the higher cults influenced the lower (Greek cults, for example, influenced the barbarian); but chiefly, no doubt, the advance was the result of that mysterious inner source of change and development that affects all civilizations, arts, religions, and human culture generally. In some instances the change was beneficial, in others it was not; we find instances where the modifications have strengthened and purified a cult, others where religion has become a burden upon society.

It is customary to define the Hellenistic age as extending from Alexander's conquest of the Persian Empire (say, his defeat of Darius at Gaugamela in 331 B.C.) to Octavian's defeat of Antony and Cleopatra at Actium in 31 B.C., or to the annexation of Egypt the following year. But some writers use the term to include the period of the early Empire, since there was no real break in the history of culture, ideas, or religion—certainly not in the East—when the Romans came.

> The East bowed low before the blast
> In patient, deep disdain;
> She let the legions thunder past,
> And plunged in thought again.

Arnold's lines are true enough, all but the last. For the vast creative activity of the East—in art, technics, literature, philosophy, and religion—would have been impossible in a world lost in thought. The words are true enough of some remoter parts of the East, but not of Asia Minor, Syria, or Egypt. Nevertheless, the main point holds, namely, the continuity of life and thought in the eastern provinces. Hellenism can scarcely be limited to the period 331–31 B.C. In a true sense the Hellenistic age continued on under Roman political domination. It was Hellenistic culture, science, art, philosophy, and religion that survived and continued to flourish, to such an extent indeed that "captive Greece captivated her conqueror."

Nevertheless, for the sake of clarity it is better to describe the culture of the earlier period (331–31 B.C.) as "Hellenistic" and that of the latter as "Hellenistic-Roman." Many persons use the term "Hellenistic" to cover both periods, when they are speaking of subjects other than political—a loose and inexact usage, but excusable and even useful as stressing the historical continuity of the two periods. It is in this general sense that they speak of "Hellenistic religions," not limiting the term to the religious cults, practices, or ideas which were known in the three centuries from Alexander to Actium. In this volume the term "Hellenistic" will be used in this broader sense to cover both Hellenistic and Hellenistic-Roman.

1. SYNCRETISM

The main characteristic feature of Hellenistic religion was syncretism: the tendency to identify the deities of various peoples and to combine their cults. Thus the Greek Zeus becomes Zeus-Amon-Re in Egypt, Zeus-Jupiter in Italy, Zeus-Hypsistos or Zeus-Baal-Shamayim in Syria, and so on. The Greek Artemis is identified with the old Italian goddess Diana of Aricia and elsewhere; Demeter is Ceres, Hephaestus is Vulcan, and so on. The identification of Greek gods with Roman—or rather of Roman with Greek—was much more thorough than that of Greek gods with Egyptian, Semitic, or others. The racial affiliation and common ancestry of some of these gods—i.e., the common racial origins of the Greeks and Italians in the dim, far-off distance of prehistory—may help to account for this. Indeed, the religions of the Hellenistic age are like a large lake with many tributaries, uniting their waters into one; or, better, like a chain of lakes with many tributaries, for the old cults, the ancient deities, the primitive hero gods, the traditional beliefs and aspirations still survived (though modified) and, while making their contribution to the common religious life, retained much of their old identity and many of their ancient peculiarities. For that reason we speak of Hellenistic *religions,* in the plural, not of a Hellenistic *religion.* These include, at least in theory, all the religions of the known world in the Hellenistic age—Greek, Roman, Anatolian, Syrian, Persian, Egyptian, Babylonian, and Assyrian, as well as the barbarian. And since at first the most influential of all these religions was the Greek (itself a composite of many cults), we ought properly to begin with a survey of the earlier history of Greek religions, prior to Alexander the Great. From this it would be clear that some of the major changes which were leading on to the Hellenistic age, including its syncretism, were already beginning to take place at the end of the fifth century, precipitated apparently by the social crisis and the political tragedy of the Peloponnesian War, which ended in 404 B.C.

But Greek religion, as we have said, was not the only nor even the exclusively dominant force among the Hellenistic cults. As time went on other religions grew in importance. The new Oriental mysteries became popular, especially in the second, third, and fourth centuries after Christ. From the first century B.C., in some circles Judaism exercised an influence upon thoughtful, religious-minded pagans, especially, it would seem, during and after the reign of Herod. This influence was chiefly to be seen in Egypt, especially at Alexandria, though it was by no means limited to that country. The originally Egyptian cult of Sarapis spread over the whole world and became of great importance long after the line of the Ptolemies had come to an end. The cult of Isis made a widespread appeal, especially in centres of culture. The cult of Mithras was spread very widely by the Roman army. Under the Roman Empire, solar monotheism, a mystical cult of Helios, spread far and wide, even in the West. Finally, a highly intellectual, spiritual, theological religion—the cultic, religious side of Neoplatonism— won numerous adherents among the educated. The old philosophies were played out: this mystical revival of Plato's teaching took their place.

Meanwhile, among these many competing or, as often, mutually amiable and cooperating cults, with their "lords many and gods many," there was rising and spreading the one significant *new* religion of the Hellenistic-Roman age—Christianity. The subject is of course important enough to require a volume by itself, and the same is true of Judaism and of other religions, such as the Greek, Roman, Egyptian, and Persian; yet it is impossible to present a complete and rounded view of Hellenistic religions without taking into account Christianity. This is not begging any question: for example, whether Christianity, as the product of its environment, was the final and most complete example of ancient religious syncretism—in this case Hebraism combined with Hellenism—or whether it was simply one more Oriental mystery cult traveling westward—the one that chanced to succeed where all the others failed. It is only to insist that any picture of the age is incomplete if it leaves out that religion which above all others was destined to influence the West during the following centuries and which, in the days of its youth, was the most disturbing and creative force at work among the ancient cults and creeds of later antiquity. It is not only the student of the general history of religions but also the student of early Christianity who finds the religious history of the Graeco-Roman world of immense interest and unending significance for his research.

The background of this earliest stage of Christianity was two-fold: first, in the immediate background, the Jewish world of the first century; and then, behind this, the widespread, in fact universal, world culture of the Hellenistic age—the Graeco-Roman civilization of the first century—to which, indeed, Judaism likewise belonged. This double background is of immense importance for the study and interpretation of the New Testament, which is, from first to last, a Greek book. Its underlying traditions were unquestionably derived from the Aramaic-speaking early Christian communities in Palestine, but they have survived only in Greek translation and as edited by the New Testament writers. Furthermore, the earliest Christian religious thought or theology was a body of religious thought which was in process of transition; it was a Christian-Jewish theology moving steadily toward expression in a very different world of ideas from that which prevailed in the original cradle of Christianity in northern Palestine.

What this new world of thought included, what were its main concepts, its attitudes toward religious practices and beliefs, what were its varied processes of logic in dealing with religious ideas— these are questions of immense importance for the study of early Christianity.

At this point, let us interject a protest. The pagan world of the first century was by no means so wholly lacking in religious and ethical ideals, nor even in noble religious and moral practice, as it has often been pictured. The early Church Fathers, for example, held the virtues of the heathen to be no more than splendid vices and worship of the gods to be inspired by devils—a perversion of the sacraments and other rites of the Church. But one must discriminate between the intolerant paganism castigated by the Fathers or the rich and degenerate high society of Rome, as reflected in the pages of Juvenal, Martial, Suetonius, or Petronius, and the faith and worship of the common people, especially of the rural population. The late Warde Fowler, a great authority on ancient Roman religion, once remarked that, in order to get at its heart one must make a thorough study of the epitaphs, specifically Franz Bücheler's *Carmina Latina Epigraphica*. Here we find despair, disillusionment, frustration in abundance; but we also find tender hope and love, and at least a dim, yearning kind of faith—faith beaten down and overwhelmed by actual experience, but still a faith, and unextinguished. Take, for example, the epitaph written by a noble lady of the fourth century for her own and her husband's tomb (page 149). The nobleman was Vettius Agorius Praetextatus, his wife Aconia Fabia Paulina. These two belonged to the group about Symmachus and, like him, were tireless champions of the old paganism. The inscription, which dates from soon after 384 A.D., begins by recounting the honors bestowed on Praetextatus during his lifetime, and then continues as follows:

> But these are nothing. Thou, O pious mystes,
> Dost hide, within that secret inmost shrine
> Of thy pure heart, what holy initiates know,
> Honoring the manifold majesty of God.

Pagan faith of this quality cannot be scorned, nor dismissed as crude or merely formal. Of course, we cannot assume that all pagan religion was on this high level; Praetextatus and his wife were exceptional persons. Nevertheless here is clear evidence of the height to which paganism was capable of rising.

The religion of the Graeco-Roman world in the first century was as manifold and variegated as the many nations and cultures that had contributed to the vast melting pot of the Hellenistic age. To us the two most familiar tributaries are the religions of Greece and Rome, but there were also Egypt with her ancient rites, Anatolia, Syria, Armenia, northern Mesopotamia, Persia, and Babylon, and the barbarians beyond the frontiers of the Empire, East, North, and South. But in the Hellenistic age, as we said, these tributaries had flowed into one common sea. Such a book as the religious romance *In Praise of Apollonius of Tyana,* by Philostratus (ca. 220 A.D.), makes it clear that more or less the same presuppositions could be carried from one end of the Empire to the other, and even beyond.[1] Wherever he goes, Apollonius lectures on the ritual and theology of the cults, "restores" their rites, and expounds a common Neopythagorean doctrine of the soul. The work is apologetic; but it must have been possible to assume considerable common ground between various cults and between the various interpretations of their rites—a compound of Homeric and post-Homeric mythology; of Orphic or Pythagorean ideas of the soul; of "primitive" beliefs in the existence of daemons, good and bad, and in the skill of the exorcist (see the magical papyri); of confidence in the efficacy of rites, both beneficent and maleficent, including curses and spells; of familiarity with the institution of mysteries; of belief in the validity of signs, portents, prodigies, and omens, and in the possibility —and the actuality—of revelation by oracles or dreams or through prophets; of faith in the art of divination and foretelling the

---

[1] See the translation by J. S. Phillimore, in the Oxford Library of Translations, or that by F. C. Conybeare, in the Loeb Classical Library.

future. Commonly shared was a religious (if not philosophical) dualism; a confidence in the significance of sacred writings, especially of those which were ancient and mysterious or cryptic, or in a foreign tongue; an unquestioning acceptance of the possibility of magical control over things and persons; an equally credulous belief in the reality of miracles; the assumption that human destiny is determined by the stars and that the individual's destiny could be discovered from his horoscope; the ascription of personal existence to the sun and stars; the equally illogical and inconsistent belief in the capricious activity of an unpredictable force, Tyche (Chance or Fortune), in the affairs of men, though the dark-visaged Fate or Destiny stood behind human fortunes and ruled the whole universe of gods, daemons, heroes, and men.

The emergence of this type of syncretism, composed of elements good and bad, high and low, old and new—some of them the recrudescence of beliefs and practices older than recorded history—has often been described and is familiar from the writings of the later classical authors, among whom Plutarch is one of the best representatives. It is sometimes described with the implication that earlier Greek religion, say before Pericles, was pure, lofty, and idealistic, that with the end of the Peloponnesian War and the downfall of the Athenian sea empire there came a "failure of nerve" which resulted in the total collapse of the earlier "Olympian" religion. Or it is said that Alexander's conquests ended the isolation of the Greek city-state, with its civic cults and rites, and that into the vacuum created by the Macedonian cyclone were drawn all manner of foreign cults, especially the Oriental mysteries. Neither of these theories is altogether sound, nor does it cover the whole case; for the Olympian religion had never been a uniform system, or even much of a "system" at all (outside the pages of Homer and the other poets), not even in the accounts of the gods. Furthermore, it lived on even after the so-called "failure of nerve." The mysteries at Eleusis and Andania were thriving in the second Christian century, as popular apparently as in the days of Pericles, while the cult of Asclepius had enjoyed a considerable expansion at the beginning of the Hellenistic age. On the other hand, foreign cults had been known to exist in Athens in the days of Plato, as the first page of the *Republic* testifies; and they had been known in the seventh and sixth centuries B.C., as well as in the fourth.

The age of Alexander and of the Successors saw great changes in the world, but the old religion survived under new conditions and circumstances, not greatly altered either for the worse or for the better. The cults had always been more or less subject to political—i.e., public—control. Thus when Ptolemy Soter, who died in 283 B.C., gave royal encouragement to the cult of Osiris-Apis, he probably had in mind the unification and loyalty of his Greek and Egyptian subjects—at least that is how his attitude has been interpreted. When the Ptolemies were worshiped as divine, it was nothing new; the Pharaohs had likewise been worshiped. Similarly when later on the Roman emperor was given divine honors, there were ample precedents not only in Roman but also in Greek religion, as well as in Egypt and the Near East. What was new was the length to which such divine honors were carried, the demand for them by living monarchs, and the opposition they aroused on the part of the intransigent "new race" of Christians. Moreover, emperor worship in the West lacked an important advantage which it had enjoyed in the East, namely, that aura of mystery and remoteness which had separated the Ptolemies from their people. Claudius and Nero, if not Domitian, could be seen any day, and their personal character was not of a kind to encourage belief in their divinity. In other words the old religion, for all its accretions and developments, was at heart still very much the same old pagan faith and practice with which the Mediterranean peoples had emerged into the light of history. Hence it was not in religion, i.e., cult and ritual, but in philosophy that the greatest changes had taken place and still were taking place at the beginning of our era.

Thus the pagan world of the first century was by no means a world "steeped in corruption and vice"; nor was its religion only a vast mass of accumulated superstition. Roman religion had broken down during the Republic, especially during the last two centuries of uninterrupted foreign and civil warfare. The Augustan restoration, for all Virgil's poetic idealization, never quite got to the heart of the matter; the beautiful ancient *pietas* and *gravitas* of the early Italian could not be restored by the simple expedient of erecting new and magnificent temples in the City nor by re-establishing ancient rites and priesthoods. But the religion of the countryside lived on; long after, it still continued to survive under a veneer of Christian doctrine and worship. And well it might, for at heart it was no mere *superstitio, Aberglaube,* but a robust, if severe, code of ritual and morals.

Since the most important of the Hellenistic religions was the Greek, it is essential to obtain a clear view of the general character of this ancient, complex, and varied faith. As we briefly view its main features, it will soon become apparent how great was their importance for the syncretism of the Hellenistic age.

2. THE OLD GREEK RELIGION

It used to be supposed that Greek religion began with Homer; that it was identical with the Homeric mythology, its cultus only the expression in ritual and song of the myths recorded or reflected in the epics and its theology the systematic exposition of their ideas, since Homer was "the Bible of the Greeks." This conception goes back to antiquity. Cornutus' *Summary of Greek Theology,* for example, was an orderly exposition and rationalization of the myths, while the Homeric "Hymns" contained the psalmody of this literary religion. Even as late as 1840, K. F. Nägelsbach wrote a book on *Homeric Theology.* When the nineteenth century became aware of the vaster reaches of religious development behind Homer, it was assumed that the gods of the "Aryans" were the prototypes of Homer's gods (so Max Müller and others); and when Schliemann first uncovered the Trojan-Mycenean remains and opened up a whole new area (the Minoan-Mycenean culture), it was at first assumed that Homer was the poet of this culture, the exponent of its religion and mythology—i.e., of the earliest stage in the history of Greek religion. But further research (e.g., Sir Arthur Evans' work in Crete) has corrected this view. Homer remains our starting point for the study of specifically Greek religion, it is true. But back of Homer lay a long development during a heroic age when the Greek spirit first began to cast off the primitive conceptions of magic, theriomorphic gods, and the whole surviving apparatus of animism. Homer, indeed, marks the end of an era; the heroic age is already past, and the religious ideas which he takes for granted have been rationalized and secularized. So thorough is this rationalization that some scholars (like Gilbert Murray) assume a late date for the "compilation" of the epics, at the end of a period of skepticism during which the separate songs of earlier balladists and minstrels had been subjected to a profane, unbelieving, even cynical and ribald "Milesian" influence.

Instead of taking Homer as the "Bible" of the Greek world (this would be true only at a far later period), the real religion of the Greek people was to be found mainly in local cults, usages, and beliefs. The myths presupposed the cultus, rather than the cultus the myths. As Professor Martin Nilsson has emphasized repeatedly in his books on Greek religion, there were two basic elements which that religion took over from earlier "primitive" religion: the conception of power, and the practice of purification. Throughout the history of classical religion, these two factors remained of primary importance, and in the later Hellenistic age they were (after a temporary eclipse) widely revived. The earliest religious worship was closely connected with the life of the family and the clan and was rooted in the mass of ancestral custom, to which appeal is constantly made, not only in early times, but throughout the history of Greek religion. It was a thoroughly Greek decision that was made at the Council of Nicaea: "Let the ancient customs prevail" (to archaia ethē krateitō).

The two main streams of early Greek religion, in cult as well as in myth, were the Minoan and the equally prehistoric Mycenaean. The latter culture was not indigenous, it appears, but grew up among those Greeks who were already settled in the southern end of the Balkan peninsula. Even some of the gods were derived from foreign sources, if we may term Cretan and other insular places of origin "foreign." In other words, syncretism is no late development of the Hellenistic age; it is to be found as far back as the history of Greek religion can be traced. In this respect Greek religion was not different from other ancient religions—the Egyptian, for example, or the Hebrew. What distinguished the syncretism of the Hellenistic age was its vast extent, its thoroughness, and the remoter origins of some of the cults and deities involved.

Into the originally local, purely cultic, largely agricultural religion of the Greek people there swept a movement, as early as the archaic age, which left behind it effects destined to survive, often underground, for many centuries. This was the secret cult of Dionysus, and in its trail the movement known as Orphism. Many of the features of Dionysiac worship (or frenzy) were plainly primitive, such as the eating of raw, sometimes even living flesh, torn from a dismembered fawn. But the ultimate form of the cult and the beliefs which gathered about it (chiefly in Orphism) were far from primitive, having to do with the attainment of immortality. With this was associated a belief in the transmigration of the soul after death and the hope of a blessed immortality after a series of lives, in each of which the soul was further purged of its grossness and sins. It was in this form that the movement appealed to such rare spirits as Pindar and Plato; and it was also in this form that the cult enjoyed widespread popularity in the Hellenistic age.

In contrast to this movement of mysticism and emotional religion, the same period saw the assertion of another important element in traditional Greek religion, namely, legalism and rationalism. Hesiod was its poet, though not its only one. Apollo was its god, and Delphi its sacred center. The famous Delphic maxim, "Know thyself," was no philosophic counsel of introspection (though it was later mystically interpreted in this sense), but meant simply, "Acknowledge that you are a mortal, and do not overstep the limits of your lowly estate; do not be guilty of pride or violence, and do not infringe upon the prerogatives of the gods." This word of wisdom has a characteristically Greek accent, one which can be traced all through Greek literature and down into the Hellenistic-Roman age. The gods resent rudeness and presumption as much as any Greek gentleman would, or any gentleman anywhere. This is the feeling at the root of the Herodotean notion of the "jealousy" of the gods, causing them to smite down every mortal who grows too lofty or proud, too fortunate or too powerful.

In the classical age, specifically in the fifth and fourth centuries, a reaction arose against the traditional cult—but more against the crude, primitive myths that surrounded it than against the cult itself. The Sophists questioned everything; this was basic to their forensic, oratorical type of education. Should not a clever young man be able to discuss any topic in the world? Why should not religious ideas also be compelled to come out of their dark corner and give a reason for their existence? To the more emancipated spirits of the time much of the inherited religion seemed superstitious—as, indeed, it was. The result of this criticism of religion was unfortunate, partly owing to political circumstances, especially after the tragic end of the long-drawn-out war between Athens and Sparta. It was a time when religion was needed more than ever before, in order to hold together a nation torn asunder and threatened with destruction not only by its external foes (Persia, for example, which still had its eyes on the Greeks) but also by internal dissension. To call religious views in question at such a time was treason, not only against the gods but against the state. This is the background of the trial and condemnation of Socrates, who died, not for his system of philosophy, nor for having a new religion, nor for a higher code of morals, but for unsettling the youth. It was a time when the political leaders of Athens needed all the support a loyal and unquestioning body of youth could give their city-state and its ruling class, and the political record of Socrates' pupils was not reassuring.

It is one of the tragedies of history that the Athenian culture which Alexander's conquests spread over Egypt and the Near and Middle East was not of the high and noble type which had reached its flower in the fifth century, but the skeptical, disillusioned, post-bellum type found in the fourth century. Criticism of religion was voiced on all sides. Added to this was the further calamity that Alexander's empire was so short-lived. At his death it broke into four great fragments, and the successors of Alexander set upon one another, each determined to wrest control of the whole empire from the hands of his rivals. It was a period of wild anarchy, of constant warfare, of powerful dictators with armies of mercenaries under their control, of sudden shifts in fortune; a city or a citizen, wealthy and at peace today, might tomorrow be impoverished or sold into slavery. No wonder if belief in Tyche, Fortune, Chance, or Luck, spread far and wide. No wonder that Athenians despaired of any intervention of the gods such as their fathers had experienced during the Persian invasion, and sang a hymn of welcome to Demetrius Poliorcetes, the newest dictator to "liberate" their city:

> The other gods are far away—
> Thee we see face to face!

As Professor Nilsson has pointed out, this widespread belief in Tyche, in an age characterized by despair of divine intervention and by an exclusive reliance upon human ingenuity or ability, was the last stage in the secularization of Greek religion. Its conception of the powers which govern the universe and the destinies of men could not possibly have been more completely undermined and still have retained any semblance of religious belief.

An age of pseudo-science and superstition succeeded an age of faith, although the continued advance of medicine did something to light up the dismal scene. It was not an age of technology (at least not in the sense in which ours is such an age), nor even of experiment, as Professor Farrington has pointed out, but only of scientific, logical thinking, and only, as often happens, in the broad outlines of a view of the world. The man in the street was no more a scientist then than he is today. But he had imbibed a few scientific ideas, e.g., that the earth was probably round. There were some persons, at any rate, who held that the earth revolved about the sun rather than the sun about the earth; that the constellations were formed by balls of fire, not mythological monsters or even gods; that the sun was not alive, but a flaming sphere. It is significant that the most popular science of the day was astronomy, not one or other of the experimental sciences.

But for all the vague rumors of mathematical hypotheses held by the experts, the ordinary man still clung to the old views. The only difference was that, just as in the modern world, the universe had expanded enormously and that natural law had to some extent supplanted the gods. For him the "science" that really mattered was astrology, rather than an experimental science (today it would be biology and, more recently, nuclear physics). And again as in modern times, superstition lived on side by side with an advanced scientific view of the world. Once more the age-old belief in the supernatural, the age-old, deep, instinctive hunger for contact with a power or powers superior to those of nature, emerged in full vigor, this time in the guise of astrology. Men believed that the powers which govern individual human life and the wide course of history reside in the heavens; that one could, if one had the skill, deduce from the position of the heavenly bodies at a particular moment (say, at the moment of a man's birth) the whole future course of events. And as a consequence of the same hunger for power, once the fatalistic domination of the stars over human life was established, it was necessary to look for ways and means of circumventing these celestial forces and the rigid, cast-iron system of determinism which they represented. Magic was cultivated far and wide, one of the most primitive of all expressions of man's attitude toward the outside world, and deeply rooted in the prehistory of the race. No modern voodoo from the darkest jungle can outbid what magic promised to men in the Hellenistic age, so that even the most cultivated and most eminent were prone to resort to magic in moments of strain or danger.

Yet along with this vast development of superstition and of pseudo-science, enveloping and eventually destroying the true sciences, like a blanket of ivy muffling and smothering an oak, there arose a tendency toward monotheism and a more spiritual conception of religion. It is part of the bewildering variety and complexity of Hellenism that this should be so. It will not do to say that the Hellenistic age was one of gross superstition, nor, on the other hand, one of spiritual enlightenment. It was both, and much else besides.

One cannot indict an age any more than he can indict a nation; nor is unqualified eulogy in place. Skepticism was to be found in wide and influential circles, especially among the educated; but there was also faith here and there. We see the same paradox in our own age: along with modern science, and side by side with the vast expansion of Christian missions, no period in all human history has witnessed such a resurgence of bestial savagery as has our "enlightened" age. Nor has astrology lost its appeal. And so the growth of monotheism in the later centuries of the Hellenistic age is only one among several features in religious development that call for attention. Above the powers in the heavens there was thought to be one supreme power, one God, one divinity; and as time went on more and more persons came to identify this power with the sun. The belief is still reflected in the names of the days of the week, which begin with Sunday. Solar monotheism in a way marked a triumph over the inherited astrological concepts, although it carried with it an almost equally deterministic view of the universe and of human life.

3. HELLENISTIC PHILOSOPHY

All of these various tendencies of religious thought and feeling were at work throughout the Hellenistic age. On the level of everyday life—i.e., in the thinking of the majority of people—religious thought was very largely conditioned by these factors. Among the educated, philosophy was of more importance, and the ideas of the philosophic schools did seep down into the language, speech, and general ideology of the man in the street. This was especially true after the Cynics and Stoics took up their mission of street preaching and conducted an almost missionary propaganda for "the philosophic life."

All later Greek philosophy was influenced, either positively or negatively, by Socrates, whom many looked upon as philosophy's great saint and martyr. Platonism was the most direct and immediate consequence of Socrates' lifework, although the teaching of

Plato went far beyond that of his master. In general—and that is
the extent of its influence upon the New Testament, for example—Platonism stood for a view of reality as spiritual, ideal, invisible; the external, visible objects in the universe being only
copies or shadows of the invisible realities. For Plato this theory
had been, certainly at first, a principle of epistemology; for Platonism as it was revived later, during the opening centuries of
our era, it had come to be an out-and-out ontological principle:
the external world is only a shadow or reflection of the real world.

The Platonism of the school, i.e., of the Academics, did not
share this subterranean mystical view; the later Academics were
notorious for their "suspense of judgment," which they pressed to
the limit of skepticism. They questioned the very capacity of the
human mind for true knowledge, as Cicero shows in his *Academics*. The impossibility of basing either ethics or metaphysics
upon such an attenuated view is obvious. The traces of "Platonism" often alleged to be found in the New Testament, as in
Paul's Letter to the Romans (1:20), in Hebrews *(passim)*, and
in John (especially 1:1–18), are of the mystical, transcendental
type, rather than epistemological, and probably owe more to cur-
rent "theosophy" than to the study of Plato or of any philosophy.

Allied to this type of thought in the first century was the doctrine of the Logos, the archetype of human reason and speech,
the demiurge, the creator of the world, the intermediary between
the Supreme God, the One, and the fleeting, insubstantial world
of things and events. The history of the Logos doctrine dates back
a long way and owes more to other sources than to Plato. Moreover, the concept took different forms and received different
emphases in various cults and systems. In general, the Logos was
the mediator between the Supreme God and the world, sometimes
conceived as independent of God, as another heavenly being like
him, with him, but not opposed to him; sometimes, on the other
hand, conceived as only a manifestation of God, as one of his
"powers." So Philo of Alexandria thought of the Logos. The conception found in John, on the other hand, seems more personal—
of a divine being, second to God, almost (as in Justin Martyr)
a "second God."

Epicureanism was a philosophy that deserved more consideration than it received as a system of hedonism and skepticism. The
noble life of Epicurus, its founder, refutes the popular caricature
of its creed; yet there were many in the ancient world, as there
are in the modern, who scorned "Epicurus' sty," having never
appreciated the philosopher's teaching. Though Epicureanism
had its followers in the Roman period (in Cicero's day), especially among the intelligentsia, its metaphysics was too subtle for
the rank and file to grasp, and its reputed ethics, "Let us eat and
drink, for tomorrow we die," alienated the best religious minds
of the day (cf. I Cor. 15:32). To be sure, there are traces of
Epicureanism in the New Testament, but they are very rare and
obviously of no importance.

Cynicism was a much more popular philosophy, which won a
wide hearing, if not a great following, in the market place. The
Cynic was indeed a rude customer; his great aim in life was to
prove that a man can do without things and still be happy,
healthy, and wise. He was a born democrat, like our American
frontiersmen or revolutionists of the Tom Paine variety. To him
a beggar was as good as a king and rank was but the "guinea
stamp," since he believed that true nobility lay within a man's
mind, not in external trappings.

Stoicism was a more systematic philosophy, with its division of
subject matter, for purposes of study and teaching, under three
main heads: logic (including epistemology), physics, and ethics.
The chief contribution of the Stoic philosophy to religious progress was in the realm of ethics, and yet its contribution to theology
(the Stoic physics, which dealt with the nature of things, of
course included theology) was almost equally important. As Paul
Wendland said, Stoicism was the hallmark (the "signature") of
the Hellenistic age. Its criticism of the myths, or rather its interpretation of them as allegories of physical phenomena, did much
to ease the burden on tender consciences of the inherited mass of
traditional religious lore—inherited now from the Greeks by the
Romans, as also by the whole eastern Hellenistic world from the
distant past in early Greece, Anatolia, Egypt, Syria, and lands
farther away. The goal of Stoic ethics was the noble one of "life

in accordance with nature," which meant, not naturalism, as some modern interpreters would have it, but doing what is appropriate to one's own nature. You are a man?—then *be* a man, and do not give way to passion, or excessive grief, or cowardice, or any of the things unbefitting and unworthy of your real nature. The ancient Stoic would have applauded Sir Richard Burton's philosophy, set forth in the famous lines of his *Kasidah*:

> Do what thy manhood bids thee do,
> From none but self expect applause;
> He noblest lives and noblest dies
> Who makes and keeps his self-made laws.

Stoicism was a philosophy for an age of tyranny and suppression of individual rights. In spite of the ceaseless power politics of the era of the Successors, in spite of Tyche's reign over the whole realm of human interests, in spite of the iniquity of judges and governors and the tyranny of mad emperors like Gaius (Caligula) or Nero or Domitian, a man could nevertheless be free within the fortress of his own mind; he need not yield to any outside circumstance or condition. The Stoics revered Socrates, and often quoted his reputed saying, "Anytus and Melitus [the accusers at Socrates' trial] may bind my leg, but Zeus himself cannot fetter my will."

Such theories as the cyclic recurrence of universes, the burning up of one and the phoenixlike emergence of its successor, and the identification of the reason or intelligence in man with the fiery ether (which they looked upon as divine) were characteristic enough of the Stoics, though perhaps they merely put into quasi-scientific or philosophical terminology ideas that were to be found elsewhere in the ancient world; but such doctrines had not the influence upon the world of religious thought which their ethical terminology and ideas came to have. Traces of Stoic ethical conceptions and terminology—at least of the terms, for the concepts were often reinterpreted—may be seen in Philo and Saint Paul, and in many later religious teachers of other schools, including even (through Cicero) some of the Church Fathers.

Neo-Pythagoreanism was "in the air" in the first two centuries, destined in the third and fourth, especially with the rise of Neoplatonism, to become very influential. There was also, it appears, a genuine survival of the old, literary, nonprofessional Platonism, which, to change the figure, had flowed like a subterranean stream through the centuries since Plato's immediate successors. This kind of Platonism—ontological rather than epistemological, as we have described it—was destined to influence Philo, the Epistle to Hebrews, Clement, Origen, and Greek Christian theology generally. According to this philosophy, "Things that are seen are transient; only things invisible are eternal" (cf. II Cor. 4:18); at the same time "The unseen things of God are apparent from the things that are seen" (cf. Romans 1:20)— the two statements are not irreconcilable. The body is only a temporary abiding place of the soul, and the less one gets attached to it the better. Hence asceticism, hence renunciation, hence the cultivation of a purely interior type of piety, in order that the soul may eventually take its flight, the "flight of the alone to the Alone." But the great period of Neoplatonism was not yet; the New Testament shows very slight traces of the influence of this circle of ideas.

Thus the Stoic ethics, especially the ethical terminology of Stoicism, and the later Platonic metaphysics prepared the way for Greek Christian, i.e., patristic, theology and helped to provide a matrix for even such early theological formulations as we find in the letters of Paul, Hebrews, and to some extent in the Gospel of John. There is even some evidence of Stoic (or Cynic) ethics in Matthew's formulation of Jesus' teaching in the Sermon on the Mount. In other words, Greek philosophy prepared the field for the spread of Gentile Christianity, partly through the medium of Hellenistic Judaism, partly more directly.

Upon Judaism during this period, on the other hand, the influence of Greek philosophy was transient and evanescent, and limited to the Greek-speaking Jews of the Diaspora. It is almost in vain that one searches the Mishnah and Talmuds, the liturgy and Midrashim, for traces of any positive influence of Greek philosophy. The *pilôsôphôs*, whenever he does appear, is usually a negative and sometimes a sinister foil to the faith in the One and Only God of Israel, and significantly he is usually an Epicurean.

The best representative of ancient religious philosophy, for the purposes of studying Hellenistic religions, is undoubtedly Plutarch of Chaeronea in Boeotia (ca. 50–120 A.D.). He was an eclectic, leaning strongly in the general direction of Platonism, and he was profoundly learned in matters of religion. Above all, he was a great moralist and believed in the "lessons" of history. He wrote forty-four parallel lives of famous Greeks and Romans from Theseus and Romulus to Philpoemen and Flamininus, and in addition four single lives (the series is unfinished), in which he pointed to the moral values and moral failings of men. This work has been a standard textbook in educating the youth of the Western world ever since, or at least until three generations ago. Plutarch's *Moral Essays* comprise an even longer series; among them the theosophical or religious essays preserve much of the best history, criticism, and interpretation of religion known in the author's time. Such essays as "Isis and Osiris," "The Failure of Oracles," "The Face in the Orb of the Moon," "The 'E' at Delphi," "Why the Pythia No Longer Gives Oracles in Verse," "The Delay in Divine Punishment," "The 'Genius' of Socrates," and "Superstition" are priceless sources for our knowledge of second-century religion and the philosophy of religion. The student of religious history should make Plutarch his "guide and familiar friend" in exploring the thoughtful, rational, even philosophic, and yet genuinely devout Greek paganism of the second century. Plutarch is a conservative, a traditionalist; therein lies his great value. He tells us men's actual beliefs—not their disbeliefs or their skepticism, their problems, or their ridicule. If one would understand Catholicism, Hinduism, or any other religion, he must study it from within and learn about it from those who really believe in it, not from its critics or from scoffers. So it is with Hellenistic religions; we must learn from someone who honestly believes in them. And Plutarch is probably our best guide and interpreter.

4. A RELIGIOUS AGE

Alexander's brief achievement of world empire, at least from the Adriatic eastward, was a prototype of the much more enduring achievement of Augustus and his successors. The profound social, political, and economic forces that led to the swift conquest of the Persian Empire, and almost at once to the disruption of Alexander's own, were still at work in the centuries that followed. It was perhaps inevitable that, with the collapse of the ancient city-state, larger political unities should take its place. In the end, it was also inevitable that the fairly unified, fairly homogeneous civilized world should be united under one master. The religious expression of this tendency was a similar longing for unity. A single world language, a single homogeneous universal culture, and a world-wide centripetal tendency observable in the political realm—all this encouraged a general tendency toward monotheism and a common longing for salvation. Never in history had questions about God and his nature been so widely discussed: *"volgata iam propter adsiduam quaestionem de deo"* (Pliny, *Historia Naturalis,* II. 27). Especially from the time of Augustus onward—i.e., from the establishment of the *pax romana,* following two centuries of almost continual warfare—a strong undercurrent of religious thought and interest is observable everywhere. Indeed, the whole Hellenistic age, after the disillusioned and cynical fourth century, and especially after the bitter third and second centuries, was in increasing measure a religious age. This fact is especially noteworthy with regard to the philosophy of this period. The main features of eclectic religious philosophy, of which Plutarch was such a noble representative, were chiefly the following:

1. There was a steady development of monotheism. The old gods and their myths were interpreted in this sense, namely, the "gods" were the powers of nature, manifestations of the one supreme deity; or they were only various "names" for the one true God, as in Apuleius's beautiful "Epiphany of Isis"; or they

(at least many of them) were only human beings who, for their virtues or achievements, had long ago been deified (this was Euhemerus' theory), but who were nonetheless far inferior to the one and only universal, eternal deity. Cleanthes' "Hymn to Zeus" is a noble and very early expression of philosophical monotheism from the Stoic viewpoint.

2. Along with the conception of the one God, there was a growing enthusiasm for ethical idealism. It is most unfortunate that the works of Posidonius have perished, but the main outline of his thought, as preserved in surviving fragments of his writings (chiefly in quotations of him by Cicero) and paraphrases found in works of later writers, is proof of the great influence he exerted in the first century before Christ and later. Although some modern scholars have been inclined to exaggerate it, his influence was vast and powerful. Posidonius represented a Stoicism that was always religious, always profoundly ethical.

But it was not only among the Stoics that ethical values were set in the foreground of philosophy or that the "practice" of philosophy (the "practical" life versus the "theoretical") received most emphasis. This emphasis is also to be seen in other movements. The general character of philosophy in the Hellenistic age is practical and ethical, rather than theoretical or metaphysical. The later Stoics—Seneca, Epictetus, Marcus Aurelius—with their high ethical outlook upon life, can be matched by the Cynic Dio Chrysostom and the Platonist Plutarch, except of course that they are all eclectics and that they all borrowed from the teachings of the earlier schools.

3. There was at the same time a notable tendency in the direction of dualism, to be seen especially in the revival of Orphic and Pythagorean doctrines and practices. It found further expression in Gnosticism and Manichaeism, and its full and final elaboration in Neoplatonism. But it had flourished for a long time before these movements arose. The archeological evidences for a revived interest in Orphism and in Pythagoreanism in Italy, even in Rome itself, go back to the first century before Christ. In the second century A.D. it is to be seen in Plutarch, who held that as long as the soul inhabits the earthly body God

cannot be fully known; one may catch glimpses of God in high moments of philosophic insight or in dreams or visions, but the open vision is reserved for another life.

4. Dualism carried with it two further requirements: the need for revelation, and the need for redemption. If man cannot, while living in the body, truly find God, then God must make himself known. And if the life of the body drags down the aspiring soul to its own level and weakens its powers of flight, then the body and its activities can never achieve their destined end without some infusion of divine power from outside, from above. How closely this view approaches the traditional Christian doctrine of man is obvious at once. The private pursuit of inner freedom and virtue by the Stoics on the one hand, and the universal longing for revelation and redemption, for a "Power not ourselves that makes for righteousness," on the other, are both alike expressions of the spiritual and moral aspiration of the age.

5. At the same time there is a marked and increasing archaism in religion. Augustus undertook to restore the old Roman religion, the ancient cults and priesthoods, and reopened eighty-two temples in the City itself (see the *Monumentum Ancyranum*). Apollonius of Tyana, both a theologian and liturgist, went about lecturing on the meaning (i.e., the theology) of ancient rites and also upon their proper observance. Plutarch was a profound student of ancient cults, even of their minute details (see his *Greek and Roman Questions*). Diogenes Laertius traced the origins of philosophy back to prehistoric, "barbarian" views of the universe. Egypt, which had always overawed the Greeks, was thought to be the repository of ancient religious wisdom superior to that of all other nations, approached only distantly by Babylon, Persia, or India.

6. The State cultus and the worship of the Roman emperor belong properly to the history of Roman religion, but the immense influence of this cultus upon popular religious ideas, especially in the East, must not be overlooked. The emperor was the representative, almost the incarnation, of the *genius* or presiding spirit of his own—the Augustan—house, his ancestry,

his line; and as *princeps* he represented Rome itself. He was the guardian of the state and the defender of the peace, the protector of civil order. Prosperity and peace depended as much upon him, in imperial Rome, as ever it had in Egypt upon the Pharaoh, or among the barbarians upon the health, vigor, and self-defensive abilities of their kings. The emperor was the *Soter* of the State, i.e., of the world empire—not merely its rescuer, but its preserver. The religious implications of this term throughout Hellenistic history, from the days of Alexander's "Successors" to the latest Roman emperors, is obvious. Equally important was the cultus offered the emperor—as the early Christians soon discovered. One might almost describe Roman imperialism, on its religious side, as a negative, secular, diabolically perverted Catholic Church. The historical justification for this comparison would be the fact that more than one external feature of later Catholicism was derived from imperial Rome.

5. THE NEW CULTS

Although the old cults survived, some of them with renewed and increasing vigor, the growing religiousness of the age and its widespread individualism made possible the further importation and spread of many new cults, especially from the East. One and all these cults met the requirements of the age for individual salvation, for revelation and redemption, for divine grace. In general, they were dualistic and promised to save man out of this present life; they were likewise in general monotheistic—the god of the cult was either the supreme deity, or the son, or the consort, or the loyal friend of the supreme god; they were individualistic, addressing the private soul in its solitariness, even if they also brought it into a religious fellowship with certain social values and interests. Finally, their implications for ethics, e.g., for ascetic renunciation or for rigid self-control, were very real.

Since the Hellenistic religions included all the cults and faiths of the known world, our survey should properly include

an account of the history of Egyptian religion, and also of Meso-
potamian, Hebrew, Anatolian, Persian, Indian, Roman, Iberian,
Gallic, German, British, Scythian, and still others—even the
nomadic religions on the very fringes of the civilized world. But
for one thing, most of these religions—except for the Hebrew,
Persian, Indian, and Roman—have little history and apparently
continued static for thousands of years. In the second place, even
in the case of the exceptions just named we know too little
about three of them, the Persian, Indian, and Roman, to trace
their course in complete detail, i.e., on a scale comparable with
that of Greek religion. Again there are exceptions: the Hebrew
and the Greek religions, for all the lacunae in our knowledge, are
to us the best-known religions in the ancient Mediterranean
world; the Roman had been static and almost without a history
until it came in contact with Greek ideas. And in our limited
period—say, from the death of Plato to the reign of the Severi, the
period during which these various religions were in a position to
contribute to the religious life of the Hellenistic-Roman world—
what do we know of their history beyond a few generalities? Fortunately it is not necessary to reconstruct the history of these foreign religions during the Hellenistic period; their influence did not
depend upon an understanding of their history. To the degree
that they met the needs of the time and satisfied some inner
hunger, whether for salvation or revelation or peace of soul
or ethical renewal or inner illumination, they spread abroad and
grew, some of them taking on a new form in their Hellenistic
manifestation. The old Persian *magus*, for example, became a
different person in the West; the Hellenistic Isis was a far more
important, far more lovable, more human deity than the old
Egyptian vegetation goddess she once had been; Mithras, the
soldier's god, was a far nobler cosmic deity than the primitive
bull slayer he once had been in Persia or in India.

The most beautiful of these cults was that of the Egyptian
Isis, with its open shrine, its daily services, lustrations with
Nile water, and its offerings of incense instead of bloody sacrifices; its hymns, liturgy, and sacred literature; its mystical theology. Virtually, Isis took the place of all other gods and god-

desses when she claimed that their names were only various epithets or titles of her own and that their functions really belonged to her; that she, and she alone, was the great Mother Goddess of the whole world, though she left room for her consort Osiris and her son Horus.

In contrast to this widespread, genteel, mystical, and very feminine cult was the wild Anatolian worship of the Mother Goddess Cybele, originating at Pessinus in Phrygia, but identical (or at least identified) with other cults of the Mother Goddess—e.g., the one at Ma in Cappadocia. As early as the third century (204 B.C.) her cult was introduced at Rome by official invitation, as a result of the exigencies of the Punic Wars, and by direction of the Sibylline Oracles. But republican Rome did not take kindly to her rites, and none but foreigners were permitted to engage in them. Associated with the worship of Cybele was the savage and probably primitive, certainly barbarous, corybantic enthusiasm of the Galli, devoted to the worship of Attis (or Adonis), young consort of the aged Mother Goddess. In their mad hypnotic dances, accompanied by the shrill scream of Phrygian flutes which drowned out their own cries, they stabbed, hacked, and mutilated themselves in honor of Cybele and her divine lover. One might think that civilized men would be utterly disgusted by the sight, but apparently it was a common practice for centuries. A society that enjoyed gladiatorial exhibitions also enjoyed such examples of primitive worship. Indeed, the two may ultimately go back to the same more primitive source, a sort of fanatical devotion to death.

Other and related cults, also originally associated with vegetation and the cycle of the seasons, were those of Tammuz (or Adonis: from the Semitic Adon, Lord), Atargatis (or Derceto, the Syrian Goddess), Baal (or Bel: Master, Owner), and many others. But the greatest of all the Oriental deities came from still farther East—from Persia via Babylon, and originally from Vedic India—the sun god Mithras. His cult had already gathered up many syncretistic features on its westward course through the Hellenized East before it gradually spread through Asia Minor and eventually arrived at Rome, and from there passed on, largely via the Roman armies, to the northern and western provinces. The period during which the cult of Mithras flourished was chiefly the third and fourth centuries—a period in which the early Christian Church was its chief competitor.

It was in this world of cults, old and new—of ancient Greek, or Hellenized, shrines, oracles, temples, priesthoods, and of new mystery rites of redemption—that Judaism and early Christianity lived and flourished. Old cults were revived and aroused widespread interest, like that of the Cabiri to which Strabo devotes space in his *Geography*, discussing its origin and meaning. A "theology" of syncretism was created which proved useful, either positively or negatively, to Christians in working out the intellectual presuppositions of their faith; it had been tried by Hellenistic Judaism, but repudiated when the great era of retrenchment began after the second fall of Jerusalem (135 A.D.). On the basis of this theology rested many ideas of the "mysteriosophical" type widely favored in later antiquity: the descent or fall and ascent of the soul; reincarnation; the cyclical view of history, and the expectation of a great world renewal, if not of a future age; the concept of a divine man, indeed of a god-man (of which Caesar, the man-god, was only a caricature); the tradition of secret, sacred wisdom from the hoary past, as transmitted by Hermes to Tat (or Thoth) and by him to the Hermetic votaries; the Gnostic cosmogony, with a vast hierarchy of aeons extending downward from the primal essence to the lowest level of foul matter; the doctrine of Fate and of its overcoming, not by magic only nor by theurgy, but by ascetic devotion and self-sacrifice, by purity of life, by knowledge, by renunciation, by fellowship with the enlightened, by love for man—and so we approach the Christian circle of ideas. Little wonder that Judaism (in Philo, for example) found itself at home in such a world—or at least in part of it—and came to be looked upon as a high philosophical religion; and that Christianity, a little later on, found a language at hand for the expression of its own highest concepts and hearts ready for the proclamation of its gospel. For increasingly throughout the later Hellenistic age (especially perhaps after 250 B.C. or thereabouts) and down through the Hellenistic-Roman age to the very end of paganism, there was a widespread, if more or less hidden, hunger for knowledge of the deity by a clear and incontestable revelation; a great desire for participation or sharing in the divine life, sacramentally or mystically; for release from servitude to the malevolent cosmic powers that hold mankind in leash; for cleansing from pollution and guilt, age-old and ingrained in human nature; and for the sure guarantee of a blessed future in the world to come or in some realm beyond this present evil one. The long process of Hellenizing the religions and cults of all mankind, with its consequent deepening and enrichment—and subjectivizing—of the religious life, viewed strictly historically, was in fact nothing less than what the Greek Fathers called it: "the preparation for the Gospel." To those who care deeply for both religion and philosophy, for the Jewish Syngogue and for the Christian Church, and at the same time for the noblest elements in the ancient religions, this fact is one of perennial interest and inexhaustible meaning.

HELLENISTIC RELIGIONS

The Age of Syncretism

I. INSTITUTIONAL RELIGION

1. SACRED HISTORIES, FOUNDATIONS, AND VOTIVE OFFERINGS

The public, institutional religion of the Hellenistic age is illustrated not only by the surviving literature but also, and most vividly, by a vast number of inscriptions and papyri. These are firsthand documents; little imagination is required to put oneself in the place of those who lived among the temples, shrines, and other sacred monuments, attended the sacrifices, listened to the prayers, and read the incised records of the sacred past. It is a great mistake to assume that the old, traditional religion was dead, and that only the secret mystery cults were alive. Instead, the whole Hellenistic and Hellenistic-Roman age was "very religious" (Acts 17:22), as its monuments testify.

In addition to the passages given here, see also Strabo's account of Olympia (VIII. 3. 30–31) and Delphi (IX. 3. 3–12) in the first century B.C. There are also many other interesting inscriptions in Dittenberger's *Sylloge Inscriptionum Graecarum;* see especially those classified under *res sacrae,* third edition, Vol. III, 977–1181. See also the votive inscriptions on the acropolis at Athens in *Inscriptiones Graecae* I. 485, 650. In the following passages we shall see how the old religious rites and usages, rules and customs, standards and requirements still prevailed. The institutional side of traditional religion was far from dead or abandoned in the Hellenistic age.

TWO WOMEN BRING AN OFFERING TO ASCLEPIUS

Herondas (or Herodas) Mime IV. The following scene, dated about 250 B.C., takes place in the temple of Asclepius at Cos, famous medical center of the Asclepiads. There is only one manuscript, a papyrus in the British Museum. Compare Theocritus' Women at the Adonis Festival.

Kynno. Hail to thee, King Paieon, who rulest over Tricca and dwellest in sweet Cos and Epidaurus; and Coronis, thy mother, and Apollo, I also hail; and Hygieia, whom thou holdest by thy right hand; and those whose blessed altars [I behold] here, Panace and Epio and Ieso I hail; and those who ravaged the house and walls of Leomedon, healers of savage sicknesses, Podalirius and Machaon, hail to them and all the gods and goddesses that dwell beside thy hearth, O Father Paieon! Come, graciously accept this cock, this herald on the walls about our house which I am sacrificing, and receive it as a side dish [?]. For 'tis but little and poor that we draw from our well [i.e., our resources are scanty], otherwise we would gladly have brought an ox or a good fat sow, and no cock, as a gift for healing of the illness which thou, O King, hast brushed away with the gentle touch of thy hand. Kokkale, put the tablet at the right hand of Hygieia.

Kokkale. My, oh my, dear Kynno, what gorgeous statues! Whoever carved this stone, and who placed it here?

Kynno. Praxiteles' sons—can't you read what it says on the base? Euthies, the son of Prexon, set it up.

Kokkale. May Paieon be gracious to them all, and to Euthies, for their good works! Look, dear, see the child gazing up at the apple—wouldn't you say if she doesn't get it she'll die? And look at that old man, Kynno. By the Fates, that child will choke the goose to death! You have to stand close, or you wouldn't know they're stone, these carvings; you might even say they could talk! Some day they'll even know how to make stones come alive. Look, Kynno, at this statue of Batale, daughter of Myttes—she's walking! If you never saw Batale herself, what of it? Her statue is just as real as she is.

Kynno. Come with me, dearie, and I'll show you something you never saw before. Kydilla, go and call the sacristan. Do you hear me talking to you?—standing there with your mouth open gawking at everything! Goodness me, she pays no attention to what I say, but stands gaping at me like a crab. *Go, I say, and call the sacristan!* You big, empty breadbasket, good for nothing either outdoors or in, lying around as idle as a rock!

I call this god to witness, Kydilla—in spite of all my self-restraint, you simply drive me frantic with rage. I say it again—I call the god to witness; some fine day you'll wake up and scratch that dull head of yours!

Kokkale. Dear me, Kynno, don't take things so much to heart! She's only a slave, and slaves always have their ears stuffed with cotton wool.

Kynno. Well, it's clear daylight now, and the crowd is getting thick. So stay here; the door is open and we can go in. [They go inside and view the famous painting of Apelles.]

Kokkale. Oh, Kynno dear, see what works of art! You might say Athena herself—hail to Thee, our Lady—had carved these beautiful things! This naked boy here—if I scratched him, wouldn't he show the welt, Kynna? His soft flesh looks so warm and alive. And this silvery roasting iron—if Myellus or Pataikiskus, son of Lamprion, saw it, their eyes would fall out of their heads thinking it was real silver! That ox, and the man leading it, and his wife trailing behind, and that man with a beaked nose, and the one with a stubby nose—how the very life and light of day shines in their eyes! If it weren't I was ashamed to act too much like a woman, I'd be even crying aloud for fear that ox might do me some harm—he's looking at me that hard with one eye!

Kynno. True enough, dearie, and the hands of our Ephesian knew how to do everything. You can't say, "That man knew how to paint one or two things as he saw them, but the next one he missed"—no; for whatever happened to come into his mind or was sent by the gods he carried out perfectly. And if anyone grudges to admire him or his works after viewing them carefully, I say let them hang him up by one leg in the fuller's shed!

Sacristan. Ladies! Your meat offerings are simply perfect, and they certainly guarantee good fortune for both of you. No one ever found more favor in Paieon's eyes than you have! *Iê, iê, Paieon!* Be thou propitious on account of these fine offerings, and likewise to their husbands and children. *Iê, iê, Paieon!* So let it be.

Kynno. So be it, Almighty One; and let us come again soon in good health, with our husbands and children—next time with bigger offerings. Kokkale, be sure you cut up the cock neatly, and give a drumstick to the sacristan, and lay the cake down gently in the serpent's den, and dip the wafer. The rest we'll eat at home—and don't forget, either, to bring along some of the health bread [?] he gave you. It is a good thing you take along some of the portion with you. [The last two lines are very obscure.]

RULES OF PURITY FOR VISITORS TO THE TEMPLE OF ATHENA AT PERGAMON

Dittenberger, Sylloge², *566, 2–9 (S³, 982); Michel,* Recueil, *730. This is a copy of a very old law which undoubtedly was still in force in the Hellenistic age.*

Whoever wishes to visit the temple of the goddess [Athene Nikephoros], whether a resident of the city or anyone else, must refrain from intercourse with his wife (or husband) that day, from intercourse with another than his wife (or husband) for the preceding two days, and must complete the required lustrations. The same prohibition applies to contact with the dead and with the delivery of a woman in childbirth. But if he has come from the funeral rites or from the burial, he shall purify [sprinkle] himself and enter by the door where the holy water stoups are, and he shall be clean that same day.

REGULATIONS FOR VISITORS TO THE TEMPLE OF ALECTRONA AT IALYSUS

Dittenberger, Sylloge ², 560 (S³, 338); Insc. Gr. XII. 1. 677; Michel, Recueil, 434. This marble tablet from the third century B.C. was found at Ialysus on the Island of Rhodes.

Law [concerning] what it is not holy [sic] to let enter or to bring into the temple and the sacred enclosure of Alectrona. No horse, ass, mule, jenny, or any other mane-growing animal may enter, and no one may bring one in hither; nor may anyone enter wearing shoes or anything made of pigskin. Whoever disregards this law, let him cleanse the sanctuary and the sacred enclosure, and in addition offer sacrifice; or else let him be guilty of irreligion [i.e, subject to the curse that haunts those who disregard, dishonor, or disobey the gods]. If sheep wander in, whoever drove them in shall pay a fine of an obol for each sheep. Whoever wills may report any infringements [of these rules] to the Mastroi [i.e., temple officials].

REGULATIONS FOR VISITORS TO A TEMPLE IN ASTYPALAEA

Dittenberger, Sylloge ², 563 (S ³, 980); BCH VII. 477. 1; Michel, Recueil, 794. This Doric inscription, of about 300 B.C., appears on a stone which presumably rested over the entrance to the temple. Later it was built into the wall of the chapel of Saint Eustathius. It is subject to various interpretations.

Into the temple let no one enter who is not pure [ceremonially] and perfect [in body], or he will be [kept] in mind [i.e., the gods will remember him for ill].

REGULATIONS FOR SACRIFICES AT MYCONOS

Dittenberger, Sylloge², *615 (S³, 1024; Michel, Recueil, 714. A white marble tablet, of about 200 B.C., found on the island of Myconos in the Cyclades. It lists the sacrifices required on specified days in the different months, with the most scrupulous and exact concern for liturgical detail. Posideon was the first month in the year on Myconos; in Attica it was the sixth month; but an island folk would naturally begin the year with the month named for Poseidon, god of the sea.*

Gods, for good fortune! [*Theoi tychei agathei:* cf. "In the Name of God, Amen!"]

Under the leadership of Cratinus, Polyzelus, and Philopron, when the cities had joined together, the Myconians decided to offer the following sacrifices in addition to those formerly offered, and the former ones were better ordered:

On the twelfth day of the month Posideon a beautiful white uncastrated ram [is to be offered] to Poseidon Temenites. The ram is not [to be] led into the city. The back and the shoulder blades are to be cut off; the shoulder blades are sacrificed; the tongue and the forequarters belong to the priest. On the same day a white uncastrated lamb is to be offered to Poseidon Phukios; no woman may be present. And from the sale of [or tax on] the fish the Council shall spend twenty drachmas for sacrificial offerings [sheep?]. On the same day two of the finest sows [are to be offered] to Demeter Chloe, one of which must be pregnant. The back of the pregnant one is to be cut off. Let the Council judge the pigs. The rulers are to give the slayer of the sacrifices the loin and thigh of the other pig, two quarts of barley groats, and three half-pints of wine. [Then follow regulations for sacrifices in other months of the year.]

A TOMB INSCRIPTION WITH A WARNING
AGAINST DISTURBERS

*Dittenberger, Sylloge[2], 888 (S[3], 1238); Insc. Gr. III. 1417.
This inscription, of about 100 B.C., was found under the ruins
of a temple near Kephisia in Attica. Note the Roman names.*

APPIA ANNIA REGILLA, WIFE OF HEROD,
THE LIGHT OF HER HOUSEHOLD

By the gods and heroes, whoever you are who [may hereafter]
own this land, never remove anything [from this tomb]. Whoever either destroys or removes the images [i.e., reliefs] and offerings, to him the earth will not bear fruit nor the sea permit
passage, but they [sic] and their progeny shall come to a miserable end. But whoever in this place guards and honors [this tomb]
in the customary way and continues to beautify it even more,
many and good things shall be his, both for himself and his
descendants. Let no one defile or damage or chip off or smash or
demolish the relief and the decoration. If anyone does so, let the
same curse fall upon them!

THE TEMPLE CHRONICLE OF LINDUS IN RHODES

*La Chronique du Temple Lindien, edited by C. Blinkenberg
(Bull. Akad. Kopenhagen, 1912, 5–6); Lietzmann, Kleine Texte,
No. 131. This inscription, of 99 B.C., was found in 1904 by the
Danish Archeological Expedition. The introduction, A, runs
across the top of the stele, like banner headlines in a news-
paper; the first two columns, B and C, list the ancient votive
offerings; and the third column, D, recounts the epiphanies of
the goddess Athena, one of which bears a striking resemblance
to the plot of the Book of Judith, in the Apocrypha. For a
modern picture of Lindus, see M. Rostovtzeff, Social and
Economic History of the Hellenistic World, Vol. II, p. 687,
pl. 76; see also Edwyn Bevan, Sibyls and Seers, pp. 72 ff.*

Introduction (A 1–12)

At the time when Teisylus, son of Sosikrates, was priest, on the twelfth of [the month] Artemisios, the Council and the People of Lindus decreed as follows: Hagesitimus, son of Timachidas, from the district of Old Lindos, proposes:

Forasmuch as the temple of Athene at Lindus, which is very ancient and most famous, has been adorned with many splendid gift offerings from earliest times on account of the epiphany of the goddess; and since most of the offerings and their inscriptions have been destroyed with age, the Council and the People of Lindus decree as follows—and may it result in a blessing:

After the passage of this decree two men shall be chosen who shall erect a tablet of stone from Lartus, following the directions of the city architect, and upon it they shall inscribe this decree; further, they shall inscribe extracts from the letter [of the priest of Athena] and from the oracles and the other testimonies, whatever relates to the gift offerings and the epiphany of the goddess; and the inscription is to be engraved in the presence of the clerk of the Council who is now in office; the temple treasurers are to pay out to the men [so] chosen, for the preparation of the stele and for the inscription, no more than the city architect, Pyrgoteles, estimates, viz., two hundred drachmas; during the coming month Agrianios, the rulers of the temple shall select a place for it in the temple of Athena at Lindus. Anyone who fails to comply with the orders contained in this decree, let him pay a fine of five hundred drachmas in sacred money of Athena of Lindus.

The men chosen were Tharsagoras, son of Stratus, from the district of Ladarma, and Timachidas, son of Hagesitimus, from the district of Old Lindos [son of the proposer of the motion?].

The Earliest Mythical Gift Offering (B 1–8)

The following have brought gift offerings to Athena: Lindos [the city hero]—a bowl, no one can find out of what it is made; upon it was the inscription, "Lindos, to Athena Polias and to Zeus Polieus." So we are told by Gorgo, in the thirtieth book of his *History of Rhodes;* by Gorgosthenes the priest of Athena, in his letter to the Council; and by the priest Hierobulus, likewise in his letter to the Council.

[Then follows a long list of forty-five or more gifts, with their inscriptions, some of them in very fragmentary form.]

Epiphanies [of Athena] (D 1–59)

When Darius, King of Persia, sent forth a great army for the purpose of enslaving Hellas, this island was the first which his fleet visited. The people in the country were terrified at the approach of the Persians and fled for safety to all the strongholds, most of them gathering at Lindus. Thereupon the barbarians set about to besiege them, until the Lindians, sore-pressed by a water shortage, were minded to hand over the city to the enemy. Right at this juncture the goddess stood over one of the magistrates in his sleep and bade him be of good courage, since she herself would procure, by intercession with her father, the water they needed. The one who saw the vision rehearsed to the citizens Athena's command. So they investigated and found that they had only enough water to last for five days, and accordingly they asked the barbarians for a truce for just that number of days, saying that Athena had sent to her father for help, and that if help did not come in the specified time they would surrender the city. . . . When Datis, the admiral of Darius, heard this request, he immediately burst out laughing. But the next day, when a great cloud gathered about the Acropolis and a heavy shower fell inside the cloud, so that contrary to all expectations [*paradoxos*] the besieged had plenty of water, while the Persian army suffered for lack of it, the barbarian was struck by the epiphany of the goddess. He took off his personal adornment and sent it as an offering—his mantle, his necklace, and his bracelets, and in addition his tiara, his scimitar, and even his chariot, which formerly was preserved here, but was burned along with most of the offerings in the priesthood of Halius Eucles, son of Astyanactidas [probably soon after 350 B.C.], when the temple caught fire. As for Datis, he set forth on the business before him, after establishing peace with the besieged and declaring publicly, "These men are protected by the gods." These events are described by Eudemus in his *Lindiaca,* by Ergias in the fourth of his histories, by Polyzelus in the fourth of his histories, by Hieronymus in Book II . . . of his *Heliaca,* by Myron in Book XXX of his *Praise of Rhodes,* by Timocritus in Book I of his *Chronological Summary,* by Hiero in Book I of his work *On Rhodes.* Xenagoras, in Book IV of his *Chronological Summary,* states that the epiphany took place, but he connects it with Mardonius, as the commander sent by Datis. Aristo also mentions the epiphany in Book XXX of his *Chronological Summary.*

Another [Epiphany] (D 60–93)

In the priesthood of Halios Pythanna, son of Archipolis in Lindus, a man got himself shut into the temple secretly at night and hanged himself on the struts between the back of the image and the wall. When the Lindians were planning to send to Delphi and inquire what they ought to do in the circumstances, the goddess stood over the priest in his sleep and bade them rest easy so far as she was concerned; however, they should uncover part of the roof immediately above the image, and leave it so till three suns had gone by and the place had been cleansed by the water falling from her father; then they were to join up the roof again as it was before and, having cleansed the temple in the regular way, offer sacrifice according to the traditional rites to Zeus. . . . [The next ten lines are broken off. Then follow six lines giving the historical authorities for the tale, beginning once more with Eudemus' *Lindiaca.*]

Another [Epiphany] (D 94–115)

When the city was being besieged by Demetrius [305–304 B.C.], Callicles, who had just vacated the priesthood of Athena of Lindus, but was still living in Lindus, thought that the goddess stood over him in his sleep and commanded him to bear a message to Anaxipolis, one of the chief magistrates [*prytaneis*], to the effect that he should write to King Ptolemy and urge him to send help to the city, for she herself would lead and would procure victory and might; if he failed to give the message to the chief magistrate, or if the chief magistrate failed to write to King Ptolemy, they would have cause to regret it. After seeing the vision, Callicles at first held his peace, but when the same thing happened again and again—for six nights running the goddess stood over him and gave him the same command—Callicles came to the city and told the whole matter to the Councilors and stated the message clearly to Anaxipolis. And the Councilors. . . . [The inscription breaks off at this point. A fourth Epiphany followed, but the inscription is too badly damaged to be legible.]

SACRAL AND LEGAL SANCTIONS FOR A MANUMISSION

Dittenberger, Sylloge² , 841; P. Caver Delectus Inscr. Gr., No. 224; Michel, Recueil, 1418; CIGS III. 42. These sanctions were found inscribed on a marble tablet, of about 250 B.C., at Steiri in Phocis. The first two lines are from an older dedication, the stone having been used twice.

PHILO THE STONEMASON TO ASCLEPIUS

God, Good Fortune! Under the archonship in Steiri of Callon, son of Ageson, in the fourth month, Praxias, son of Theon, set free Eupraxis and her child, whose name is Dorion. No one shall in any manner whatsoever reduce them [again] to slavery. They are to remain with Praxias and his wife Aphrodisia as long as they live, and shall afterward bury them and perform their funeral rites. But if they do not bury them and perform their funeral rites, as specified above, the release is to be null and void, and in addition they are to pay a fine of thirty silver minas. If anyone lays a hand upon them or enslaves them, their consequent enslavement shall be null and void, and the one who attempted it shall pay a fine of thirty minas—half shall go to their protector and half to Asclepius. It is permitted any Phocian who wishes to do so to be their protector.

A DECREE RELATING TO DIONYSIAC ARTISTS

Dittenberger, OGIS 50; BCH IX, 140. No. 2; Michel, Recueil, 1018. This inscription, of about 240 B.C., was found in 1884 near ancient Ptolemais in Egypt. Note the sacral relationship of the guild players to Dionysus. This guild was famous throughout the Hellenistic age.

Be it resolved by the guild of artists devoted to Dionysus and the Brother Gods [Ptolemy Philadelphus, and his departed sister and wife, Arsinoe], and by those who share membership in the guild, that Dionysius, the son of Musaeus, who is a Prytanis for life, is hereby authorized to adorn himself, in accordance with native custom, with the crown of ivy, in recognition of his generosity to the city of the Ptolemaeans and to the guild of artists devoted to the great Dionysus and the Brother Gods. The crowning shall take place publicly at the Dionysia [i.e., the festival], and this resolution shall be inscribed upon a stele and set up in front of the temple of Dionysus. The cost of the stele shall be paid by the treasurer [i.e., of the guild], Sosibius.

ERETRIA DECIDES TO CELEBRATE THE FREEING OF THE CITY

Dittenberger, Sylloge², 277 (S³, 323); Insc. Gr. XII. 9. 192; Michel, Recueil, 343. This incomplete inscription is probably from the year 308 B.C.

The priest of Dionysus, Theodotus, son of Theodorus, and the polemarchs Sosistratus, Protomenes' son; Aeschylus, Antandrides' son; Ithaigenes, Aeschylus' son, have made the following proposal: Since at the festival procession on the Dionysia the [Macedonian] garrison has [now] gone away and the people have regained their freedom, and the ancestral laws and the democracy are restored once more, therefore the Council and the People have decreed, in order to keep this day in memory, that all the

Eretrians and those who dwell there shall wear a crown of ivy at the festival procession of Dionysus; the citizens shall be provided the crowns at public expense, and the treasury shall pay for the supply of crowns [or farm out the concession to the highest bidder?]. The dances shall begin . . . [a lacuna] like the dances in honor of Dionysus, [when the] wine is sent . . . [The inscription breaks off at this point; it is uncertain how much of it is missing.]

HONORS TO FAITHFUL STEWARDS OF THE MYSTERIES

Dittenberger, Sylloge², *650 (S³, 540); Insc. Gr. II. 5. 385 (I.G.² 847); Michel, Recueil, 132. This inscription was discovered at Eleusis and belongs between 216 and 201 B.C. It begins with the date and names of the officers being honored and then proceeds as follows.*

The Council and the People have decreed: Democrates, son of Sunieus of Colonus, proposed the motion: Whereas, the chosen stewards [?] of the mysteries for the year of the archon Diocles have offered to Demeter and Kore and the other gods, as is customary, for the Council and the People and the children and wives, all the offerings which are appropriately to be made during the year, and also the preliminary offering . . . ; and have further provided, at their own cost, the conveyance for the use of the sanctuaries, and have voluntarily turned over to the Council the amount set aside for their use as the expense of the conveyances, and have also provided for the procession to the sea and for the reception of Iacchos in Eleusis, and similarly for the mysteries before Agra, which took place twice in this year, during the celebration of the Eleusinian games; and have moreover sent a steer as sacrifice for the Eleusinian games, giving the six hundred and fifty members of the Council their share of the flesh; and beyond all this have delivered the accounts to the office of the treasury and the *metrōion* [the Athenian state archives in the temple of Cybele], and have rendered their account before the court, in accordance with the laws; and out of their own funds have provided for everything else connected with the sacrifice, in order to show themselves agreeably disposed toward the Council and the People, thus setting an example for those who are ready to sacrifice themselves for the public welfare and showing that they can count upon the proper [measure of] gratitude, by good fortune.

Let the Council decree that the presiding officers who are to preside at the next assembly of the People shall place this matter on the agenda and present the decree of the Council to the People, [viz.] that the Council has agreed to honor the stewards of the mysteries in the year of the archon Diocles, [viz.] Thrasykles [son of . . .] of Auridae, and Nicetes, son of Nicetes of Pergase, and to crown them both with myrtle because of their piety toward the gods and their unselfishness toward the Council and the People; and to set before them other popular honors in the future, if they show themselves to be worthy of them; finally, that the secretary for the Prytany is to have this decree inscribed upon two columns of stone and set them up, one in the court of the sanctuary at Eleusis, the other on the Acropolis. For the [cost of] inscribing. . . .

THE INSTITUTION OF A HERO CULT

Epigrammata Graeca ex Lapidibus Conlecta (1878), edited by G. Kaibel, No. 774. This account from Priene was written in the third or fourth century B.C.

Sleeping, Philios, a Cypriot by origin from Salamis, son of Ariston, saw in a dream Naulochus [a hero] and the pure, gay Thesmophorae [Demeter and Kore] in white garments. In three dreams they commanded that this hero be honored as guardian of the city, and pointed out the place. Therefore Philios erected a statue in honor of this god.

THE GENESIS OF A HERO CULT

Pausanias Guide to Greece *VI (Elis II). 11. 1–9. This passage
is a bit of popular antiquarianism, throwing light upon the real
day-by-day religion of ordinary folk in the Graeco-Roman world.
Note the possibilities assumed—e.g., the paternity of Theagenes—and the importance of athletics in Greek religion; also
the primitive law involved, exacting penalties from inanimate
objects (though a Hellenistic Greek might have insisted that
the statues of the gods were living images), and the fine distinction between sacrifice to a hero and sacrifice to a god. (See
E. Rohde, Psyche, Ch. V.) Pausanias describes another cult,
that of Artemis Laphria, in VII (Achaia) 18. 8–13, showing
how tenaciously the primitive cults were rooted in everyday
religious life, not only in a back-country district like Arcadia,
but even in an up-to-date city like Patrae.*

(1) Next to these are votive offerings of the people of Elis,
[representing] Philip, the son of Amyntas, and Alexander, the
son of Philip, and Seleucus, and Antigonus. The statues of all
but Antigonus are on horseback; he alone is on foot.

(2) Not far from these kings is a statue of Theagenes of
Thasos, the son of Timosthenes. But the Thasians say that he
was not the son of Timosthenes, who was a priest of the Heracles
of Thasos, but that Heracles disguised as Timosthenes had an
intrigue with the mother of Theagenes. And when the lad was
nine years of age, and was going home from school, they say he
was attracted by the bronze statue of one of the gods in the
market place, and picked it up and put it on his shoulder and
carried it home. (3) The citizens were angry with him for what
he had done, but a man of repute and of advanced age ordered
them not to kill the lad, but bade him take the statue back to the
market place. This he did, and immediately became famous for
his strength, his exploit being talked about all over Greece.
(4) The most notable of his successes at Olympia I have already
recorded [*supra*, 6. 5], and how he beat Euthymus in boxing, and
how he was fined by the people of Elis. At that time Dromeus of
Mantinea won the victory in the pancratium, for the first time

on record without a contest. But he was beaten by Theagenes the following Olympiad in the pancratium. (5) Theagenes also won three victories in the Pythian games for boxing, and nine at Nemea and ten at the Isthmus for the combined pancratium and boxing. At Phthia in Thessaly he gave up boxing and the pancratium, and tried to win fame among the Greeks in racing; he beat all comers in the long race. I cannot but think he was desirous of rivaling Achilles, by winning a prize for racing in the country of the swiftest of those who are called heroes. The total number of the crowns he won was fourteen hundred. (6) When he died, one of his enemies went up to his statue every night and flogged the bronze as if it were Theagenes himself he was maltreating. But at last the statue fell over on him and killed him, and so stopped this outrage, whereupon the sons of the dead man prosecuted the statue for murder. Therefore the Thasians threw the statue into the sea, following the law of Draco, who in his Athenian penal legislation banished even lifeless things if they had killed anyone by falling upon him. (7) But in the course of time, as the earth yielded no fruit to the Thasians, they sent envoys to Delphi, and the god bade them receive back from exile those that had been banished. Some were accordingly recalled from exile, but the scarcity still continued. So they went a second time to the Pythia, saying that, although they had done what the oracle had ordered, the wrath of the gods still continued. Then the Pythian priestess answered: "But you have forgotten your great Theagenes." And when they could not think of any device for recovering the statue of Theagenes, some fishermen, they say, putting out to sea for a catch of fish, caught the statue in their net and brought it to land. The Thasians set it up again where it used to be, and offer sacrifice to it as to a god. (9) I know that there are statues of Theagenes in many different parts of Greece, and also among the barbarians; and that he cures diseases and receives [divine] honors from the people of the neighborhood. His statue is in the Altis and is by Glaucias of Aegina.

DEDICATION OF A STATUE OF ARTEMIS

Dittenberger, Sylloge², *552A. This inscription, made soon after 150 B.C., was found at Magnesia on the Maeander.*

In the year that Polycleides, son of Pythodelos, was bearer of the crown [*stephanephoros,* i.e., eponymous official of Magnesia], in the month Hagneon: concerning the setting up of the statue of Artemis Leucophryene in the Parthenon built for her, and concerning the offerings and gifts assigned to her each year in the month Artemision on the sixth day, and likewise that offerings shall be made by every inhabitant before the doors, in proportion to his ability, upon the altars erected by them.

The Council and the People have decided: Diagoras, son of Isagoras, proposed the motion: Whereas, divine inspiration and divine compulsion having led the entire people of this state to restore the temple, the Parthenon having now been completed, and indeed upon such a scale that by its increased size in all parts and by its splendor it has surpassed in the greatest degree the temples left by our ancestors from earlier times; and since it is customary with the people to present with pious care the gifts appropriate in every season to the deity of all the gods, above all to the protectress of the city, Artemis Leucophryene, for the welfare and continuance of the people and of all those who are favorably disposed toward the people of the Magnesians with their wives and children: Therefore let the Council and the People decree that the temple warder and the priestess of Artemis shall on the sixth day of the month Artemision effect the removal of the goddess to the Parthenon, with the most splendid offerings; and that this day shall forever hereafter be proclaimed as a festival, with the name Feast of Entry; and on it shall prevail everywhere the truce of God [i.e., it shall be a universal holiday]; and that there shall be a procession of women to the temple, and they shall tarry there and present to the goddess the proper honors and attentions. The temple warder shall further engage choirs of maidens to sing hymns to Artemis Leucophryene; the children shall be excused from school and the slaves (both men and women) from their work for the day on which this festival occurs. The priestesses of Artemis, who bear this office from the year of the crownbearer [*stephanephoros*] Polycleides, and the future *stephanephoroi*, each in his year, shall provide offerings and processions. Moreover, on this day the market shall also be held, after the year of the crownbearer Polycleides; this takes place on the first day of the year. The sacrificial herald, the one for the present year like the one for the following year, shall always, during this month, on the day appointed for the festival, when the market place has filled up, in the presence of the following officers in festival garments and crowned with laurels— the polemarch, the oeconomicus, the secretary of the Council, the general, the chief cavalry officer, the crownbearer, and the controller—he shall then command a sacred silence and before the Councilhouse offer, with the youth, the following prayer and bidding addressed to the assemblage:

I bid all the dwellers in the city and on the land of the Magnesians to bring this day to the beautiful Feast of Entry an acceptable gift offering to Artemis Leucophryene, in proportion to the ability of each household, and to pray that Artemis Leucophryene will give to the Magnesians themselves and to their wives both health and wealth, and that all may be well with the generation now living, and that posterity may likewise be blessed. . . . [The rest of this part is lost.]

THE INSCRIPTION OF KING ANTIOCHUS I
OF COMMAGENE

Dittenberger, OGIS, 383; O. Puchstein, Reisen in Kleinasien und Nordsyrien (1890), pp. 259 ff.; Michel, Recueil, 736. This inscription, set up probably between 50 and 35 B.C., was discovered in 1881 on the high mountain of Nimrud-Dagh, in the Taurus range, within the borders of ancient Commagene. Compare Fritz Krüger, Orient und Hellas in den Denkmälern und Inschriften des Königs Antiochos I von Kommagene, "Greifswalder Beiträge zur Literatur und Stilforschung," No. 19 (Greifswald, 1937).

The Great King Antiochus, the God, the Righteous One, the Manifest [Deity], the Friend of the Romans and the Friend of the Greeks, the Son of King Mithradates the Victorious and of Laodice the Brother-loving Goddess, the Daughter of King Antiochus Epiphanes, the Mother-loving, the Victorious, has recorded for all time, on consecrated pedestals, [and] with inviolable letters, the deeds of his clemency.

I have come to the conclusion that, for mankind, of all good things piety is both the most secure possession and also the sweetest enjoyment. This conviction became, for me, the cause of fortunate power and its blessed use; and during my whole life I have appeared to all men as one who thought holiness to be the true guardian and the incomparable happiness of my reign. By this means I have, contrary to all expectations, escaped great perils, have easily become master of hopeless situations, and in a blessed way have attained to the fullness of a long life.

After taking over my father's dominion, I announced, in the piety of my mind, that the kingdom subject to my throne should be the common dwelling place of all the gods, in that by means of every kind of art I decorated the representations of their form, as the ancient lore of Persians and of Greeks (the fortunate roots of my ancestry!) had handed them down [to us], and honored them with sacrifices and festivals—as was the primitive rule and the common custom of all mankind; in addition to which I have myself, in my upright intention, thought up still other and especially brilliant honors. And as I have decided to lay the foundation of this tomb—which is to be indestructible by the ravages of time, in closest proximity to the heavenly throne, wherein the fortunately preserved outer form of my person, preserved to ripe old age, shall, after the soul beloved by God has been sent to the heavenly thrones of Zeus Oromasdes, rest through immeasurable time—so I undertook to make this holy place a common throne room of all the gods; so that not only the heroic company of my ancestors, whom you behold before you, might be set up here by my pious devotion, but also that the divine representation of the manifest deities [daimones] might be consecrated on the holy hill and that this place might likewise not be lacking in witness to my piety.

Therefore, as you see, I have set up these divine images of Zeus-Oromasdes and of Apollo-Mithras-Helios-Hermes and of Artagnes-Heracles-Ares, and also of my all-nourishing homeland Commagene; and from the same stone, throned likewise among the gracious daemons, I have consecrated the features of my own form, and thus admitted a new Tyche [Fortune] to a share in the ancient honors of the great gods, since I thereby, in an upright way, imitated the example of the divine Providence [Phrontis], which as a benevolent helper has so often been seen standing by my side in the struggles of my reign.

Adequate property in land and an inalienable income therefrom have I set aside for the ample provision of sacrifices; an unceasing cultus and chosen priests arrayed in such vestments as are proper to the race of the Persians have I inaugurated, and I have dedicated the whole array and cultus in a manner worthy of my fortune and the majesty of the gods. I have decreed the appropriate laws to govern the sacred observances thus established for everlasting, so that all the inhabitants of my realm may offer both the ancient sacrifices, required by age-old common custom, and also new festivals in honor of the gods and in my honor. The birthday of my natural body, the sixteenth of Audnaios, and the tenth of Loos, the day of my accession to the throne, I have consecrated to the manifestation of the great deities, who were my leaders in a good beginning and have been the source of universal blessings for my whole kingdom. Because of the multitude of offerings and the magnificence of the celebration I have consecrated two additional days, and each of them indeed as an annual festival. The population of my empire I have divided up for the purpose of these assemblies, festival gatherings, and [common] sacrifices, and directed them to repair by villages and cities to the nearest sanctuaries, whichever is most conveniently located for the festival observance. Moreover, I have appointed under the same title that, in addition to the observance just named, my birth on the sixteenth and my accession on the tenth shall be observed every month by the priests.

Now that these regulations have been established, to be observed continually as the pious duty of men of understanding, not only in my honor but also in the blessed hope of their own good fortune, I have, in obedience to the inspiration of the gods, ordered to be inscribed upon sacred, inviolable stelae a holy law, which shall be binding upon all generations of mankind who in the immeasurable course of time, through their special lot in life, shall successively be destined to dwell in this land; they must observe it without violation, knowing that the stern penalty of the royal daemons will pursue equally the impiety occasioned by neglect as that occasioned by folly, and that disregard [even] of the law decreed for the honor of the heroes brings with it inexorable penalties. For the pious it is all a simple matter, but godlessness is followed by back-breaking burdens. This law my voice has proclaimed, but it is the mind of the gods that has given it authority.

The Law

The priest who is appointed by me for these gods and heroes, whom I have dedicated at the monumental tomb of my [mortal] body, [here] on the topmost ridge of the Taurus range, and [or] who shall at a later time hold this office, he, set free from every other duty, shall without let or hindrance and with no excuse for evasion keep watch at this memorial and devote himself to the care of these images and their proper adornment. On the birthdays which I have established forever as monthly and annual festivals of the gods and of my own person, throughout the whole year he shall, himself decently garbed in Persian raiment, as my dedication and the ancestral custom of our race have provided, crown them all with the gold crowns which I have dedicated as the sacred honors due the daemons; and out of the income from the villages, which I have designated for the sacred honors of the heroic nature [i.e., in addition to daemons and gods], he shall offer on these altars rich additional offerings of incense and aromatic herbs, and also splendid sacrifices in honor of the gods and in my honor, in worthy [and appropriate] wise. Holy tables he must set up with appropriate foods and fill jars from the wine-press with precious mixed drink [i.e., wine and water], and he shall hospitably welcome the whole of the assembled people, both the natives and the foreigners who stream hither, and he shall provide for the common enjoyment of the feast by the assembled multitudes, in that, as is the custom, he shall take for himself a portion, as a gift in honor of the priestly office, and then distribute the rest of my benefaction to the others for their free enjoyment, so that during the holy days everyone may receive a never-failing sustenance and may thus be able to celebrate the festival without running the risk of malicious calumny, whatever he chooses to take. The drinking cups, which I have dedicated, are to be used by them as long as they remain in the holy place and participate in the general assembly for the feast. The group of musicians whom I have chosen for the purpose and those who may later be consecrated to the same office, their sons and daughters, and also their descendants [in turn] shall all learn the same art and be set free from the burden of every other responsibility; and they are to remain present throughout the observances which I have established, to the [very] end, and without any evasion [or excuse] are to continue their services as long as the assembly requests it. No one, no king or ruler, no priest or official shall ever make slaves of these *hierodules,* whom I have, in accordance with the divine will, consecrated to the gods and to my own honor, or their children or the descendants of their children, who carry on their family to all later time; he shall not enslave them, either to himself or to anyone else, nor alienate them, nor injure one of them, nor deprive him of this ministry; but the priests shall take care of them, and the kings, officials, and all private persons shall stand by them, since the favor of the gods and heroes will be laid up [as a reward] for their piety. Similarly it is not permitted, by divine law, for anyone to appropriate or to alienate the villages which I have dedicated to these gods, to sell them or to devote them to some other purpose, or in any way to injure those villages; or to reduce the income from them, which I have dedicated to the gods as an inalienable possession. Nor, in accordance with our honor, shall anyone go unpunished who shall devise in his mind some other scheme of violence or of reducing or suspending the sacrifices and festal assemblies which I have established. Whoever shall presume to rescind or to injure or sophistically to interpret the sacred force of this regulation or the heroic honors which the [i.e., this] immortal decree has sanctioned, him the wrath of the daemons and of all the gods shall pursue, both himself and his descendants, irreconcilably, and with every kind of punishment.

[Since] a noble example of piety, a testimony to gods and ancestors, is a matter of sacred duty, I have set [one] before the eyes of my children and grandchildren, as in many others, so in this work; and I believe that they will emulate this beautiful example by continually increasing the honors appropriate to their line and, like me, in their riper years adding greatly to their personal fame. For those who do so I pray that all the ancestral gods, from Persia and Macedonia and from the native land of Commagene, may continue to be gracious to them in all clemency. And whoever, in the long time to come, takes over this reign as king or dynast, he also shall, if he observes this law and guards my honor, enjoy, through my intercession, the favor of the daemons and all the gods. But whoever, in his folly of mind, undertakes measures contrary to the honor of the gods, he shall, even apart from my curse, suffer the full animosity of the gods.

2. SACRED LAWS: RULES FOR PRIESTHOODS, INITIATIONS, AND SACRIFICES

Greek religion was formal, and did not leave the procedures of worship and sacrifice to the choice of the individual; the cultus had its strictly prescribed rules. See M. P. Nilsson, *Geschichte der griechischen Religion*, Vol. II (1950), pp. 64–78. As a rule, the sacred laws were handed down by tradition and, when written out, were often inscribed on stone for all to read. In addition to the following passages, see also Aristotle's account of the duties of the King Archon, in his *Constitution of*

Athens 56–57, and also what he says of the regulations concerning sacred things in *Politics* III. 9. 2, V. 9. 15, VI. 5. 11, VII. 8. 6, 9. 7, 11. 1–3.

RULES OF PURITY FOR THE PRIESTESS OF DEMETER OLYMPIA AT COS

Archiv für Religionswissenschaft, Vol. X (1907), p. 402, ll. 22–27; M. P. Nilsson, Lesebuch, p. 5. The date is unknown, but presumably the regulations continued in force down through the Hellenistic and Hellenistic-Roman age. Cos was a famous literary and medical center throughout antiquity. See Nilsson, Geschichte der griechischen Religion, *Vol. I, p. 82 note.*

The priestess must be pure from the following: She must in no wise come in contact with anything filthy [ceremonially unclean?]; she must not participate in a hero meal [i.e., a meal for the dead]; she must not touch a grave; she must not enter a house where a woman has given birth to a child, whether a live birth or a still one, during the preceding three days; nor during the three days following a burial shall she enter the house in which someone has died; and she must not eat carrion [i.e., meat of any animals that have perished or been suffocated].

RULES FOR THOSE ABOUT TO BE INITIATED IN THE MYSTERIES AT LYCOSURA

Dittenberger, Sylloge[2]*, 939 (S*[3]*, 999); Insc. Gr. V. 2. 514. The date is unknown, but the primitive character of the rules is obvious. Such regulations survived long after their original promulgation, especially in as conservative a region as Arcadia. Even in Rome the similar taboos governing the* flamen dialis *continued in force as late as the second century* A.D., *and probably later.*

It is not permitted to enter the temple of the Lady Goddess with any object of gold on one's person, unless it is intended for an offering; or to wear a purple or bright colored or black garment, or shoes, or a finger ring. But if one enters wearing any forbidden object, it must be dedicated to the temple. Women are not to have their hair bound up, and men must enter with bared heads. No flowers are to be brought in at the mysteries; no pregnant women or nursing mothers are to have any part. If anyone wishes to make an offering, let it be of olive, myrtle, honey, grains of barley clean from weeds, a picture, a white poppy, lamps, incense, myrrh, spice. But if anyone wishes to offer the Lady Goddess sacrificial animals, they must be female and white. . . .

AN EXAMPLE OF APOLLINE PIETY

Theopompus, in Porphyry De Abstinentia II. 16. *The general subject of Porphyry's work is abstinence from animal food. Theopompus is probably the fourth-century historian. Clearchus' date is unknown.*

[To a man from Magnesia who was accustomed to bring the gods rich offerings] the priestess replied, "It is Clearchus, who lives at Methydrion in Arcadia, who honors the gods best of all." He was amazed at this, and desired to see the man and to meet him personally in order to learn in what manner he offered sacrifice. Having soon arrived at Methydrion, he was full of scorn for the tiny, poverty-stricken place; for he could not believe that even the whole town itself, let alone a single man in it, could be in a position to offer the gods nobler or more magnificent honors than he. Nevertheless he sought out the man and begged him to explain in what way he honored the gods. Then Clearchus said that he performed the offerings with great care at the appointed times; that every month on the day of the new moon he crowned and decorated the pillars of Hermes and of Hecate, and the other shrines which his forefathers had erected, and that he honored them with incense and crushed barley and offering cakes; and that year by year he held public sacrifices, not neglecting any of the festivals.

RULES OF A PRIVATE RELIGIOUS ASSOCIATION IN PHILADELPHIA

Dittenberger, Sylloge [3], *985. This marble stele, dating from the first century* B.C., *was found at ancient Philadelphia and was edited by Keil and von Premerstein in* Dritte Reise in Lydien, *p. 18. Compare Weinreich in* S.B.A. Heidelberg, *1919, XVI. The high ethical standard which these rules enforced reminds one of the Graeco-Jewish writers, especially of Pseudo-Phocylides, and such early Christian books as the* Didache *and the* Apology *of Aristides, and also of the New Testament. See also Pliny's letter to Trajan about the early Christians in Bithynia (Pliny X. 96 f.; ca. 110* A.D.*). Cf. A. D. Nock,* Conversion *(1933), pp. 216 f.; "Early Gentile Christianity and its Hellenistic Background," in* Essays on the Trinity and the Incarnation *(1928), edited by A.E.J. Rawlinson, pp. 72 ff; U. von Wilamowitz-Moellendorff,* Der Glaube der Hellenen, *Vol. II (1932), p. 369. The owner of the house, which was once a shrine of Agdistis, is Dionysius. But the cult, which he himself appears to have established, is dedicated to other gods as well.*

Good Fortune! They were written for the health and common welfare and the noblest thought, the commandments given to Dionysius [by Zeus], granting access in sleep to his own house both to free men and women, and to household slaves. For here are the altars of Zeus Eumenes, Hestia who is seated beside him, and the other Savior Gods: Eudaimonia, Plutus, Arete, Hygiaea, Tyche Agathe, Agathos Daimon, Mneme, Charites, Nike.

To him Zeus gave commandments: To observe the purifications and cleansing rites, and offer the sacrifices in accordance with ancestral rites and as now practiced. Those who enter this house [i.e., temple], both men and women, both bond and free, are to take oath before all the gods that, conscious of no guile toward man or woman, they will not [administer] an evil drug to men, nor will they learn or practice wicked charms, nor [give] any philter, or any abortive or contraceptive drug, nor [commit] robbery or murder, either carrying it out themselves or advising another or acting as witness [for his defense], nor overlook complacently those who rob [or withhold—i.e., offerings] in this house; and if anyone shall do any of these things or advise them, they will not consent or pass over it in silence, but will bring it out into the open and see that [the crime] is punished.

A man [is not to take] another woman in addition to his own wife, either a free woman or a slave who has a husband, nor is he to corrupt either a child [boy] or a virgin, nor is he to counsel another [to do so]; but if he should witness anyone [doing this], he must not hide it or keep silent about it. Woman and man [alike], whoever does any of the things above written, let them not enter this house. For the gods who dwell here are mighty and watch over these things and will not hold back [punishment] from those who transgress [their] commandments. A free woman is to be pure and is not to know bed or intercourse with any other man except her own [husband]. If she does know it, she shall not be pure [as before], but is defiled and full of corruption within her family [i.e., she has corrupted the family line] and is unworthy to worship this god for whom these rites were established, or to offer sacrifices, or to . . . [about twelve lines are missing] to stumble upon or to see the mysteries observed. If anyone does any of these things with which the commandments here copied have to do, terrible curses from the gods will come upon those who disregard them. For God does not by any means will that these things should come to pass, nor does he desire it, but to obey [i.e., God wills that men should obey the commandments, and not be punished for disobedience].

To those who obey, the gods will be gracious and will always be giving them everything good, such as the gods are wont to give to men whom they love. But if any transgress, they will hate such persons and will lay upon them great penalties.

These commandments were placed [here] by Agdistis, the most holy Guardian and Mistress of this house, that she might show her good will [or intentions] to men and women, bond and free, so that they might follow the [rules] written here and take part in the sacrifices which [are offered] month by month and year by year, even those, both men and women, who believe within themselves [i.e., are faithful to] this writing in which the commandments of God are written, so that those who follow the commandments may become known openly, and also those who do not.

O Zeus the Savior, graciously and favorably accept this account and . . . [about eighteen lines are missing] provide a good requital, health, safety, peace, security by land and sea . . . [about twenty-one lines are missing] likewise.

A LAW REGARDING THE SALE OF THE PRIESTHOOD OF ASCLEPIUS AT CHALCEDON

Dittenberger, Sylloge[2], 594 (S[3], 1009); Michel, Recueil, 732. This inscription comes from about 200 A.D.

[The priest of Asclepius] shall wear a crown during the festival and shall attend the public banquets. He may also use the plaza [space?] in front of the sanctuary, which belongs to the state, as he will, except when part of this space is in use by the community [for the erection of public buildings or some such purpose]. In order to be eligible to buy the priesthood, one must be physically without blemish and possess the right to be clothed in public office. It is permitted for a man to buy the priesthood for his son; in no other case may anyone purchase it save for himself. If anyone makes an offer or tries to obtain a pledge [of sale] in advance, whether in the Council or in the Popular Assembly, or wherever else it may be, they shall take away the priesthood from the purchaser and he shall pay a fine of one thousand drachmas into the treasury of Asclepius. The buyer shall pay down one half, plus $1/130$ [ca. three-quarters of 1 per cent, as a sales tax] before the tenth day of the month Metageitnios, the remainder before the tenth day of the month Dionysius. When he has paid the full amount, he shall be installed in his office; he himself must bear the costs of the installation ceremony. The priest must open the temple every day. He shall also see to it that the portico of the temple of Asclepius is kept clean. The income shall be his from the month Machaneios onward. The price of the priesthood, including the [additional tax of] a one-hundred-thirtieth part, amounts to 5,038 drachmas, 4 obols.

The purchaser is Matris, son of Menios.

THE FESTIVAL PROCESSION AND TENTS AT THE MYSTERIES IN ANDANIA

Dittenberger, Sylloge², 653, 28–37 (S ³, 736); Michel, Recueil, 694. In addition to the inscription, dated 92 B.C., see also the account which Pausanias gives in his Guide to Greece, IV (Messenia). 1. 5—2. 7; 26. 6—27. 8; 33. 4–6. Pausanias' interest is archeological, like that of every good tourist guide; but he also compares the mystery with that at Eleusis, which sets the standard for the whole Greek world, and he recognizes the principle of liturgical reform and the authorized mode of revision of sacred rites—matters of real concern in the Hellenistic age.

Regarding the festival procession. The procession is to be led by Mnasistratos; then follows the priest of the gods whose mysteries are being celebrated, together with the priestess, then the director of the games, the sacrificing priests, and the flute players; following them the sacred virgins draw the cart, their order of precedence being determined by lot, and in the cart is the chest containing the sacred objects. Following these come the stewardess of the temple of Demeter and her assistants, who have already begun their work [?], then the priestesses of Demeter of the Hippodrome and of Demeter in Aigila; then come the holy [consecrated?] women, one by one, as the lot has determined their order, and the holy [consecrated?] men, in the order assigned them by the Council of Ten. The overseer of the women is to determine by lot the order of precedence of the consecrated women and virgins, and shall take care that they have the place in the procession assigned to them by the lot. Sacrificial animals shall be led along with the procession, to be offered as follows: to Demeter a pregnant sow, to Hermes a ram, to the great gods a young sow, to Apollo Karneios a wild boar, to Hagna a sheep.

Regarding the tents, the consecrated men shall not be permitted to have a tent larger than thirty feet square, or to have coverings and curtains about it; nor shall anyone not belonging to the consecrated men be permitted to have a tent within the boundary drawn by the consecrated men. No unconsecrated person shall intrude within the area which they have marked off.

They are also to set vessels with holy water [water for consecration] at a [specified] place. They must also set up a notice stating from what one must be pure, and what one may not take with him, if he wishes to enter [the consecrated area, or the tent].

STATEMENT OF ACCOUNT OF SALES OF SACRIFICIAL ANIMALS

Dittenberger, Sylloge ², 620, 4–29 (S ³, 1029); Insc. Gr. II. 741; Michel, Recueil, 824. From this inscription, dating from 334– 333 B.C. and found in Athens, we learn what became of the sacrificial animals after the offering had been made. Part of the flesh was burned and part sold in the market (cf. I Cor. 8); the hides were also sold (see the parallel in Lev. 7–8).

Proceeds from the sale of hides under the Archon Ktesikles

From the Dionysians in Piraeus, per ox buyers........311 [drachmas]
Balance left from purchase of oxen................280
From the Dionysians at the Lenaion, per leaders
of the mysteries.........................   ....
From the sacrifice for Agathê Tyche, per supervisor of the sacrifice................160
From the Asclepians, per supervisor of the sacrifice 281
From the Dionysians in the city, per ox buyers.....808
From the Olympians, per conveners of the people...721
From the sacrifice for Hermes the Leader, per
army commanders ....
From the Bendideans, per supervisors of the sacrifice 457
From the sacrifice for Zeus the Savior, per ox
buyers 1,005

Total money from hides under the Archon
Ktesikles ....5,099 drachmas,
4 obols

3. RELIGIOUS PRACTICES AND BELIEFS

ORACLES

Among the various cult practices, none was more universal than the consultation of oracles. People in all walks of life consulted them for help with every type of problem. Many of the questions asked reflect the wistful, utterly human character of the problems submitted.

Oracles apparently were not as sacred as the mysteries. The demands of popular religion did not require that a hero with a cult, a shrine, and an oracle must have led an exemplary life. The basis of cult observance and of oracle consultation was pragmatic: results were obtained, whatever the character of the hero. The revival of interest in oracles early in the Hellenistic age and their decline and eventual failure by the time of Plutarch is well known. For an account of oracles in the Hellenistic and Hellenistic-Roman age, see M. P. Nilsson, *Geschichte der griechischen Religion*, Vol. II, pp. 97–107, 447–465; also S. Eitrem, *Orakel und Mysterien am Ausgang der Antike* (Zürich, 1947), and F. W. H. Myers, "The Greek Oracles," in *Essays: Classical* (1883).

QUESTIONS ASKED AT DODONA

Dittenberger, Sylloge², *794–797 (S³, 1160–1163).*

Heracleidas asks Zeus and Dione good Fortune, and inquires of the god concerning a child, if he is to have one by Aigle, his present wife.

Nicocrateia says [i.e., asks] to which of the gods she had better and more advantageously offer sacrifice and [i.e., so] that the illness may cease.

Whether we [ought to] go around in Elina . . . or in An-
actorium . . . or sell the . . .
Lysanias asks Zeus Naios and Deona if the child which
Annyla is bearing is his.

INQUIRY AT AN ORACLE REGARDING
THE BUILDING OF A TEMPLE

*Dittenberger, Sylloge*², *555 (III), (S*³*, 977); CIG 2477; Insc.
Gr. XII. 3. 248; Michel, Recueil, 853. This inquiry, recorded
in an inscription from the first century* A.D., *from the island
of Anaphe, was presumably addressed to Apollo at Delphi.*

Timotheos inquired of the god whether it would be better
and more appropriate to request the city to build a temple to
Aphrodite, to remain the property of the city, in the sacred
enclosure of Apollo of Asgelata, as planned, or in the sanctuary
of Asclepius, as [was also] planned. The god replied that he
should ask [to have it built] in the sanctuary of Apollo; and
when the temple was finished the decree of the Council and
the oracle and the [account of the whole] proceeding should be
inscribed on a stone stele. The Council concurred.

THE ORDER OF PROCEDURE AT AN ORACLE

*Dittenberger, Sylloge*², *790 (I–II), (S*³*, 1157); Michel, Recueil, 842. The inscription is fragmentary—three pieces of
white stone were found at Demetrias on the Pegasean Gulf.
The date is about 100* B.C. *The procedure is different from
that described in the preceding passage. Compare Lucian's
satirical account of the oracle founded by Alexander of
Abunoteichos. (See below, pp. 95 ff.)*

In the year of the priest Krinon, son of Parmenion, on the
tenth of the month Areios, a motion was presented by Krinon,
son of Parmenion of Homolion, priest of Zeus Acraios; and by
Dionysiodorus, son of Euphraios of Aeolia, commander of the

Magnesians; and by the commanders Aetolion, son of Demetrius of Pagasae, Kleogenes, son of Amytas of Halae, Menes, son of Hippius of Aeolea; and by the guardians of the law Menelaus, son of Philip of Iolcus, Aeneas, son of Nicasibulus, Alexander, son of Meniscus of Spalanthra, and Menander, son of Nicius of Korope:

Whereas our city is piously devoted not only to the other gods but also, not least, to Apollo of Korope, and honors him with the highest honors because of the benefactions for which it is indebted to the god, since through his oracle, the right course is indicated in matters both public and private, in everything that concerns health and welfare; whereas it is accordingly right and proper, especially since the oracle is ancient and was held in high esteem by our forefathers and since many foreigners come here to visit the oracle, that the city should take most serious measures for the worthy maintenance of the oracle:

Let the Council and the People decree [i.e., be it resolved] that, whenever an oracular communication takes place, the permanent priest of Apollo appointed by the city, and from among the commanders and law guardians one chosen from each group, and one from the Prytanies, and the treasurer and the secretary of the god and the prophet shall proceed [to take action]. If any of those just named be sick or outside the country, he shall send another [in his place]. The commanders and the law guardians shall also enroll staffbearers [*rhabdouchoi*] from the citizens, three men below thirty years of age, who shall have the right to punish anyone who is disorderly. These [staffbearers] shall be paid their wages out of the collected funds, two days at a time, at [the rate of] a drachma per diem. If one of the appointed staffbearers is intentionally absent from his post, he shall pay [a fine of] fifty drachmas to the city, as the commanders and law guardians assess his fine. When those named above are present at the oracle and the sacrifice has been offered in accordance with ancestral custom, and with favorable result, the secretary of the god shall, after the offering of the sacrifice, take up the list of those who wish to inquire of the oracle, write all their names on a white tablet, set this up at once before the temple, and then admit them, calling them in the order of [their names on] the list, except when one or another has permission to enter first. If the person called is not present, he [the secretary] shall admit the next following, until the one who was called arrives. In the sanctuary the persons named [on the list] shall be seated, properly clad in festival garments, crowned with laurel crowns, [ceremonially] clean and sober; and they shall receive the [question] tablets from those inquiring of the oracle. When the oracle begins [literally, is completed], they are to toss [the tablets] into a vessel and seal it with the seal of the commanders and law guardians, and also with that of the priest, and shall permit [the inquirers or the tablets?] to remain in the sanctuary. At dawn the secretary of the god shall bring in the vessel, display the seals to the above-named, open it, and, calling off the names in the order of the list, return to each his [question] tablet [with] the oracle [i.e., reply]. . . .

The staffbearers shall take thought beforehand about [maintaining] order, whenever it is necessary. When the Assembly of the People takes place in the month Aphrodision, before everything else the examiners shall, in the presence of the People, obtain from each of the above-named men the following oath: "I swear by Zeus of Akra, and by Apollo of Korope, and by Artemis of Iolcus, and by all other gods and goddesses that I have performed everything as ordered by the decree which was ordained relatively to the oracle in the year of the priest Krinon, son of Parmenion."

When they have so sworn they shall be released from their responsibility. If anyone does not take oath, the examiners, and every citizen who so desires, will be justified in bringing complaint against him on the ground of this failure. If the examiners fail in any particular to do as enacted above, they are to be held responsible to their successors in office and to others who wish [to prefer charges]. That the decree may be binding for all time, the ten annually chosen *strategoi* [commanders] and the law guardians shall regularly deliver this decree to the officers chosen by them. Also, a copy of the decree shall be inscribed upon a stone stele, to be provided by the wall builders [i.e., the officials appointed to repair the city walls] and is to be erected in the sanctuary of Apollo of Korope.

[Part III has to do with the restoration of the grove in the sanctuary.]

THE ORACLE OF AMPHIARAUS

Pausanias Guide to Greece *I (Attica) 34. In describing an oracle which is still active and another which is now "the most trustworthy," Pausanias enables us to see how oracles were viewed by the rank and file, and how they maintained their popularity. See also what this same author has to say about another second-century oracle which he visited, the Oracle of Trophonius, in* Guide to Greece *IX (Boeotia). 37. 1—40. 2, quoted below. What Pausanias says of the popularity of oracles must be balanced against what Plutarch says of their decline.*

(1) The land of Oropus between Attica and Tanagra, which originally belonged to Boeotia, is now Athenian. The Athenians always fought for it, but did not get firm hold of it until Philip gave it to them after the capture of Thebes. The city is on the sea, but has played no great part in history: about twelve stades [a mile and a half] from it is the sanctuary of Amphiaraus. (2) It is said that when Amphiaraus fled from Thebes, the earth opened and swallowed him up with his chariot; but they say it did not happen here, but at a place called Harma [Chariot], on the way from Thebes to Chalcis. The Oropians are thought to be the first who made Amphiaraus a god; afterward all the Greeks so esteemed him. I can mention others who then were men but who now receive among the Greeks the honors paid to the gods, and even have cities dedicated to them, such as Eleüs in the Chersonnesus, which is dedicated to Protesilaus, and Lebadia in Boeotia, which is dedicated to Trophonius. The Oropians have both a temple of Amphiaraus and also a statue of him in white marble. (3) The altar is divided into five parts:

one belongs to Heracles, Zeus, and Apollo the Healer; another is dedicated to heroes and wives of heroes; a third belongs to Hestia and Hermes and Amphiaraus and the sons of Amphilochus—though Alcmaeon, because of what he did to Eriphyle, is not honored either with Amphiaraus or with Amphilochus; the fourth division of the altar belongs to Aphrodite and Panacea, and also to Iaso and Hygeia [Health] and Athena the Healer; the fifth has been set apart for the Nymphs and Pan, and the rivers Acheloüs and Cephisus. The Athenians also have an altar to Amphilochus in the city; while at Mallus in Cilicia there is an oracle of his which is the most trustworthy of those now in existence. (4) The Oropians have a spring near the temple, which they call the spring of Amphiaraus, but they neither sacrifice in it nor use it for purifications or for washing their hands. But when any man has been cured of a disease by means of the oracle, it is customary to throw a gold or silver coin into the spring; for it was by this route, they say, that Amphiaraus rose up after he had become a god. Iophon the Cnossian, who was one of the interpreters [exegetes], produced some oracular responses in hexameter verse, saying that Amphiaraus gave them to the Argives who were sent to Thebes. These lines had an irresistible attraction for the public. Except for those who are said to have been inspired of old by Apollo, none of the seers uttered oracles, but they were good at explaining dreams and interpreting the flights of birds and the entrails of sacrificial victims. (5) Amphiaraus was, I think, especially skillful at divination by dreams, and it is certain that when he became a god he set up a dream oracle. And whoever comes to consult Amphiaraus must first, according to custom, purify himself; that is, he must sacrifice to the god. They sacrifice not only to him, but also to all the other gods whose names are on the altar. And after all these preliminary rites, they sacrifice a ram and, spreading its skin under them they go to sleep, expecting to receive divine direction in a dream.

THE ORACLE OF TROPHONIUS

Pausanias Guide to Greece *IX (Boeotia) 39. 5–14. Here we learn more details about the origin, history, and modus operandi of oracles. This oracle was in Plutarch's neighborhood (Chaeronea), and one should bear the passage in mind in reading Plutarch's essay on the decline of oracles (see below pp. 41 ff.). For a modern description of the site, see J. G. Frazer's* Pausanias and Other Greek Sketches *(1900), pp. 359–361.*

(5) What takes place at the oracle is as follows: When a man has decided to descend to the oracle of Trophonius, he first stays a fixed number of days in a certain building, this being sacred to the Good Spirit [Agathos Daemon] and to Fortune [Tyche]. While he stays there, he practices various regulations for purity, including warm baths and bathing in the river Hercyna [or, he abstains from warm baths, and bathes only in the river]. He has plenty of meat from the sacrifices, for everyone who descends sacrifices to Trophonius himself and to his children, to Apollo also and to Kronos, to Zeus surnamed King, to Hera the Charioteer, and to Demeter, whom they surname Europa and of whom they say that she was the nurse of Trophonius. (6) At each sacrifice a diviner [*mantis*] is present, who looks into the entrails of the victim, and after an inspection prophesies to the person descending whether Trophonius will receive him kindly and graciously. The entrails of the other victims do not show the mind of Trophonius so much as a ram, which each inquirer sacrifices over a pit the night when he descends, invoking Agamedes [Trophonius' brother]. Even though the previous sacrifices have appeared propitious, no attention is paid to them unless the entrails of this ram give the same indications; but if they agree, then the inquirer descends full of hope. The descent is as follows. (7) First, during the night he is taken to the river Hercyna by two boys, sons of citizens, about thirteen years old, named *hermae* [guides]; after taking him there, they anoint him with oil and wash him. These

are the ones who wash the descender and do all other required services as his attendant boys. After this he is taken by the priests, not at once to the oracle, but to springs of water very near to each other. (8) Here he must drink water called the Water of Forgetfulness, so that he may forget all that he has been thinking of hitherto; afterward he drinks of another water, the Water of Memory, which causes him to remember the things seen during his descent. After looking at the image which they say was made by Daedalus (it is not shown by the priests to any except those who are going to visit Trophonius), having seen it, worshipped it, and offered prayer, he proceeds to the oracle, dressed in a linen tunic, girded with ribbons, and wearing the boots of that country. (9) The oracle is on the mountain, above the grove. It has a circular foundation of white marble, in circumference about that of the smallest threshing floor, while its height is just under two cubits. On this foundation stand spikes, which are of bronze, and so are the crossbars that hold them together; through them gates have been made. Inside the enclosure is a chasm in the earth, not a natural one, but skillfully constructed from a most accurate design. (10) The shape of this structure is like a bread oven. Its breadth across the middle one might guess to be about four cubits; its depth can hardly be estimated to extend to more than eight. They have made no way of descent to the bottom; but when a man gets to Trophonius, they bring him a narrow, light ladder. Going down [farther] he finds a hole between the floor and the structure. Its breadth appears to be two spans and its height one span. (11) The descender lies with his back on the ground, holding in his hands barley cakes kneaded with honey, and pushes his feet into the hole; himself following, he tries hard to get his knees into the hole. After his knees, the rest of his body is at once swiftly drawn in, just as the largest and swiftest of rivers will seize a man in its whirling and drag him down. It is after this that those who have entered the shrine learn the future, not always in one and the same way, but sometimes by sight and at other times by hearing. The return upward is the reverse of the descent, through the same mouth, the feet being pushed out first. (12) They say that no one who has made the descent has ever been killed, except one of Demetrius' bodyguards. But they say that he performed none of the required rites in the sanctuary and that he descended, not in order to consult the god, but hoping to steal gold and silver from the inner shrine. It is said that the body of this man appeared in a different place, and was not cast out at the sacred mouth. There are other tales about this fellow, but I have given the one most worthy of consideration. (13) After his ascent from Trophonius, the inquirer is again taken in hand by the priests, who seat him upon a chair called the Chair of Memory, which stands not far from the shrine, and they ask of him, when seated there, all he has seen or learned by his inquiry. After obtaining this information, they then turn him over to his relatives. These lift him up and carry him to the building where he formerly stayed with Fortune and the Good Spirit, though he is still paralyzed with terror and is wholly unconscious, both of himself and of his surroundings. Afterward, however, he will be no less able to think than formerly, and will even be able to laugh once more.

(14) What I write is not hearsay; I have not only seen other inquirers but I myself have inquired of Trophonius. Those who have descended into the shrine of Trophonius are required to dedicate a tablet on which is written all that each has heard or seen. The shield of Aristomenes is also still preserved here. That story I have already told, in an earlier part of this work [IV. 16. 7 ff.].

ON THE DECLINE OF ORACLES

Plutarch On the Failure of Oracles 10 (415a). *Briefly stated, Plutarch's theory is that the responses at the oracles were given by daemons, semi-divine beings whose supernatural knowledge enabled them to foretell the future, explore secrets, read the minds of men, unravel the processes of nature. But the daemons were not wholly divine, and hence were subject to mortality—in brief, they, like us, grow old. Hence the decline in the wisdom, accuracy, and even ability to hear of these great spirits. Just as for the early Christians, the world*

*was for Plutarch very old, and the daemons, who had begun
giving responses in early times, were now advanced in age.
See the whole work, with F. C. Babbitt's translation, in Vol.
V of the Loeb Classical Library edition of Plutarch's* Moralia.
See also Robert Flacelière, Plutarque: Sur la Disparition des
Oracles *(1947). For another theory of oracles (viz. dreams),
see Plato* Timaeus *71a–72b.*

"You are quite right," said Cleombrotus; "but since it is hard
to comprehend and to define in what way and to what extent
the idea of Providence must be brought in, those who make the
god responsible for nothing at all, and also those who make him
responsible for everything, both miss what is reasonable and
appropriate. They speak well who say that Plato, since he discovered the element that underlies all created qualities—what
we now call 'matter' and 'nature'—has relieved philosophers of
many and great difficulties. But it seems to me that those men
have resolved even more and greater problems who have set
the race of daemons halfway between gods and men, and so
have discovered a way to draw them together and unite them in
our common fellowship. [It makes no difference] whether this
doctrine comes from the Magi who followed Zoroaster, or
whether it is Thracian and goes back to Orpheus, or is Egyptian or Phrygian, as we may infer from observing that many
things in the rites connected with death and mourning are in
both lands combined in the ceremonies so fervently celebrated
there. Among the Greeks, moreover, Homer appears to use both
names indifferently, and sometimes speaks of the gods as daemons; but Hesiod was the first to set forth clearly and distinctly
the four classes of rational beings: gods, daemons, heroes, and
last of all men. It was on this basis, apparently, that he pos-
tulated the transmutation [which he describes], many of the
golden race becoming daemons, and many of the demi-gods
being chosen to become heroes.

"Others assume a transmutation of bodies and souls alike.
Just as water is seen to be derived from earth, air from water,
and fire from air, as a result of their substance being borne upward, so from men into heroes and from heroes into daemons the

better souls experience the transmutation. But from the daemons a few souls, in a long course of time, being cleansed by virtue, come to partake wholly in divinity. But some of these souls fail to maintain control over themselves, but yield to temptation, and so are clothed once more with mortal bodies and have a dark, dim life, like mist or vapor. Hesiod even thinks that after long periods of time the daemons themselves succumb." [From this the argument develops that the oracles, being the utterances of daemons, grow feeble and indistinct as the source of their inspiration becomes weak with advancing age.]

BELIEFS ABOUT THE DEAD AND THE OTHER WORLD

The belief in ghosts is probably older than history. Certainly the Hellenistic age had its quota of ghost stories—some of them amusing, some tragic, some terrifying. In addition to the passages here, see the fragment of Democritus' book *Concerning Those in Hades;* it is preserved in Stobaeus and is given in translation in E. Bevan, *Sibyls and Seers,* p. 53. See also the fragment of Heraclides Ponticus, which Bevan gives on pp. 54 f. The great passage in Pausanias' *Guide to Greece* X (Phocis, etc.). 28. 1—32. 1 is worth looking up; here Pausanias describes the famous eschatological painting by Polygnotus, which was to be seen at Delphi. It was one of two pictures that decorated the Lesche, or Common Room; the first depicted the fall of Troy and the departure of the victorious Greeks (X. 25. 1—27. 4); the other pictured Odysseus' descent to Hades, based upon Book XI of the *Odyssey.* The latter was looked upon throughout later antiquity as the classical portrayal of the orthodox eschatology, the great artistic commentary on the Homeric Nekyia. Compare with this passage not only *Odyssey* XI but also Virgil's "Vision of the Other World," in *Aeneid* VI. On beliefs about the dead held in later antiquity see especially Franz Cumont, *Lux Perpetua* (1949).

EUTHYNOOS

Plutarch Consolation Addressed to Apollonius *14. 109. Compare E. Bevan,* Sibyls and Seers, *pp. 92 ff.*

They tell the following story of the Italian [i.e., South Italian-Greek] Euthynoös. He was the son of a certain Elysius, a man of Terina, foremost of the citizens in virtue, wealth, and reputation. Euthynoös died very suddenly from some unknown cause. Then it occurred to Elysius, as it might have occurred to anyone under such circumstances, that perhaps his son had been poisoned; for Euthynoös was his only son, and heir to his vast property and wealth. Being perplexed as to how he might put the matter to a test, he visited a soul oracle [*psychomanteion*, a place where the spirits of the dead are conjured up]. Having first offered a sacrifice, according to the rule, he lay down to sleep and saw the following vision. He thought his own dead father had come to him; and so Elysius told him the misfortune that had happened to his son, and prayed and begged him to help him find out what had caused his son's death. "It is for this very purpose," replied the ghost, "that I have come; but take from the hand of my companion what he brings you; from that you will know the whole truth of the event over which you are sorrowing." The person he pointed to was a young man following him, who closely resembled Euthynoös, and was like him in both age and stature. "Who are you?" Elysius asked. And he replied, "I am your son's guardian spirit [daemon]," and with that he handed Elysius a little scroll. When Elysius had unrolled it he found written within it these three lines:

Of a truth the minds of men wander in ignorance;
Ethynoös died by a natural death, in accordance with destiny;
For it was not well that he should live, either for him or for
    his parents.

Such, you will observe, is the meaning unfolded by these tales told by ancient writers.

BATTLE OF THE SPIRITS ON THE CEMETERY HILL AT MARATHON

Pausanias Guide to Greece *I (Attica). 32. 3–4.*

There is a parish [*deme*] called Marathon equidistant from the city of Athens and from Carystus in Euboea. This was the point in Attica where the barbarians landed, were defeated in battle, and lost some of their ships when they withdrew. Here on the plain is the grave of the Athenians, and upon it are tablets giving the names of those who died, arranged by their tribes. There is also another grave for the Boeotian Plataeans and for the slaves; for then for the first time slaves fought [side by side with their masters]. There is also a private monument to one man, Miltiades, the son of Cimon, although he died later, after he had failed to take Paros and had therefore been brought to trial before the Athenians. Here [at Marathon] every night you can hear horses neighing and men fighting. No one who has purposely undertaken to see this vision has ever gained any good from it, but the spirits are not angry with those who innocently happen upon it. The Marathonians worship those who died in the battle, naming them heroes; and also Marathon, from whom the parish derives its name; and finally Heracles, saying that they were the first of the Greeks to recognize him as a god.

MAGIC, INCLUDING CURSES

The border line between religion and magic was often difficult to draw in the Hellenistic age, and especially, perhaps, in the Hellenistic-Roman age that followed. The step from the oath, which is a self-imprecation ("May such-and-such happen to me if it is not so or if I do not do so-and-so!") to a curse hung over the head of others is only a short one. The following passages illustrate the religious side of magic, though most magic is not religious at all and has no connection with religion. See M. P. Nilsson, *Geschichte der griechischen Religion*, Vol. II (1950), pp. 498 ff. See "Magic," in *Oxford Classical Dictionary* (1949), with bibliography.

THE MAGICAL PAPYRI

Karl Preisendanz, Papyri Graecae Magicae (Leipzig, 1928, 1931). The religious quality of these prayers and invocations is obvious. See M. P. Nilsson, Die Religion in den griechischen Zauberpapyri (Lund, 1949), reviewed in The Review of Religion, XIV (January 1950), 160–163; see also Kurt von Fritz, "Greek Prayers," in The Review of Religion, X (November 1945), 5–39.

Draw near to me, thou from the four winds, thou all-ruling God, who hast breathed into men the breath of life, Lord of the world's beauty. [XII. 237; also XIII. 762.]

Who hath fashioned the forms of [living] beings, who hath formed the paths? Who is the begetter of fruits, who hath fashioned the towering mountain heights? Who hath commanded the winds to continue at their yearly labors? Which Aion hath sustained the aion [age, *durée*] and ruleth over the aions? An immortal god; the begetter [creator] of all art thou, and impartest to all their souls, and rulest all, King and Lord of the aions [ages], before whom the hills and the plains tremble, and the waves of streams and rivers, the hollow places of the earth, and the daemons, even everything that exists; the shining heaven above trembles before thee, and every sea—O Lord, the holy and almighty one, the ruler of all. [XII. 245 ff.]

I invoke thee, the Eternal and Uncreated, thou who art One, who alone sustainest [or holdest together] the whole creation, whom no one knoweth, whom the gods adore, [but] whose name even the gods are unable to utter. [XIII. 842.]

I call upon thee, who encompassest all, in every voice and in every thought which has first praised thee, established by thee and by thee entrusted with all authority—Helios. [XIII. 138.]

Thee, the one and blessed among the aions and Father of the world, I invoke with cosmic prayers. [IV. 1169.]

I invoke thee, who art greater than all, who hast created all, thee the self-begotten, who seest all but art thyself unseen: thou hast given the sun its splendor and all its power; thou hast ordained that the moon should wax and wane and move in steady paths, and hast not diminished the former darkness, but hast given it equal measure. When thou appearest, the cosmos and the light appear. To thee all things are subject; thy true form none of the gods can behold. Thou who canst transform thyself into all things art the unseen Aion of aions. [XIII. 62; cf. XIII. 571.]

Open, open, ye four quarters of the cosmos, for the Lord of the world goeth forth. The archangels rejoice, [the rulers of] the decans, the angels; for he himself, the Aion of aions, the only and supreme [one] passes invisibly through the world. [XIII. 327.]

I call upon thee who hast created earth and bone and all flesh and spirit, and hast fixed the bounds of the sea and nailed fast the heaven, who hast separated light from darkness. Thou, great Spirit, who as guardian of law rulest all things; eternal Eye, Daemon of daemons, God of gods, Lord of spirits, unerring Aion, Iao—hearken to my cry! I call upon thee, Lord of the Gods, Zeus who thunderest in the heights, Zeus the Ruler, Adonai, Lord Iao. [V. 460.]

DEVOTION TO PUNISHMENT
BY DEMETER AND KORE

Dittenberger, Sylloge², 815, 812 f., (S³, 1180, 1178); Michel, Recueil, 1327. The lead tablets on which the following inscriptions were recorded were found in the temple of Cnidus.

I devote to Demeter and Kore the one who said of me that I was preparing a deadly poison for my husband. By [order of]

Demeter may he be sold [or burned] with what he possesses, confessing all, and may he find Demeter and Kore not easily reconciled [with him], nor the gods that are with Demeter. But let purity and freedom remain with me, rather than that I should ever dwell with him under one roof or in any way have dealings with him [?]. And I likewise curse the one who has written against me or has directed it. May he find Demeter and Kore and the gods that are with Demeter not easily reconciled, but may he and all that he possesses be burned up [consumed?] by [order of] Demeter.

I devote to Demeter and Kore and the gods with Demeter those who laid hands on me, beat me, and bound me, and also those who enticed me out. May they not escape, but let me be clean . . . [The rest is missing.]

Let him be devoted to Artemis, Demeter, Kore [and] all the gods that are with Demeter—whoever does not return to me the mantles, clothing, and [other] apparel I left behind, after I have asked for them. Let him be brought before Demeter, and if anyone else has anything of mine let him be burned [by fever? or perhaps "sold," i.e., into slavery], confessing it. But me—let me be pure and free, and drink and eat [with others], and dwell under the same roof. I have been treated unjustly, Lady Demeter!

MIRACLES, INCLUDING HEALING CULTS

Healing cults were commonly found throughout the ancient world. It is evident from their writings that philosophers as well as ordinary men recognized the validity of miracles. The great shrine of Asclepius continued to be popular for many centuries. That new methods of healing were expected to result in marvelous cures was as insistent a hope in ancient as in modern times. Great physicians were even expected, like the gods, to raise the dead.

Thessalus of Tralles, a contemporary of Saint Paul, visited temples in Egypt in order to find out more about the secrets of medicine. (See the interesting account of him by E. Bevan, in *Sibyls and Seers*, pp. 78 ff. Compare R. Reitzenstein, *Hellenistische Mysterienreligionen*, third edition, p. 128; A. D. Nock, *Conversion*, pp. 108 ff.) In his *Natural History* (XXVI. 7), Pliny describes the new methods of Asclepiades (ca. 40 B.C.) and the latter's raising of the dead (VII. 124). (See also Apuleius *Florida* 19.) The Emperor Vespasian was credited with miracles of healing, even with the "king's touch." (See Cassius Dio *Roman History* LXV. 8; Tacitus *Histories* IV. 81; Suetonius *Vespasian* 7.) Such a popular ascetic philosopher and liturgiologist as Apollonius of Tyana not only described exorcisms and instances of healing the blind, the lame, and the sick among the Indians (Philostratus *For Apollonius of Tyana* III. 38 f.) but was himself credited with performing similar miracles, and even with raising the dead (IV. 45). Even the skeptical Lucian told of incredible recoveries, like that of the vinedresser Midas who had been bitten by a serpent while at work in the vineyard and was brought back to life by a "Babylonian, one of the so-called Chaldeans," who drove out the poison by means of a spell and by fastening to his foot a piece of stone which he broke off the tomb of a dead maiden (*Philopseudes* 11).

On the general subject of miracles and healing cults, see M. P. Nilsson, *Geschichte der griechischen Religion*, Vol. II (1950), pp. 207–220. See also Otto Weinreich, *Antike Heilungswunder* (1909); *Gebet und Wunder*, from *Genethliakon Wilhelm Schmid* (1929). Paul Fiebig collected a group of ancient miracle stories in his *Antike Wundergeschichten, Kleine Texte* No. 79 (Bonn, 1911, reprinted 1921). J. Tambornino's *De Antiquorum Daemonismo* (Giessen, 1909) is a fascinating collection of texts. On the occultism, theosophy, and theurgy of the late Hellenistic and Hellenistic-Roman age, see M. P. Nilsson, *Greek Piety* (1948), Chs. VII-X; also Shirley Jackson Case, *Experience with the Supernatural in Early Christian Times* (1929), and *The Origins of Christian Supernaturalism* (1946); S. V. McCasland, *By the Finger of God* (1951).

THE NEOPLATONIC BELIEF IN MIRACLES

From Eunapius Lives of the Philosophers, *pp. 466 ff. Boissonade; K. Latte, Lesebuch, No. 43; edited and translated by W. C. Wright in Loeb Classical Library, pp. 400 ff. Eunapius lived in Sardis; he was born in 346 A.D. and died about 414.*

Thus the eloquent Eustathius married Sosipatra, who outshone her husband in wisdom and cast him in the shadow. So widely famous was this woman that I ought to speak of her at greater length, even in this catalogue of wise men. She was born in Asia, near Ephesus, where the river Cayster flows into and crosses a plain and gives its name to it. Her ancestors and her family were rich and well known; and while she was still a child everything she did seemed to prosper, such beauty and decorum brightened her tender years. She was just five years old when two old men, both of them past middle age and one of them considerably older, bearing huge knapsacks and clad in skins, arrived at one of the estates belonging to Sosipatra's parents. They induced the steward to entrust to them the cultivation of the vineyard, which they succeeded in caring for without any special labor. When the vineyard presently brought forth fruit in unexpected abundance—the owner was there at the time, and with him the child Sosipatra—it caused no end of astonishment, and a divine activity was suspected. The owner of the estate himself invited them [the two men] to dine with him and showed them great honor, and he found fault with the other cultivators of the estate for not doing equally well.

The old men, who were thus enjoying Hellenic hospitality and entertainment, were struck by the beauty and sprightliness of the child Sosipatra, and were simply captivated by her. So they said, "Our other secrets and skills we keep to ourselves; this much-lauded fruitfulness of the vineyard is only a pastime or jest, to which we assign no importance compared with other things we can do. If you wish us to make a really worthy return for your hospitality and entertainment, not with money or with any perishable benefits, but with something that is quite beyond you and your rank, a heavenly gift and one reaching the stars, then let us take charge of this Sosipatra, whose teachers or rather fathers we already are. For five years you need have no fears for the maiden, neither her death nor any disease, but rest content and have confidence. Only you must not visit the estate until, in the sun's course, the five years have elapsed. Wealth will come to you of itself from the estate, increasing and flourishing; and your daughter will be not merely like a woman or a man, but you will yourself discern in the child something more [than mortal]. If you trust us, take with open hands what we offer you; but if you entertain doubts, then we have said nothing." At this the father bit his tongue, and quickly took the child and delivered her to them; and he called the steward and gave him orders: "Supply the old gentlemen with whatever they ask, and do not try to pry into their affairs." Soon the gray dawn appeared, and he hurriedly left both his daughter and the estate. They took the child—they may have been heroes or daemons, or of an even more divine origin—and no one knew into what mysteries they initiated her or with what religious rites they consecrated her; this could not be ascertained, even by those most eager to find out.

At last the time came, and everything was fulfilled in regard to the produce, and the father came back to the farm. He did not know his child, she had grown so much, and her beauty seemed to him passing strange. She for her part hardly knew her father. He even greeted her with reverence, since he fully believed he was looking at someone else. When the teachers came in and they all sat at table, they said, "Ask the young lady any questions you wish." And she added, "Yes, Father, ask me what *you* have been doing on the way here." When he asked her to tell it—he had come, like a rich man, in a four-wheeled carriage, and that kind of a journey is often accompanied by accidents—she related the whole thing exactly, the cries and the dangers and the anxiety, just as if she had been with him in the carriage. Her father was so astonished that he not only marveled but was utterly amazed, and concluded that the maiden was a divine being. He threw himself down before the men and implored them to tell him who they were; finally they told him, reluctantly—as a god would—that they were initiated into the wisdom of the so-called Chaldeans; but even this they acknowledged enigmatically, while looking down at the ground. Then Sosipatra's father clung to their knees in supplication, begging them to become masters of the estate, and to keep his daughter with them and initiate her into still more sacred mysteries. They nodded their agreement to do so, but said not a word more. He then took courage, as if he had received [their] promise, or rather an oracle, though he could not fathom its meaning. And in his heart he praised Homer exultantly for having sung of such a supernatural and divine event:

> For the gods disguise themselves as strangers from abroad
> And assuming the most varied shapes wander through the
> cities. [Odyssey XVII. 485 f.]

For he certainly believed that he had fallen in with gods in the guise of strangers.

While he [the father] was thinking about all this, he was overcome by sleep, and the others left the table, taking Sosipatra with them. Then they very kindly and tenderly handed over to her the vestment in which she had been initiated and also some other vessels [symbols? *organa*], and bade Sosipatra seal up her chest, tossing into it some little books. And she was just as greatly pleased with these men as her father was. When day began to dawn and the courtyard gates were opened, and men began going to work, these [two men] likewise went out with the others, just as they usually did. Then Sosipatra ran to her father to bring him the good news, one of the servants carrying the chest. The father took all the money he happened to have with him, and took from the stewards all they had in the way of expense money, and sent to call the men. But they had disappeared! Then he asked Sosipatra, "What does this mean, my child?" After a moment's thought she replied, "Now at last I understand what they said. For when they handed me these things, weeping, they said to me, 'Take care of them, child, for we are journeying to the Western Ocean [the home of heroes], and soon we will return again.'" This is the clearest of proofs that those who thus manifested themselves were daemons. So they departed and went on their journey, wherever it was they were going. But Sosipatra's father took charge of the girl, who was now fully initiated and inspired with divinity, though she was still prudent and circumspect, and he let her live as she chose, never prying into her affairs, though he was sometimes vexed with her silence. [Further evidences of her gift of second sight are recorded in what follows.]

HEALINGS PERFORMED BY ASCLEPIUS IN DREAMS

Aelius Aristides Sacred Orations (Hieroi Logoi) *II. 30–36, 74–77 (Oration 48 Keil, Oration 24 Dindorf); W. Haussmann, ed.* Pantheion *(1948), pp. 48 ff. Compare K. Latte,* Lesebuch, *pp. 34 f. Aristides, one of the leading orators of the second century* A.D., *visited the sanctuary of Asclepius at Pergamum in search of healing. From then on his whole life was governed by Asclepius, who manifested himself in dreams. In gratitude to the god, Aristides published his* Sacred Orations, *some of which are written in the manner of a diary. The warm personal devotion of Aristides to Asclepius reminds us of other examples of personal religion. See also other passages from Aristides in E. J. and L. Edelstein's* Asclepius, *Vol. I.*

(30) One of the two ministers in the temple was named Philadelphus. He had the same dream that I had one night, with only the slightest variations. Philadelphus dreamed—at least I remember this much—that in the sacred theater were a number of men clad all in white who had come to visit the god. In their midst stood I, and delivered a panegyric in honor of the god [Asclepius], in which, among other things, I told how he had often intervened in my course of life. Only recently he had ordained that I should drink vermouth [wormwood] in thin vinegar, in order to be relieved of my complaint. He [Philadelphus] also told me of a sacred stairway, if I rightly remember, and of an epiphany of the god and his wondrous deeds.

(31) This is what Philadelphus dreamed. What happened to me was as follows: I dreamed that I stood in the entrance to the sanctuary, where also some other people were gathered, as at the time of the sacrifice for purification; they wore white garments and were otherwise festively garbed. Then I spoke about the god and named him, among other things, Distributor of Destiny, since he assigns to men their fate. The expression came to me out of my own personal experience. Then I told

about the potion of wormwood, which had somehow been revealed [to me]. The revelation was unquestionable, just as in a thousand other instances the epiphany of the god was felt with absolute certainty. (32) You have a sense of contact with him, and are aware of his arrival in a state of mind intermediate between sleep and waking; you try to look up and are afraid to, lest before you see him he shall have vanished; you sharpen your ears and listen, half in dream and half awake; your hair stands up, tears of joy roll down, a proud kind of modesty fills your breast. How can anyone really describe this experience in words? If one belongs to the initiated, he will know about it and recognize it.

(34) When morning came, following this vision, I called in the physician Theodotus, and when he came I told him about the dream. Its divine character astonished him, but he did not know what to do about it, since it was winter and my bodily weakness somewhat alarmed him; for I had already been in bed for months. (35) It seemed to us desirable to call in the sacristan Asklepiacus, in whose house I was then living; I was used to telling him most of my dreams. The sacristan came, but before we could say a word he began speaking [as follows]: "I have just come from my colleague"—he meant Philadelphus—"who had sent for me; for last night he had a wonderful dream, which had to do with you." And so Asklepiacus related what Philadelphus had dreamed; and Philadelphus himself, whom we called in, related the same things. Since the dreams agreed, we applied the remedy and I drank more of it than anyone had ever drunk before, and on the following day, at the god's direction, an equal quantity. The relief it brought me and the good it did me simply cannot be described. (36) . . . Many other things of the same kind took place both before this and afterward and showed [me] the same kind of help.

[Here follows an account of further cures, or at least temporary relief. Finally Aristides proceeds to describe the great climactic experience of his life at the shrine:]

(74) It was during the spring equinox, when in honor of the god people were accustomed to smear themselves with mud;

but I was unable to do so, unless he gave me some sign of command. So I hesitated, though I remember that it was a nice warm day. A few days later there came a storm; the north wind swept across the sky, thick black clouds gathered, and it was winter once more. Such was the weather when he now commanded me to smear myself with mud from the sacred spring and to wash there. I was surprised, since the ground and the air were so cold, to find myself eager to go to the spring and [to discover] that the water really helped to warm me. That was only the beginning of miracles! (75) The following night he ordered me again to smear myself with mud, in the same way, and then to run around the temple three times; the north wind was indescribably fierce, and the cold was increasing; one could not find a garment thick enough to protect him from it—it went right through and stabbed one in the side like a knife. (76) Some of my companions decided to help me by going along, though they were under no obligation to do so, and by performing [the same rite] with me. So I smeared myself and ran, and let the north wind thoroughly blow me about, and finally came to the spring and washed myself off. As for my two companions, one of them soon turned back, while another fell into convulsions and had to be hurriedly carried into a bath, and got warm again only with the greatest difficulty. The next day was a real spring day. (77) But when winter temperature returned, with frost and ice-cold wind, he [the god] bade me take mud and put it on me, then sit in the court of the sacred gymnasium and call upon Zeus, the highest and best of gods; and there were many persons who saw me do this. . . .

HEALINGS AND MIRACLES AT EPIDAURUS

Dittenberger, Sylloge² 802–803 (S³, 1168–1169); Insc. Gr. IV. 951–952; Michel, Recueil, 1069; Lietzmann, Kleine Texte, No. 79. For an account of the Asclepius sanctuaries, see Pausanias Guide to Greece II (Corinth) 11. 1—12. 1 (in which he describes the sanctuary at Titane) and 26. 1—28. 2 (in which he describes the sanctuary at Epidaurus). The ac-

count is the more interesting in that the votive tablets referred to have been rediscovered in modern times; some of them are given here. They throw considerable light on the popular religion of the time and on the age-old connection between religion and health. See R. Herzog, Die Wunderheilungen von Epidauros *(1931);* O. Weinreich, Antike Heilungswunder *(1909);* E. J. *and* L. Edelstein, Asclepius, 2 vols. *(Baltimore, 1945);* P. Kavvadia, To Hieron tou Asklepiou en Epidauroi kai he Therapeia ton Asthenon *(Athens, 1900).*

God!   *Good Fortune!*
Healings of Apollo and Asclepius

I. *Cleo was pregnant for five years.* When she had now been pregnant for five years, she turned for help to the god and slept in the holy of holies [*abaton*]. As soon as she came out again and had left the sacred precincts she bore a son, who, as soon as he was born, washed himself at the spring and walked around with his mother. Having found such favor, she inscribed upon the gift offering:

It is not the greatness of the tablet that is wonderful, but the god!
Cleo bore for five years the burden beneath her heart,
Until she slept here, and the god made her well.

III. *A man whose fingers, all but one, were paralyzed.* He came to the god looking for help, but when he read the tablets set up in the temple he gave no credence to the healings and made fun of the inscriptions. But as he slept, he had the following dream. It seemed to him that he was playing dice in the temple and was about to make a throw. The god appeared to him, and sprang upon his hand and stretched out his fingers. Then he got up and, still in his dream, the man clenched his fist and opened it, stretching out one finger after another. After he had stretched them all out, the god asked him if he still refused to believe what the inscriptions related, and he said "No." "Well then," answered the god, "since you formerly refused to believe what is not unbelievable, you shall henceforth be known as 'the Doubter.'" When it was day, he came out cured.

IV. *Ambrosia from Athens, who was blind in one eye.* She came to the god seeking help, but as she went about the temple she mocked at the many records of cures: "It is unbelievable and impossible that the lame and the blind can be made whole by merely dreaming!" But in her sleep she had a dream. It seemed to her that the god came up and promised to make her whole; only in return she must present a gift offering in the temple—a silver pig, in memory of her stupidity. After saying this he cut open her defective eye and poured in some drug. And when it was day, she went forth cured.

V. *A Dumb Boy.* He came to the sanctuary seeking to recover his voice. As he was presenting his first offering and performing the usual ceremony, the acolyte who bears the fire [for the sacrifice] to the god turned and said to the father of the boy, "Will you promise, if you get your wish, between now and the end of the year to bring the offering you owe as a fee for the healing?" At once the boy cried out, "I promise!" The father was greatly astonished, and told him to say it again. The boy said it again and was made whole from that moment.

VI. *Pandarus a Thessalian, who had branding marks on his forehead.* He slept [in the sanctuary] and had the following dream. It seemed to him as if the god bound up the brand marks with a bandage and commanded him to take it with him when he left the holy of holies and place it in the temple. When it was day, he went out and took the bandage off, and he saw that his face was free from the marks. In the temple he dedicated the bandage, which had the branding marks transferred to it from his forehead.

VII. *Echedorus received the branding marks of Pandarus in addition to his own.* This man had received money from Pandarus to present to the god here at Epidauros on his behalf, but he did not deliver it. In his sleep he had the following dream. He dreamt that the god came and stood over him and asked him if he had received certain money from Pandarus for an offering [?] to the temple. He replied that he had received nothing of the kind, but that if he would heal him he would set up a statue for him. Thereupon the god fastened upon him the bandage of Pandarus, which had covered the branding marks, and bade him take it off when he had left the holy of holies, wash his face at the spring, and then look in the water. When it was day, he came out of the holy of holies and took off the bandage. The bandage no longer bore the brand marks. Instead, as he looked in the water, he saw that his face was marked not only with his own stigmata but also with the letters which once had been on Pandarus' forehead.

VIII. *Euphanes, a boy of Epidaurus.* This one was suffering from stone, and slept in the temple. And it seemed to him as if the god stood by him and said, "What will you give me if I make you well?" He replied, "Ten dice." Then the god laughed and promised to relieve his sufferings. When it was day, he came out cured.

IX. *A man who was so blind that only the lids were left,* while the hollows of his eyes were completely empty, came seeking help from the god. Some of those who were present in the temple held forth on his stupidity in believing that he could ever see again, in spite of the fact that nothing was left of his eyes but only the empty sockets. But as he slept a vision came to him. He dreamed that the god prepared some drug, opened his eyelids, and poured it in. When day came, he came forth seeing with both eyes.

THE TESTIMONY OF M. JULIUS APELLAS

Dittenberger, Sylloge [2], *804 (S [3], 117); Insc. Gr. IV. 955. This inscription of the second century A.D. came from Epidaurus. Compare E. J. and L. Edelstein,* Asclepius *(1945), Vol. I, p. 248; Vol. II, Index, s.v.* Apellas.

In the priesthood of Publius Aelius Antiochus

I, Marcus Julius Apellas, from Idrias and Mylasa, was sent [for] by the god, since I was often ill and suffered from digestive upsets. On the journey, at Aegina, he commanded me not to lose my temper so much. When I entered the sanctuary, he commanded me to go about for two days with my head covered since it was raining; to eat bread and cheese, celery with lettuce; to bathe without an attendant; to run for exercise, to drink citron juice thinned with water; to rub myself after the bath beside the wall at [the place called] The Ears; then to take a walk on the upper balcony; to swing myself [in the gymnasium?]; to strew sand over myself; to walk about without shoes; to rub myself with wine before I entered the warm bath; to bathe [there] alone, and to give the bath steward a drachma; to present a joint offering to Asclepius, Epione, and the goddesses of Eleusis; and to drink milk with honey in it. One day I drank only milk, and he said to me, "Put honey in the milk, so that it can get through." When I besought the god to relieve me more quickly, I felt as if my whole body had been rubbed with salt and mustard, and that I had left the sanctuary at The Ears, while a boy went ahead of me with a smoking incense burner and the priest said to me, "You are healed, and now you must pay the honorarium." I did as I had seen [in the vision], and when I had rubbed myself with salt and mustard, it smarted, but not in the bath. This began within nine days after my arrival. He touched my right hand and also my [right] breast. On the following day, at the sacrifice, the flame rose up high and burned my hand, so that blisters formed; but in a short while the hand was well again. As I stayed longer, he said to me that I should apply anise and oil for a headache; but I had no headache. Then it happened that while I was studying I suffered a rush of blood to the head, and after applying the oil I was free from the headache. With cold water [I was to] gargle for inflammation of the uvula—I had already besought the god for relief—and likewise for inflammation of the tonsils. He also commanded me to write down this [prescription]. Restored and grateful, I took my journey homeward.

ASTROLOGY

The pseudo-science of the Hellenistic age produced—or imported, chiefly from Babylonia—a belief that was destined to rule men's minds for hundreds of years, down to the rise of modern science; and it is true that many persons still accept and practice the art of reading the stars. Vettius Valens gives a good exposition of the theory underlying the so-called science, and the little poem preserved by Stobaeus illustrates the psychological ramifications of the belief. For fuller accounts of the Babylonian or Chaldean system, see Diodorus Siculus, II. 29. 1—31. 9, and Censorinus, *De Die Natali*, 8 (quoted in Cochrane, *Christianity and Classical Culture*, p. 158). The religious element in astrology paved the way for solar monotheism, on which see Macrobius, *Saturnalia*, I. 17. 2–6, XXIII. 21–22; and Orphic *Fragments*, p. 238 Kern. The worship of Aion is discussed in Epiphanius *Panarion*, LI. 22, and in C. A. Lobeck, *Aglaophamus*, Vol. II, p. 1227, note z (also given in K. Holl's edition of Epiphanius, in *Griechische christliche Schriftsteller*, Vol. II, p. 286). See also A. Jacoby, *Die antiken Mysterienreligionen und das Christentum* (1910), pp. 42–44.

For Hellenistic astrology in general, see M. P. Nilsson, *Greek Piety* (1948), pp. 110–115; *Geschichte der griechischen Religion*, II (1950), pp. 256–267, 465–485; Hugo Gressmann, *Die hellenistische Gestirnreligion* (Leipzig, 1925). For Solar Monotheism, see Nilsson, *Geschichte der griechischen Religion*, Vol. II, pp. 486–497; W. Nestle, *Griechische Religiosität*, Vol. III, pp. 82–86; F. Cumont, *La théologie solaire* (1909).

THE BENEFITS OF ASTROLOGY

Vettius Valens, Anthologies V. 9. 2 (p. 219. 26 Kroll). Valens lived in the second century A.D. *Compare K. Latte, Lesebuch, pp. 32 ff.*

Fate has decreed as a law for each person the unalterable consequences of his horoscope, controlled by many causes of good and evil; and their results are watched over by two self-begotten deities who are her ministers, Hope [Elpis] and Chance [Tyche]; these rule over life, and by both deception and compulsion see to it that everyone obeys the law. The one [Hope] makes herself apparent to all through the results of what has been decreed in advance, now good and favorable, now dark and cruel. She raises up some, only to cast them down; and she flings down others into obscurity, only to raise them up in greater splendor. The other [Chance] is neither dark nor serene; she always goes about secretly in disguise and smiles at all like a flatterer, and points out various encouraging prospects, which however no one can attain. Thus deceiving them, she rules over the majority; and even though they have been fooled by her in their pursuit of enjoyment, still she always draws them back again; trustingly they believe [they will get] what they desire, and then they experience what they do not expect. And if once she has awakened a permanent expectation, suddenly she seems to be close to everyone, but she remains steadfast with none.

Whoever, then, is ignorant of foreknowledge [i.e., astrology] and is uninfluenced by it will accordingly be led into error and driven hither and yon by the afore-named goddesses; he suffers every mistreatment and suffers cheerfully. Some find a part of their expectations fulfilled, and so they put up higher stakes and keep on looking for a permanent and favorable outcome, without recognizing how easy it is for things to go wrong and how unprotected they are from change. But some whose expectations have gone all awry, not only for a while but permanently give themselves up soul and body to passion, dishonored and without any aim in life; or else they live without achieving anything, until they die as slaves of inconstant Chance and of deceitful Hope.

But whoever takes the trouble to learn about the future [i.e., the forecasts of astrology] and to know the truth will possess his soul in freedom from this servitude, disregarding Chance and assigning no importance to Hope, not fearing death and living without distraction, having disciplined his soul to courage, and neither rejoicing over good fortune nor depressed by misfortune, but giving himself contentedly to the present. Since he does not long for things beyond his reach, he bears what is decreed for him with self-discipline and, renouncing both pleasures and penalties, becomes a good soldier of Fate.

For it is impossible by means of prayer or sacrifice to overcome the destiny fixed from the beginning and create for oneself another in accordance with his own wishes. Whatever is in store for us takes place apart from any prayer of ours; whatever is not decreed for us will not take place even if we pray. Like players on the stage, who change their masks as the poet's drama requires and calmly take the parts, now of kings, now of robbers, now of peasants, common folk, or gods, so we too must don the masks and play as Fate requires of us, and accept the parts which time's conjunctions bring about, even when they do not suit us. If anyone refuses, "he does badly, but he must nevertheless submit" [quoting Cleanthes, Fragment 527, Arnim].

HUMAN FACULTIES (HUMORS) AND THE SEVEN PLANETS

Stobaeus Eclogae I. 5. 14 (p. 176 Heeren, I. 45 Meineke). The author of the following poem is unknown; Stobaeus attributes it to Hermes (Trismegistus). Compare K. Latte, Lesebuch, p. 33.

Seven wide-wandering stars across the Olympian threshold
Are rolled, where among them ageless Time [Aion] forever mingles:
Night-shining Mene, and gloomy Kronos, and the sweet Sun,
The bride-guiding Paphian, bold Ares, and well-winged Hermes,
And Zeus, best and noblest, from whom all nature is derived.
And they by lot have received a race articulate, for in us are
Mene, Zeus, Ares, Paphie, Kronos, Helios, Hermes;
Hence our lot, to draw into ourselves from the ether

Weeping and laughter and wrath, life, reason and sleep and
  desire.
Kronos gives us tears, Zeus gives us birth, Hermes gives
  understanding,
Ares sends wrath, Mene sends sleep, the Cytherean sends
  us desire.
Yet from the Sun comes laughter; for by the Sun all nature
  smiles,
And the mind of man, and even the boundless sum of
  things.

DIVINE HONORS PAID TO KINGS

One of the most striking features of the Hellenistic age was
the cultus paid to rulers, a feature of great political as well
as religious significance. In the Orient, kings had long been
looked upon as divine or inspired, as sons of God by adop-
tion if not by descent; and even in Homer they were described
as "Zeus-descended." Alexander made a great point of his
divine ancestry; and after conquering Egypt, and before his
final assault upon the Persian Empire, he had himself recognized as the son of Zeus-Amon. Only a divine ruler could
succeed to the reign of the "Great King." The Successors likewise claimed divinity, and applied divine titles to themselves
and to their children, such titles as Euergetes, Epiphanes, and
even Theos. In time the Romans took over the administration
of the East, and it was in this part of the world that Roman
emperor worship originated and found its chief support. (See
the chapters in Nilsson's Geschichte der griechischen Religion,
Vol. II, on "Religion in the Service of the Kings," pp. 125–
175, and on "Emperor Worship," pp. 366–376. A very full
bibliography will be found in the notes.)
  As early as the end of the fifth century, Lysander had
claimed divine honors (see Plutarch Lysander 18). He was the
Spartan general who defeated the Athenians at Aegospotami
in 405 B.C. and ended the Peloponnesian War the following
spring. Plutarch quotes Duris as saying: "He was the first
Greek to whom cities erected altars as to a god and offered
sacrifice; he was also the first to whom songs of triumph
[paeans] were sung." Plutarch then quotes four lines from one

of the songs. But the most striking example of ruler worship in early Hellenistic times is that of Demetrius Poliorcetes at Athens.

DIVINE HONORS PAID ANTIGONUS AND DEMETRIUS

Plutarch Demetrius *10–12. 4. Demetrius I of Macedonia was given the surname Poliorcetes, Sacker of Cities. He undertook to reunite Alexander's empire, but his genius was military rather than administrative, and his career ended in failure. When he liberated Athens in 307 B.C. he was hailed as Savior and Benefactor* (Soter *and* Euergetes). *See W. S. Ferguson,* Hellenistic Athens *(1911), pp. 63–65.*

Returning to Munychia [on the east side of Piraeus] and laying siege to it, he cut off the garrison and razed the fort; whereupon the Athenians were ready to receive him, and so at their invitation he entered the city, assembled the people, and gave back to them their ancestral form of government. He also promised them from his father [Antigonus I] one hundred and fifty thousand bushels of grain and enough suitable timber for shipbuilding to lay down a hundred triremes. It was now the fifteenth year since the Athenians had lost their democratic form of government, and in the meantime, following the Lamian War and the battle at Crannon, their government had been formally an oligarchy, but really a monarchy, owing to the power of [Demetrius] the Phalerean. And now that Demetrius [i.e., Poliorcetes] had shown himself to be a great man and magnificent in his benefactions, the Athenians proceeded to render him odious and obnoxious by the extravagance of the honors which they voted him. For they were the first people to give Demetrius and Antigonus the title of King, although both had up to that time piously avoided using the word, as the one royal honor still left to the lineal descendants of Philip and Alexander which it was thought no others could assume or share. Moreover, the Athenians were the only people to give them the title of Savior Gods; and they gave us the custom of designating the year by the name of the annual archon and elected each year a priest of the Savior Gods, whose name they now placed at the head of their decrees and contracts. They also decreed that the figures of Demetrius and Antigonus should be woven into the sacred robe [at the Panathenaic Festival], along with those of the gods; and they consecrated the spot where Demetrius first alighted from his chariot, and set up there an altar, which they named the altar of Demetrius the Alighter [*Kataibatos*]. They also created two new tribes, Demetrias and Antigonis; and they increased the membership of the Council, which had been five hundred, to six hundred, as each of the tribes provided fifty councilors.

(11) But the most monstrous notion that entered the head of Stratocles (for it was he who devised these ingenious and extravagant flatteries) was his proposal that envoys who were sent by public decree and at public expense to Antigonus or Demetrius should be called sacred deputies [*theōroi*], rather than ambassadors, like those who conducted to Delphi and Olympia the customary national sacrifices on behalf of the cities at the Hellenic festivals. In other ways as well Stratocles was a reckless fellow; he lived a licentious kind of life, and was thought to imitate the base flattery and utter want of shame that had characterized old Cleon in his familiarity with the people. He had a mistress named Phylacion; and one day when she had bought at the market some brains and neck bones for his supper, he said, "So—you've bought the very things we politicians play ball with!" Another time, when the Athenians suffered their naval disaster near Amorgus [in 322 B.C.], before the news of the defeat could reach the city he [hastily returned], placed a garland on his head, and drove through the Ceramicus; and after announcing that the Athenians had been victorious presented a motion that a sacrifice of [thanksgiving for] good tidings should be offered and also that a generous distribution of meat should be made to the people by tribes. Presently, when the wrecks were coming in from the battle and the people angrily called for him, he coolly faced the mob and said, "What terrible thing have I done, please tell me, if I let you be happy

for a couple of days?" Such was the bold effrontery of Stratocles. (12) But there are some things hotter than fire, as Aristophanes says. For somebody else, trying to outdo Stratocles in servility, proposed that whenever Demetrius visited the city he should be received with the welcoming honors which were paid to Demeter and Dionysus; and that whoever surpassed everyone else in the splendor and expensiveness of his reception, to him should be granted a sum of money from the public treasury for a sacred offering. Finally, they changed the name of the month Munychion to Demetrion and the name of the last day of every month, the Old and New, to Demetrias, and the festival called Dionysia they renamed Demetria. Most of these changes were marked with the divine displeasure. The sacred robe, for instance, into which they had decreed that the figures of Demetrius and Antigonus should be woven, along with those of Zeus and Athena, as it was being carried in procession through the Ceramicus was torn by a violent wind which struck it. All around the altars [of these new Savior Gods] the soil produced an abundance of hemlock, a plant which grew in no other part of the country. And when the day came for the celebration of the Dionysia, the sacred procession had to be omitted because of the severe and unseasonable cold. A heavy frost followed, which not only froze all the vines and fig trees, but also destroyed most of the grain in the blade. For this reason Philippides, who was Stratocles' enemy, attacked him in a comedy with the following verses:

It was through him the hoarfrost blasted all your vines,
Through his impiety Athena's robe was rent in twain—
The gods' own honors he has given unto men.
That is what wrecks a nation, not its plays!

HYMN TO DEMETRIUS POLIORCETES

From Athenaeus Deipnosophists VI. 63. 253 d-f. The following hymn to Demetrius, the so-called liberator of Athens in 307 B.C., has been preserved in this work of Athenaeus (The Scholars at Dinner), written about 200 A.D.; it was quoted by him from Duris of Samos (ca. 340–260 B.C.). Demetrius apparently arrived in September, the month of the Eleusinian mysteries. "The Aetolian" refers to the Aetolian League, which threatened Athens.

Now the greatest and dearest of the gods have come to our
    city!
For hither the propitious hour [*kairos*] has brought both
    Demeter and Demetrius:
She comes to celebrate the solemn mysteries of the Daughter,
But he, as is right worthy of the god, has come with glad-
    ness, fair and smiling.
How reverend he appears; his friends all gathered about him,
    with himself in their very midst,
His friends how like the stars, himself the sun!
O offspring of the mightiest of gods, Poseidon, and of
    Aphrodite, hail!
The other gods are either far away or have no ears,
Or are not, or pay no slightest heed to us; but thee we see
    face to face,
Not in wood and not in stone, but verily and in truth!
And so we pray to thee:
First bring us peace, thou dearest [of the gods]! For thou art
    Lord [i.e., it is within thy power].
That dread Sphinx which crushes not only Thebes but all
    of Hellas [restrain],
The Aetolian who sits upon his cliff, even as sat the Sphinx
    of old,
Snatching up and carrying off all our men—and against it I
    cannot fight.
For it is the Aetolian way to carry off their neighbors' things,
    and now things even more distant.
Best were it for thyself to punish him; but if not, then find
    some Oedipus
Who will either dash him down the cliff or turn him into
    stone!

DIVINE TITLES OF PTOLEMY V EPIPHANES

Dittenberger, OGIS, 90. This inscription, dated 196 B.C., is the famous Rosetta Stone which provided the key to the ancient Egyptian hieroglyphics. See Gilbert Murray, Five

Stages of Greek Religion, *pp. 187–192; Paul Wendland,*
Hellenistisch-römische Kultur (1912), pp. 123–127; E. Bevan,
A History of Egypt under the Ptolemaic Dynasty (1927), pp.
262–268.

In the reign of the young king, who has received the kingdom from his father, who was Lord of the [ten] diadems, great
in glory, the stabilizer of Egypt, and also pious in matters relating to the gods, superior to his adversaries, rectifier of the
life of men, Lord of the thirty-year [festival] periods like Hephaestus the Great, King like the Sun, the Great King of the
Upper and Lower Lands [i.e., of Egypt], offspring of the Parent-
loving Gods [Ptolemy IV Philopator and Arsinoë III], whom Hephaestus has approved, to whom the Sun has given victory, living image of Zeus, Son of the Sun, Ptolemy the ever-living,
beloved by Ptah;

In the ninth year, when Aëtus, son of Aëtus, was priest of
Alexander and of the Savior Gods and the Brother Gods and
the Benefactor Gods and the Parent-loving Gods and the God
Manifest and Gracious; Pyrrha, the daughter of Philinus, being
athlophorus for [the deified Queen] Berenice Euergetis; Areia,
the daughter of Diogenes, being *canephorus* for [the deified
Queen] Arsinoë Philadelphus; Irene, the daughter of Ptolemy,
being priestess of [the deified Queen] Arsinoë Philopator: on
the fourth of the month Xandicus, or according to the Egyptians the eighteenth of Mecheir.

THE DECREE: The high priests and prophets, and those who
enter the inner shrine in order to robe the gods, and those who
wear the hawk's wing, and the sacred scribes, and all the other
priests who have assembled at Memphis before the king, from
the various temples throughout the country, for the feast of his
receiving the kingdom [i.e., his coronation], even that of Ptolemy
the ever-living, beloved by Ptah, the God Manifest and Gracious, which he received from his Father, being assembled in
the temple in Memphis this day, declared:

Since King Ptolemy, the ever-living, beloved by Ptah, the God
Manifest and Gracious, the Son of King Ptolemy and Queen

Arsinoë, the Parent-loving Gods, has done many benefactions to the temples and to those who dwell in them and also to all those subject to his rule, being from the beginning a god born of a god and a goddess—like Horus, the son of Isis and Osiris, who came to the help of his Father Osiris—[and] being benevolently disposed toward the gods, has consecrated to the temples revenues both of silver and of grain, and has generously undergone many expenses in order to lead Egypt to prosperity and to establish the temples. . . . the gods have rewarded him with health, victory, power, and all other good things, his sovereignty to continue to him and his children forever.

II. THE CRITICISM OF
TRADITIONAL RELIGION

The criticism of traditional religion probably began before the time of the Sophists, but they were the ones who carried it to the farthest extreme. Their views were characteristic of the tragic *fin de siècle* that followed the conclusion of the Peloponnesian War in 404 B.C. Criticism did not end with the Sophists, however; it continued throughout the rest of antiquity, as long as the traditional religion, with its rites and ceremonies, its myths and sacred legends, continued to be observed and taught. Valiant efforts were made by Stoics, Eclectics, Neoplatonists, and other philosophers to give a morally and spiritually satisfying explanation of the cults and myths, but without much success. The final conclusion of many persons was the "suspense of judgment" advocated by Empiricus.

In addition to the passages given below, see also Pausanias' criticism of the ancient legend of Lycaon (*Guide to Greece* VIII. 2. 1–7) and that of Delphi (X. 5. 5—6. 7), and also of misleading oracles (VIII. 11. 10–12). Heraclitus' criticism of religion is given in Fragment 5 (Diels); see also Xenophanes, Fragments 11, 14, 15, 16, 23. Diopeithes' proposal against those who have denied the gods is given in Plutarch's *Life of Pericles,* 32. The utilitarian explanation of the origin of religion offered by Prodicus is in Sextus Empiricus *Adversus Mathematicos* IX. 18 (or *Adversus Physicos* I. 18); see also §§ 50–194. Cicero gives some anecdotes of the atheist Diagoras in his work *On the Nature of the Gods* III. 89, and recounts the eight gods of Xenocrates in I. 34. Finally, see the criticism of the theory of the sacred disease in the treatise under that title, "On the Sacred Disease," in the Hippocratean medical corpus (in Volume II of the Loeb Classical Library edition). On the general subject, see Paul Decharme, *La Critique des Traditions religieuses chez les Grecs des Origines au Temps de Plutarque* (1904).

THE SUPERSTITIOUS MAN

Theophrastus Characters *XVI. Theophrastus (ca.* 370–288 B.C.) *was Aristotle's successor as head of the philosophical school he had founded, and was very successful. It is said that two thousand students attended his lectures. His* Characters *is a collection of thirty sketches of various human types. The Greek term for "superstition" is "deisidaimonia."*

Superstitiousness, it is scarcely necessary to say, seems to be a kind of cowardice in relation to the divine. The superstitious man is one who will not set out for the day before he has washed his hands and sprinkled himself at three springs, and put in his mouth a little bayleaf gathered near a temple. And if a cat runs across his path, he will not go any farther until someone else has gone by or he has cast three stones across the street. And should he see a snake in his house, if it is reddish-brown, he will call upon Sabazius; if one of the sacred variety, he will build a shrine right there and then. Whenever he passes one of the shiny stones set up at the crossroads, he anoints it with oil from his flask, and kneels down and worships it before he goes on. If a mouse gnaws into a bag of barley meal, off he goes to the wizard [*exegete*] to ask what must be done; and if he tells him, "Send it to the harnessmaker's to be patched," he pays no attention but frees himself of the evil by rites of aversion. He is continually purifying his house on the plea that dread Hecate has been drawn thither. If owls hoot when he is taking a walk, he is much disturbed and goes along saying, "Athena defend me!" He will never set foot on a tomb, nor come near a corpse or a woman in childbed; he says he must keep himself unpolluted. On the fourth and seventh days of the month he has wine mulled for the household and goes out to buy myrtle boughs, frankincense, and holy pictures; and when he returns he spends the whole day offering sacrifice to the Hermaphrodites and putting garlands about them. Whenever he sees anything in his sleep, off he goes to the diviners or the soothsayers or the interpreters of dreams, to ask which of the gods or goddesses he should appeal to. And when he is about to be initiated into the mysteries of Orpheus, he visits the priests month by month, taking his wife with him; or, if she has not the time, then the nurse and the children. He seems to be one of those who are forever going to the seashore to cleanse themselves; and if he ever catches sight of one of those figures of Hecate at the crossroads wreathed with garlic, home he goes to wash his head and summon priestesses, whom he has purify him by marching around him with a squill or a puppy. And if he ever sees a madman or an epileptic, he shudders and spits in his bosom.

THE ORIGIN OF RELIGION

Aristotle (Fragment 10 Rose) quoted in Sextus Empiricus, Adversus Dogmaticos III. 20–22 (or Adv. Physicos I. 20–22). With Aristotle's view compare the oft-quoted saying of Immanuel Kant; on the other hand, contrast it with the skeptical view of Critias in the surviving fragment of his tragedy, Sisyphus (Fragment 25 Diels, or Nilsson, Lesebuch, No. 143). See also the allegorical and scientific explanation of the gods given by Theagenes of Rhegium on the battle of the gods in Iliad XX (scholion to line 67, Fragment 2 Diels or Nilsson, Lesebuch, No. 144).

And Aristotle said that the conception of the gods arose among mankind from two sources, namely, from events which affect the soul and from the phenomena of the heavens. (1) It arose from events which affect the soul because of the things that occur in sleep, viz., its inspirations and its prophecies. For when, he says, the soul is alone in sleep, then it takes its real nature, and prophesies and predicts things to come. It is also in this same state when it is being separated from bodies [i.e., the body] at death. He certainly agrees with the observation of the poet Homer, for Homer told how the dying Patroclus predicted the slaying of Hector and how Hector foretold the end of Achilles [Iliad XVI. 850 ff.; XXII. 358 ff.]. For these reasons, then, he says, men came to suspect the existence of something divine, in itself like the soul and of all things the most intelligent. (2) But they also derived this conception from the phenomena of the heavens, for when they saw the sun circling about [the celestial poles] in the daytime and at night observed the orderly motion of the other stars, they assumed that some god was the cause of such motion and order.

ON THE ORIGIN OF THE GODS

Euhemerus, Sacred History VI. About 300 b.c. Euhemerus of Messene wrote this book in which he pictures a political utopia (see Diodorus III. 56–61, V. 41–46) and also sets forth his famous explanation of the origin of the gods. The following is all that remains of Book VI, as quoted by various authors, Eusebius, John Malalas, Eustathius, Tertullian, and others. Modern editors have cleverly put these fragments together, and the result is a restoration of what Diodorus borrowed from Euhemerus in Book VI of his Library of History; he has also used him elsewhere. In the first fragment, Eusebius is quoting Diodorus, who had himself quoted Euhemerus "word for word." On Picus, see the note in M. P. Nilsson, The Minoan-Mycenaean Religion and Its Survival in Greek Religion, p. 483 (1950 edition, pp. 554 f.).

Regarding the gods, the ancients have handed down to later generations two different ideas. They say that some of them are eternal and incorruptible, such as the sun and moon and other stars in the heavens, and also the winds and other things of similar nature, for each of these has an eternal generation and duration; but others, they say, are earthly beings who became gods, having received honor and glory because of their benefactions to mankind, and such are Heracles, Dionysus, Aristaeus, and the others who are like them. Concerning these terrestrial gods, many and various are the accounts (*logoi*) handed down by historians and mythographers. Among the historians Euhemerus, the author of *The Sacred History,* has devoted special attention to them; among the mythologists Homer and Hesiod and Orpheus and others of their ilk have fabricated the most marvel-laden myths about the gods. But we will endeavor to run over briefly the views of both groups of writers, while trying to observe a proper proportion in our analysis.

Euhemerus, who was a friend of King Cassander [of Macedonia, ca. 301–297 B.C.], and was required by him to perform certain matters of state and to make distant journeys, is said to have traveled southward as far as the ocean. For he set sail from Arabia Felix and voyaged many days across the ocean, and came upon islands in the open sea, one of which was called Panchaea. Here he saw how their inhabitants, the Panchaeans, excel in piety, and honor the gods with most magnificent sacrifices and praiseworthy votive offerings of silver and gold. The island is sacred to the gods. Besides this are many other marvelous things, remarkable for their antiquity and for the technical skill required in their construction; about these we have already said something in the preceding books [e.g., V. 41–46]. There is also a majestic sanctuary of Zeus Triphylius [i.e., of the three tribes], located upon a great hill; it was established by him while he was king of the whole inhabited earth and was still a man among men. In this temple there is a gold stele, on which is inscribed, in Panchaean characters, a summary of the deeds of Uranus, Kronos, and Zeus.

After this [Euhemerus] says that Uranus was the first king, a gentle and benevolent man, familiar with the movements of the stars; he was the first to honor the heavenly gods with sacrifices, and that is why he is called Uranus, or Heaven. By his wife Hestia he had two sons, Titan and Kronos, and two daughters, Rhea and Demeter. Kronos succeeded Uranus as king and, marrying Rhea, became the father of Zeus, Hera, and Poseidon. When Zeus succeeded to the kingship, he married Hera, Demeter, and Themis; his children by the first were the Curetes, by the second Persephone, by the third Athena. Journeying to Babylon, he was the guest of Belus and afterward visited the island of Panchaea, lying in the ocean, where he erected an altar to his own ancestor, Uranus. Returning thence by way of Syria, he visited Casius, then its ruler, for whom

Mount Casius is named. Arriving in Cilicia, he conquered the toparch Cilix in battle and then visited many other nations, being honored by them all and publicly acknowledged as a god. . . .

Ninus' brother, Picus, who was also called Zeus, ruled over Italy, being sovereign of the West for a hundred and twenty years. He had many sons and daughters by the most beautiful women, for he produced [in them] various mystical fantasies and then took advantage of them. These very women took him for a god, though they were corrupted by him. This same Picus, who is also Zeus, had a son named Faunus; he also called him Hermes after the wandering star [i.e., the planet Mercury]. And when Zeus was about to die, he ordered that his remains should be buried on the island of Crete; there his sons built a temple and buried him. The tomb still exists and bears this inscription: "Here lies Picus, who is also called Zeus." . . .

As tradition relates, Castor and Polydeuces, i.e., the Dioscuri, were far superior to all other men in valor and performed the most brilliant exploits in the expedition on which they accompanied the Argonauts. Moreover, they have been the helpers of many persons in distress. Generally speaking, by their courage and their military skill, and above all by their virtue and their piety, they have come to be honored by almost all of mankind, since they manifest themselves as helpers to those who find themselves in unexpected dangers. And it is because of their exceptional character that they are deemed to be sons of Zeus and, having departed from among men, to have achieved everlasting honors.

THE EXPLANATION OF THE MYTH OF CERBERUS

Pausanias Guide to Greece III (*Laconia*) 25. 4–6. *This explanation is in the Euhemerist tradition. (See the preceding selection.)*

The cape of Taenarum juts out into the sea one hundred and fifty stades [nearly twenty miles] from Teuthrone, and has two harbors, Achilleius and Psamathus. On the cape is a temple like a cave, with a statute of Poseidon standing before it. Some of the Greek poets say that here is where Heracles brought up the hound of Hades, though there is no underground road leading through the cave; nor is one prepared to believe that the gods possess some subterranean dwelling where the souls are gathered. But Hecataeus of Miletus found a plausible explanation, saying that a dreadful serpent once lived on Taenarum and was called the hound of Hades, since anyone bitten by it was sure to die at once of its poison; and it was this snake, he said, that was brought by Heracles to Eurystheus. But Homer, who was the first to call the creature brought by Heracles the hound of Hades [*Iliad* VIII. 368 ff.], did not give it any name or describe its form, as he did the Chimaera. But later poets invented the name Cerberus; and though in other ways they made him resemble a dog, they said that he had three heads. But Homer certainly no more implies that he was a dog, the friend of man, than that he was a serpent, when he calls him the hound of Hades.

CRITICISM OF THE RULE OF THE GODS

Cercidas in Oxyrhynchus Papyri *Vol. VIII, No. 1082. Compare H. von Arnim, Wiener Studien, No. 34 (1912.) Cercidas was a Cynic philosopher and poet in Megalopolis, about 250 B.C. Only a few lines of his poetry survive. The Oxyrhynchus fragment quoted here is of the second century.*

Why does she [Tyche, the Goddess of Luck] not reduce the . . . intemperate Xenon to a beggar's staff and give us his gold for our necessities? He only squanders it uselessly! And what is there to prevent—if any [of the gods] cared to do anything about it, since it is easy for a god to bring to pass whatever he will as soon as it enters his mind—[taking] either the vile, cunning usurer and the wretched miser, or on the other hand the wastrel who throws his wealth away, and stripping him of his filthy money and giving it to the man who eats his simple meal with healthy appetite and, in fellowship with others, tilts the flowing bowl with lavish hand at slight expense?

Or is the eye of Dike [Justice] blind like a mole's? And does Phaëthon see badly with his single eye? And is the vision of impartial Themis distorted? How can they be looked upon as gods if they possess neither sight nor hearing?

Yes, even the exalted Zeus, who hurls the lightning and sits enthroned in the midst of Olympus, [merely] holds the scales in even balance and does not himself render any decision [of his own accord]. When the day of destiny arrives, says Homer in the *Iliad,* the scale sinks down even for brave men.

How does it happen then that, if it is accurate, the balance never tips in my favor, or to far-off Phrygia, among the Mysians? The truth is, I hesitate to tell how unjust is the scale of Zeus in dealing with them!

To what kind of rulers or to which of the sons of heaven can one turn in order to get what is coming to him, when the son of Kronos, who begat us all and created all things, treats one like a stepfather and another like a real father?

It is better to leave the answer to such questions as these to the stargazers; they can handle them easily enough! For our part we will concern ourselves with Paean and kindly Metados, for she is a goddess and the nemesis [i.e., the right divider] upon earth.

As long as the daemon blows you a favoring breeze, honor this goddess, you for whom life is easy! [Then, when the wind shifts around in another direction, you will be compelled to spit out all this wealth and all these gifts of Fortune, even to the tiniest crumb. (The closing lines are very fragmentary, and their reconstruction is guesswork.)]

THEOLOGICAL REINTERPRETATION
OF THE MYTHS

Cornutus Summary of Greek Theology *§19 (33. 14 Lang). Cornutus was a Roman Stoic of the first century* A.D. *The allegorical explanation of the myths was characteristic of Stoicism, though not peculiar to this philosophy. For the Neopla-*

tonic explanation of myths, see below, Sallustius, Concerning the Gods and the Universe. *For a theological explanation of rites, see below, Plutarch,* On Isis and Osiris.

The ether and the pure translucent fire is Zeus; that [fire] which is in common use, mixed with air, is Hephaistos, named from "enkindle" (*hephthai*); so it is said that he is the offspring of Zeus and Hera, or of Hera alone. For the flames, which rise from thicker matter, draw their substance almost exclusively from the warm air. It is said that he is lame, probably because his course through matter is a difficult one, like that of one who limps; probably also because he can make his way only with the help of something wooden—with a staff, so to speak. Some think that he limps because his way upward does not take as long as his way downward, when he leans backward. He was flung out of heaven and down to earth by Zeus, because the first men to make use of fire discovered it after a stroke of lightning, since they had not yet arrived at the use of fire-kindling apparatus. Aphrodite is described as his wife in the same sense as one of the Graces. For just as we speak of "charm" being in works of art, so we also say that beauty "belongs to" them. It is also possible that this [feature in the myth] is due to the fact that the fiery element plays a great part in the endeavor to achieve sexual union. The myth relates that he bound Ares when he seduced his wife—the story is found in Homer; it is extremely old—since by the power of fire even iron and brass are conquered. The invention of the [story of their] adultery is due to the fact that the military and masterful [temperament] and the gay and affectionate do not match very well and do not ordinarily come together, but when they do they produce a beautiful and noble child [Harmonia], the "harmony" of the two. Hephaistos is also said to have delivered Zeus, when he bare Athena and she sprang out of his head, since he [Hephaistos] split it open. For fire, of which the arts make use, helps men to reveal their inborn cleverness and, so to speak, brings what is hidden out into the light; so we say of those who make some new discovery that they first "conceive" it and then "bring it to birth."

ON ISIS AND OSIRIS

Plutarch Concerning Isis and Osiris. *This essay is a capital example of the study of an influential foreign religion (a "mystery" religion) by the most learned Greek of his generation. It is addressed to Clea, a priestess of Isis at Delphi (where Plutarch was also a priest), to whom Plutarch had dedicated his* Bravery of Women *(Moralia 242e–263c). In spite of certain repetitions and inconsistencies, it contains some of the author's profoundest observations on religion and is a classical expression of the growing syncretism of the early Empire. Before modern archeology deciphered the Egyptian hieroglyphs, this essay was one of the chief sources for knowledge of Egyptian religion; it still contains much information— e.g., about the myth of Osiris—which has to be fitted together piecemeal in other sources. The religion of Isis, and especially that of Osiris (under the form of Sarapis), was widely influential throughout the Graeco-Roman world, and probably appealed far more strongly to intellectuals and esthetes than did the savage rites of Attis or the military cultus of Mithras. To countless men and women this dual cultus (of Isis and Osiris) brought a sense of freedom and release from the burdens of human mortality and personal transgression.*

The latest edition of the text of Plutarch's essay is that of W. Sieveking in the new Teubner series, Moralia, *II. 3 (1932). A valuable annotated translation is that of Mario Meunier (Paris, 1924); see also the translation in the Loeb Classical Library. Léon Parmentier's* Recherches sur le Traité d'Isis et d'Osiris de Plutarque *(1913) is an interesting collection of notes on selected passages, chiefly etymological. See also Guy Soury,* La Démonologie de Plutarque *(1942); John Oakesmith,* The Religion of Plutarch *(1902); Moses Hadas, "The Religion of Plutarch,"* The Review of Religion, *VI (1942), 270– 282.*

[In the introductory sections (1–3) Plutarch insists that the intelligent person must ask the gods for all the knowledge he can obtain, especially for knowledge about the gods themselves. He insists also that the gods are superior to men by virtue of their knowledge, a view decidedly at variance with the traditional one, which stressed their immortality as the distinguishing mark. The very name of Isis suggests her true nature; this is the first step toward knowledge.]

(1) All things good, O Clea, intelligent persons should ask from the gods. And especially now that we are seeking a knowledge of themselves, as far as such knowledge is attainable by men, we pray to obtain it from them with their own consent. For there is nothing more important for a man to receive, or more noble for a god to grant, than the truth. For of all other things God grants what people require, but of mind and intelligence he grants only a portion, since these are his own special possessions, kept for his own use. For the Deity is not blessed by reason of his possessing silver and gold, nor is he almighty because of his thunders and lightnings, but by his knowledge and intelligence. And this is the finest thing that Homer ever said about the gods:

Both have one lineage, and both the same homeland;
But Zeus was the firstborn, and his knowledge is greater.
[*Iliad XIII* 354 f.]

He thus declares the sovereignty of Zeus to be superior [to that of Poseidon] because of his knowledge and wisdom, since he was the elder. And I also believe that the happiness of the eternal life which belongs to God consists in the fact that events do not escape his [fore]knowledge; for if the knowledge and understanding of events were taken away, then immortality would be not life but mere duration.

(2) For this reason a desire for the truth, especially about the gods, is in reality a yearning for the Deity. For the study and the search is a reception, as it were, of things sacred—an occupation more pious than any practice of abstinence or service in a temple, but particularly well pleasing to this goddess whom you worship; for she is both exceedingly wise and a lover of wisdom, inasmuch as her very name appears to indicate that, more than any other, knowledge and understanding belong to her. For *Isis* is a Greek word, and so is *Typhon,* her enemy; for he is "puffed up" by ignorance and deceitfulness; he tears in pieces and buries out of sight the sacred word which the goddess again gathers up and puts together, and gives into the care of those who are initiated; for by means of a continually

sober life, by abstinence from many kinds of food and from the desires of the flesh, she checks intemperance and the love of pleasure, and accustoms people to endure the hardship of service in her shrines, the object of which is the knowledge of the First, the Lord, and the Intelligible. Him the goddess exhorts you to seek after, for he is with her and at her side, and is united with her. The very name of her temple clearly promises both the communication and the understanding of Reality, for it is called the Iseion, inasmuch as Reality will be understood if we enter with a reasonable and devout mind into the sacred rites of the goddess.

[Plutarch next describes her cultus at Hermoupolis, and gives the meaning of the vestments worn and the food regulations in force at her shrines. Wine and fish are forbidden (6–7), onions and pork, the reason being that the ancient Egyptians lived very simply (8). The Egyptian kings were chosen either from the military class or from the priesthood (9), and the truths of the philosophy were veiled in symbols. The wisest of the Greeks (10) have testified to the profound wisdom of the Egyptians; their myths of the gods and their strange statues are therefore to be understood symbolically (11). Then follows an account of the cult myth:]

(12) The myth will now be told as briefly as possible, omitting everything unnecessary and superfluous. They say that the Sun, having discovered Rhea's intercourse with Kronos, laid a curse upon her, that she should not bring forth a child in any month or year; that Hermes, being in love with the goddess, consorted with her, and that afterward, playing checkers with the Moon and winning from her the seventieth part of each of her periods of light, he put these together and made five days, which he added to the three hundred and sixty [days of the year]—these days the Egyptians now call "additional," and celebrate them as the birthdays of the gods; that on the first of these days Osiris was born, and that as he was being born a voice came forth saying, "The Lord of All is entering into light." But some say that a certain Pamyles, when drawing water at Thebes, heard a voice coming out of the temple of Zeus, ordering him to proclaim with a loud cry, "A great king, Beneficent

Osiris, is born"; and for this reason Kronos placed the child in his care, and so he brought up Osiris. Accordingly, the festival Pamylia is celebrated in his honor, one that resembles the phallic processions. On the second of these days Arueris was born, whom some call Apollo, some the elder Horus. On the third, Typhon was born, neither in due time nor in the right place, but by breaking through with a blow and leaping out of his mother's side. On the fourth day Isis was born, in the regions that are always moist. On the fifth day Nephthys was born, whom they call the End and Venus, and some even call Victory. They say that Osiris and Arueris were begotten by the Sun, Isis by Hermes, Typhon and Nephthys by Kronos. For this reason the kings looked upon the third of these additional days as inauspicious and would do no business on it, and would not even attend to their bodily needs until evening. Nephthys, they say, became the wife of Typhon; but Osiris and Isis fell in love with each other and had intercourse with each other in the darkness in their mother's womb; and some say that this is how Arueris was begotten, and hence is called by the Egyptians the elder Horus, but by the Greeks Apollo.

(13) As soon as Osiris became king, he made the Egyptians give up their destitute and brutish mode of life, showing them the fruits produced by cultivation, and giving them laws, and teaching them how to worship the gods. After doing this he traveled over the whole earth, civilizing it; instead of using weapons, he won over the masses by persuasion and reasoning, combined with song and with all kinds of music which he introduced. The Greeks, accordingly, identify him with Dionysus.

During his absence Typhon made no attempt at revolution, because Isis was on her guard and was able to keep vigilant watch of him. But after Osiris returned home, Typhon devised a plot against him, taking seventy-two men into the conspiracy and having as a helper a queen who came from Ethiopia, whom they call Asô. He secretly measured the body of Osiris and made to the proper size a beautiful and highly ornamented chest, which he carried into the banquet hall. Everyone was delighted with its appearance and admired it greatly, and so

Typhon promised in jest that whoever should lie down inside it, and fit it exactly, him would he make a present of it. After the others had all tried it, one after another, and no one had fit it, Osiris got in and lay down; at this the conspirators rushed up, slammed down the lid, and fastened it with nails on the outside, pouring melted lead over them. Then they carried the chest to the river, and let it drift down the Tanitic mouth into the sea, and for this reason even now the Tanitic mouth [of the Nile] is called hateful and unlucky by the Egyptians. These things are said to have been done on the seventeenth day of the month Athyr, when the sun is passing through Scorpio, Osiris then being in the twenty–eighth year of his reign; but some say that he had lived, not reigned, for that many years.

(14) The first to discover the crime and report it were the Pans and Satyrs that lived in the country around Chemmis; that is why, even now, sudden terrors and alarms of a crowd of people are called "panics." When she heard the news, Isis sheared off one of her tresses and put on a garment of mourning, hence the city, even to the present day, has the name of Kopto; but others think the name signifies bereavement, since *koptein* also means "to deprive." As she wandered about everywhere, not knowing what to do, she met no one without speaking to him; even when she met some little children she asked them about the chest. And they, it so happened, had seen it, and they told her the mouth of the river [the Nile] through which Typhon's accomplices had let the chest drift into the sea. From this circumstance the Egyptians believe that little children possess the power of prophecy, and they try especially to foretell the future from their [children's] cries when they are playing in the temple courts and calling out whatever it may be.

Having learned that, in ignorance, he [Osiris] had fallen in love and consorted with her sister [Nephthys], thinking that she was Isis, and seeing proof of this in the garland of melilote flowers which he had left with Nephthys, she [Isis] tried to find the child; for its mother had exposed it at once, because of her fear of Typhon. She found it at last, with great trouble and difficulty, by the help of dogs which guided her to the place. So Isis brought up the child, and he became her guardian and attendant, and bore the name Anubis; and he is said to guard the gods just as dogs guard men.

(15) Soon thereafter she learned by inquiry that the chest had been washed up by the sea at a place called Byblus, and that the surf had gently lodged it in a patch of heather. This heather is a most lovely plant, growing up very large in a short time, and it had enfolded, embraced, and concealed the chest within itself. The king of the country was astonished at the size of the plant, and having cut away the clump that concealed the chest, he set it up as a pillar to support his roof. They say that Isis learned all this by the divine breath of Rumor, and came to Byblus. Sitting down at the side of a spring, dejected and weeping, she spoke not a word to anyone, except that she welcomed and made friends with the maidservants of the queen, plaiting their hair for them and infusing into their bodies a wonderful fragrance which came from herself. When the queen saw her maids again, a longing came over her to see the stranger whose hair and whose body breathed of ambrosial perfume, and so she [Isis] was sent for and became so intimate with the queen that she was made the nurse of her infant. The king's name, they say, was Malcander; the queen some call Astarte, others Saosis, others Nemanus, which is the same as the Greek Athenais.

(16) Isis is said to have nursed the child by giving it her finger to suck, instead of her breast, and at night she burned away the mortal parts of his body. She turned herself into a swallow and flew around the pillar with a wailing cry until the queen, who was watching her, cried out when she saw her child all afire, and so took away the boy's immortality. Then the goddess, manifesting herself, asked for the pillar of the roof, and having removed it with the greatest ease, she cut away the heather that surrounded it. This plant she wrapped up in a linen cloth, pouring perfume over it, and entrusted it to the care of the kings; and to this day the people of Byblus venerate the wood, which is preserved in the temple of Isis. She then threw herself down upon the chest and wailed so loudly that the younger of the king's sons died of fright; the elder son she took with her, and placing

the chest on board a ship, put to sea; but when toward dawn the river Phaedrus sent forth too rough a gale, she grew angry and dried up the stream.

(17) As soon as she found privacy and was left to herself, she opened the chest and laid her face upon the face of the corpse, caressing it and weeping; but when the little boy observed this, coming up quietly from behind to spy, she noticed his presence and, turning around, gave him a dreadful look of anger. The child could not stand the fright and died. Some say it was not so, but that he fell into the sea [from the boat mentioned above]. He receives honors for the sake of the goddess; for they say that Maneros, whom the Egyptians sing about at their feasts, is this child. Others say that the boy is called Palaestinus, or Pelusios, and that the city founded by the goddess was named for him. The Maneros they sing about, so they say, was the first inventor of music. But some pretend that "Maneros" is not the name of a person, but an expression used by people drinking and keeping holiday, and signifies "May good luck be ours, like this!" and that this is what the Egyptians mean whenever they use the word. In the same way the likeness of a dead man in his coffin which is carried around at their feasts is no reminder of the mourning for Osiris, as some interpret it, but is merely intended to warn them to make use of the present and enjoy it, as very soon they themselves will be like the corpse; and that is why they bring it in at the feast.

(18) But when Isis had gone to see her son Horus (who was being brought up in the city Buto) and had put the chest away, Typhon, being out hunting by moonlight, came upon it and, recognizing the corpse, tore it into fourteen pieces and scattered them about. Isis heard of this and went looking for the fragments, sailing through the swamps in a papyrus boat, and that is why people who sail in papyrus boats are never harmed by the crocodiles, because these animals either fear or respect the goddess.

The consequence of Osiris' dismemberment is that there are many places all over Egypt called tombs of Osiris; for whenever Isis came upon a fragment of his body, she celebrated a funeral there. Some deny this and say that she made images and gave

them to the several cities, pretending that they were the actual
body, in order that he [Osiris] might receive honors from more
cities; and that, if Typhon should get the better of Horus, he
might be baffled in looking for the real tomb by having so many
[tombs] pointed out to him as the tomb of Osiris.

Of the parts of Osiris' body the only one Isis was unable to
find was the genital member, for this had at once been thrown
into the river; and the lepidotus, the phagrus, and the oxyrhynchus had fed upon it, which kinds of fish the natives strictly re-
fuse to eat. Instead, Isis made a model of the organ and consecrated it, namely the phallus, in honor of which the Egyptians
even at the present day hold a festival.

(19) Afterward Osiris came to Horus from the other world and
trained and exercised him for war, and then asked him what he
thought to be the finest thing possible. When Horus replied, "To
avenge one's father and mother when they are ill-treated," he
asked him secondly what he considered to be the most useful
thing to anyone going into battle; and when Horus answered, "A
horse," Osiris was surprised and asked why he had said a horse
instead of a lion. But Horus explained that a lion is indeed useful
[to guard] anyone needing help, but that a horse can both cut
off the flight of the enemy and also destroy him. On hearing this
Osiris was greatly pleased, supposing that Horus was adequately
provided [with horses]. And as many persons were coming over
from time to time to the side of Horus, Typhon's concubine
Thueris also came; a serpent that was pursuing her was cut to
pieces by the friends of Horus, and in memory of this event they
even now throw down a rope in the midst of all and chop it to
pieces.

The battle lasted for many days, and Horus was victorious; but
Isis, after receiving from him Typhon bound in chains, did not
destroy him, but on the contrary released him and let him go free.
Horus could not endure this with patience, and so laid hands on
his mother and tore the royal diadem from her head; whereupon
Hermes gave her a cow's head for a helmet.

When Typhon brought a charge of illegitimacy against Horus,
Hermes acted as his counsel and Horus was pronounced legiti-

mate by the gods. After this Typhon was defeated in two other battles. Isis had intercourse with Osiris after his death, and brought forth a child prematurely born and weak in his lower limbs, Harpocrates.

[Such, then, is the myth—abhorrent as a literal narrative, but demanding an allegorical interpretation (20). The many tombs of Osiris require explanation and can be explained: his body lies at Busiris, but the souls of the gods live in the stars and so does his (21). The Euhemerist explanation, namely, that the gods were originally men, is a questionable theory, and the instances of various historical persons disprove it (22–24). Plutarch offers a better explanation in the following sections.]

(25) Far better is the judgment of those who hold that the legends told about Typhon, Osiris, and Isis do not refer to either gods or men but to great daemons, whom Plato, Pythagoras, Xenocrates, and Chrysippus, following the ancient theologians, assert to have been far stronger than men, greatly surpassing our nature in power, but that not having their divine part entirely unmixed or unalloyed, but combined with the nature of the soul and the senses of the body, they were susceptible to pleasure and pain, and to whatever other experiences result from these and by their changes cause disturbance—to some more severely, to others less. For as among men so among daemons there are different degrees of virtue and of vice. The deeds of the giants and titans, celebrated by the Greeks, the atrocious acts of Kronos, the pitched battle between Python and Apollo, the flights of Dionysus, the wanderings of Demeter, do not fall short in absurdity of the legends about Osiris and Typhon and others that one may hear freely told by mythologists. Moreover, the things that are concealed in mystic ceremonies and rites, and are kept secret and out of sight of the multitude, have a similar explanation.

(26) We also hear Homer, in various places, describing the good as "godlike" and "equal to gods" and "having prudence learned from the gods," whereas the epithet derived from the daemons he applies indifferently to good and bad alike; for example:

Come on, you daemon-possessed! Why are you vainly trying to scare the Argives? [*Iliad* XIII. 810.]

And again:

When for the fourth time he rushed upon him like a daemon [*Iliad* XX. 447];

and:

O daemon-like! what harm is Priam doing you,
Or Priam's sons, that you are ever raging
The well-built town of Ilium to destroy? [*Iliad* IV. 31–33]

It is assumed that the daemons have a complex and inconsistent
nature and disposition. For this reason Plato [*Laws* 717A] attributes to the Olympian deities all right-hand qualities and the odd
numbers, but the opposite of these to the daemons. And Xenocrates thinks that the unlucky days of the month and whatever
festivals are accompanied with beatings and lamentations, fasting,
or abusive or obscene language have nothing to do with honor
paid to the gods or to the good daemons; but that in the space
around us there are certain great and powerful beings, stubborn
and bad-tempered, which take delight in such things and, if they
obtain them, betake themselves to nothing worse.

But the kind and good ones, on the contrary, Hesiod calls "holy
daemons" and "guardians of men":

Givers of wealth, and conferring a royal reward [*Works
and Days* 126].

And Plato calls this class "hermeneutic" [interpreting] and "dia-
conic" [ministering], a middle class between gods and men, conveying up thither the prayers and petitions of men, and bringing
down from thence to earth the oracles and gifts of good things.

Empedocles even says that daemons suffer punishment for their
sins, both of commission and omisssion:

Celestial wrath pursues them down to the sea;
The sea spits them out on the land, the earth to the rays
Of the unwearied Sun, and he to the whirling ether—
Each receives them in turn from the other,
And all receive them with loathing [Fragment 115],

until, having been thus chastened and purified, they obtain once more their natural place and position.

(27) Stories like these and others that are related to them, they say, are the legends told concerning Typhon: how he committed dreadful crimes out of envy and spite; and [how,] by throwing all things into confusion, he filled with evils the whole earth and the sea as well, and finally was punished for it. But the avenger of Osiris, his sister and wife [Isis], after extinguishing and putting a stop to the madness and fury of Typhon, did not forget the contests and struggles she had gone through nor her own wanderings, nor did she permit oblivion and silence to cover up her many deeds of wisdom, her many feats of courage; but by intermingling with the most sacred ceremonies certain images, reminders, and portrayals of her experiences at that time, she consecrated at once both a lesson in piety and a consolation in suffering for men and women likewise overtaken by misfortune. And she, together with Osiris, having been translated for their virtue from the rank of good daemons to that of gods—as later were Heracles and Dionysus—receive, not inappropriately, the united honors of gods and of daemons, since they exercise the greatest power everywhere, both in the regions above the earth and also in those beneath it. For they say that Sarapis is none other than Pluto, and Isis Persephone, as Archemachus of Euboea has said; so also Heraclides of Pontus, when he maintains that the oracle at Canopus belongs to Pluto.

(28) Ptolemy Soter saw in a dream the colossus of Pluto at Sinope (though he had never before known or seen what it looked like), ordering him to bring it as soon as possible to Alexandria. He was ignorant and at a loss as to where the statue then stood, but as he was relating the vision to his friends there was found a man, a great traveler by the name of Sosibius, who declared he had seen at Sinope just such a colossus as the king thought he saw. Ptolemy accordingly sent Soteles and Dionysius, who after much time and with considerable difficulty (but not, however, without divine providence) stole the statue and carried it away. And when it was brought [to Egypt] and examined, then Timotheus the exegete and Manetho of Sebennytus [the priestly historian]

and their associates, conjecturing that it was a statue of Pluto, drawing this inference from the Cerberus and the serpent [that were with it], made Ptolemy believe that it was the statue of no other god than Sarapis. It certainly did not come bearing such a name from the other place [Sinope]; but after it had been brought to Alexandria, it acquired the name which Pluto bears among the Egyptians, viz., Sarapis. And since Heraclitus, the natural philosopher, asserts that "Hades and Dionysus are one and the same, in honor of whom they rage and rave," people tend to slip into the same belief. For those who explain that Hades means the body, the soul being out of its senses and drunk when confined therein, are not very reliable allegorists. It is much better to identify Osiris with Dionysus and Sarapis with Osiris, who received this name when he changed his nature. Accordingly Sarapis is a god common to all men, as those who have partaken of the sacred rites know Osiris to be.

(29) It is not worth while to pay any attention to the Phrygian sacred books, in which it is said that Sarapis was the son of Heracles and Isis his daughter, and that Typhon was the son of Alcaeus, another son of Heracles. We must also disregard Phylarchus when he says that Dionysus first brought two oxen from India to Egypt, the name of one being Apis, of the other Osiris, but that Sarapis is the name of the one who sets the universe in order and that it comes from *sairein* [sweep], which some say means "to beautify and arrange." The remarks of Phylarchus are absurd enough; even more absurd is the opinion of those who say that Sarapis is no god at all but the name of the coffin of Apis, and that there are certain bronze doors at Memphis called the Gates of Oblivion and Wailing which, when opened for the burial of Apis, give out a deep harsh sound, and that for this reason we [always silence by a] touch any sounding vessel of brass. More tenable is the explanation of those who derive it from *seuesthai* [shoot] or *sousthai* [lunge], referring to the motion of the universe. Most of the priests say that Osiris and Apis are joined in one, explaining it and teaching us that we should consider Apis as the beautiful image of the soul of Osiris. But for my part I believe that if the name Sarapis is really Egyptian, it means

"cheerfulness" and "rejoicing," basing my view on the fact that the Egyptians call the festival of rejoicing Sairei. In fact, Plato says that Hades is so named because he is a beneficent and kindly god, benevolent to those who come to dwell with him. Moreover, among the Egyptians many other proper names are descriptive; for example, the subterranean place to which they believe the souls go after death [the West] they call Amenthes, the name signifying "the one who receives and gives." But whether this is one of the names carried over from Greece in ancient times and then brought back again we will consider further on; at present let us consider the remaining beliefs we set out to examine.

[Isis and Osiris passed from the rank of good daemons to that of gods. Typhon did not; yet he is often worshiped (30–31). Plutarch now proceeds with his allegorical interpretation of the myth, already hinted at and announced (32–44); Osiris is the Nile, Isis the land, Typhon the sea; or, more profoundly, Osiris is the lifegiving moisture, Typhon the fatal heat and dryness of the desert. Various details of the myth are shown to fit this explanation, e.g., the chest, the battle with Typhon, and other incidents. Still another explanation is then considered, namely, the astronomical (41–44). No one explanation exhausts the full meaning of the sacred myth; all must be taken together if we are to get at the truth (45). In any case, Typhon stands for all that is hostile to and destructive of life.

The existence of evil thus forces us to a dualistic view of the world, and Plutarch turns next to a consideration of that theory as found in the teaching of Zoroaster (46 f.), the Chaldeans (48), and also in Greek myths and philosophy. The Academic interpretation points in this direction: In the soul, Osiris is the nous and the logos; in the material world, he is the principle of order; in both, Typhon is the opposite (49 f.). Symbols and ceremonies alike prove that Osiris is the sun god and Isis the moon goddess (51–53). Now follows a metaphysical and mathematical explanation of the myth of Osiris-Isis-Horus (not Typhon), with a similar explanation by Hesiod and Plato and a note on the word "matter" (54–58). Further supporting etymological evidence is adduced in §§59–62, and a defense is made of the principle of giving Greek etymologies to Egyptian names. In §63 the symbolism of the sistrum is explained. Then follows the climactic passage on the real nature of Osiris, Isis, and Typhon (64–67).]

(64) To speak briefly, it is not right to believe that water or
the sun or the earth or the sky is Osiris or Isis, nor that fire or
drought or the sea is Typhon, but only if we credit Typhon with
whatever in these elements is either immoderate or disordered by
reason of excesses or deficiencies, while all that is well-ordered
and good and beneficial we must reverence and honor as the
work of Isis and as the image, imitation, and reason of Osiris; if
we do so, we shall not go wrong. Moreover, we shall make an end
to Eudoxus' disbelief and perplexity as to why the supervision of
love affairs is given, not to Demeter, but to Isis, and why Dionysus cannot raise the Nile or rule over the dead. For, by a common
principle, we hold that these two gods were appointed over every
allotment of good and that whatever there is in nature that is
beautiful and good exists by them, the one [Osiris] supplying the
origins, the other [Isis] receiving and distributing them.

(65) In this way we shall also handle those numerous and
boresome people who rejoice in identifying the legends concerning these deities with the seasonal changes in the atmosphere or
with the growth of the crops, with sowing and ploughing; and
those also who say that Osiris is being buried when the grain
is sown and hidden in the ground, and that he comes to life again
and shows himself again when plants begin to sprout. So, too,
they say that when Isis perceived that she was pregnant, she tied
an amulet round her neck on the sixth day of the month Phaophi,
and that Harpocrates was born about the winter solstice, imperfect and premature, in the plants that spring up and flower early.
For this reason they make an offering to him of first fruits of
growing lentils, but they celebrate the days of Isis' confinement
after the vernal equinox. When they hear all this, people love it
and believe it, deriving their conviction from things close at hand
and familiar.

(66) And there is nothing alarming about it if, in the first
place, men maintain that the gods are common to us all, and not
the exclusive possession of the Egyptians; and if they do not re-
strict these names to the Nile alone and the land watered by the
Nile; and if they do not talk as if the marshes [of Egypt] and the
lotus were the only creations of God, thereby depriving the rest

of mankind of the great gods, since they have no Nile or Buto or Memphis. As for Isis and the gods associated with her, all men own and acknowledge them, although some indeed have only recently learned to call them by the names given them by the Egyptians; nevertheless from time immemorial they have recognized and honored the power belonging to each of them.

In the second place, and something far more important, let men take special care and beware lest unwittingly they degrade and dissolve divine beings into winds and streams, sowing and ploughing, the travail of the earth, and the changes of the seasons, like those who say that Dionysus is wine, Hephaestus flame, or as Cleanthes says somewhere that Persephone is the air that is carried through [pheromenon] the crops and then dies [phoneuomenon]. A certain poet has said of the reapers, "What time the young men cut Demeter limb from limb." Such persons do not differ in the least from those who regard sails, ropes, and anchor as a pilot, or yarn and thread as a weaver, or a cup and a mixture of honey and some barley gruel as a physician. Yet they produce terrible atheistic doctrines when they apply the names of gods to natural products and to things that are senseless, lifeless, and necessarily destroyed by men whenever they need to use them.

For it is impossible to think of these things as gods, (67) since we cannot conceive God to be lacking in mind, or an inanimate thing, or subject to man. Accordingly we have concluded that those who make use of these things and bestow them upon us, and dispense them to us constantly and unceasingly, are gods— not different gods among different people, not barbarian or Greek, nor of the South or of the North; but just as the sun, the moon, the sky, the earth, the sea are the common property of all men, yet are given different names by different peoples, so too the one Reason which regulates all these things and the one Providence which supervises all, and the subordinate Powers that are appointed over all things, have different honors and titles assigned to them by custom among the different peoples. So also men use various consecrated symbols, some obscure, some more intelligible, in order to guide the understanding toward things divine, but never without a certain amount of risk. For some have completely missed their meaning and have slid into superstition; while others, flying from superstition as from a quagmire, have unwittingly fallen over a precipice into atheism.

[The remainder of the essay offers explanations of various symbols (68); fasts and sacrifices offered the vegetation deities (69); the identification of the gods with their statues or with animals sacred to them, which really leads to atheism (70); theories designed to explain theriomorphic gods (72) and their relation to Typhon (73); and the cult of certain animals, such as the crocodile and the ibis (74 f.). Animal worship was the most vulnerable aspect of ancient Egyptian religion and was often criticized, especially by the Jews (see The Wisdom of Solomon*), but Plutarch goes all the way and justifies animal worship, since the deity is to be found in all living things (76). The last four sections of the essay deal with supplementary matters, as a kind of appendix: the sacred vestments of Osiris and Isis, and their meaning (77; cf. 3–5 above); the identification of Osiris with Hades (78; cf. 29); the meaning of the repeated offering of incense (79); and the correct recipe for preparing* kuphi, *the goddess's own perfume (80).]*

ALEXANDER OF ABUNOTEICHOS

Lucian Alexander the False Prophet *12–16. This is a fascinating account of a homemade oracle in the second century* A.D. *Alexander, as we know from coins and other sources, was a person of importance in Paphlagonia, but Lucian's account is the only surviving literary record. The cult here described survived for at least a century. See A. D. Nock,* Conversion, *pp. 93–97; Francis G. Allinson,* Lucian, Satirist and Artist *(1926).*

(12) And so, upon invading his native land with all this *éclat* after a long absence, Alexander was a man conspicuous and brilliant; he affected occasional fits of madness and foamed at the mouth. This he easily contrived by chewing soapwort, the plant which dyers use; but some thought even the foam supernatural and awe-inspiring. The two of them [Alexander and his accomplice Cocconas] had long before got ready and fitted up a ser-

pent's head made of linen; it had more or less of a human look, was well painted, and seemed very lifelike. Its mouth could be opened and closed by means of horsehairs; and a forked black serpent's tongue, also controlled by horsehairs, would dart out. Moreover, the [living] serpent brought from Pella was also ready in advance, but was being kept safe at home, destined in due time to manifest himself to them and to take a part in the drama —in fact, the leading part.

(13) When at last it was time to begin, he [Alexander] thought up a clever scheme. He went at night to the foundations of the temple, which were still being dug. Here a pool of water had collected—either from underground springs or from rain—and in it he deposited a goose egg, which he had previously blown and in which he had inserted a newborn snake; after burying it deep in the mud, he went away. Early next morning he ran out into the market place, naked except for a gold brocaded loincloth, carrying his scimitar and tossing his long, unbound locks like the devotees who collect money for the Great Mother and fall into fits of frenzy. Climbing up on a high altar, he made an address and congratulated the city because it was about to receive the god in a visible manifestation. Those present—for almost the whole city, women, old men, and children, had come running—were overcome with amazement, prayed, and made obeisance. He uttered a few meaningless sounds, which may have been Hebrew or Phoenician, but he dazzled the people, who did not get what he was saying except that he constantly worked in the names of Apollo and Asclepius. (14) Then he ran off to the future temple, went down into the excavation and found the previously arranged spring of the oracle, entered the water, sang hymns to Asclepius and Apollo with a loud voice, and invoked the god to come with his blessings to the city. Then he asked for a libation bowl, and when someone handed it to him he neatly slipped it down underneath and brought up, along with some water and mud, the egg in which he had enclosed the god; the hole about the plug had been closed over with white wax and lead. Taking it [the egg] in his hands, he announced that he was now holding Asclepius! The crowd gazed steadily to see what was going to happen; they had

already been overcome with astonishment at the discovery of the egg in the water. But when he broke it and received the tiny snake in the hollow of his hand, and the crowd saw it crawling and winding about his fingers, they at once raised a shout, hailed the god, congratulated the city, and greedily began, each of them, to stuff himself with prayers, begging him for treasures and wealth and health and every other good gift. But Alexander went running home again, taking with him the newborn Asclepius, "twice born, when other men are born but once," and born not from Coronis, by Zeus, nor yet from a crow [corone] but from a goose! And after him followed all the people, inspired with frenzy and mad with fanatical hopes.

(15) For the next few days he stayed at home, expecting—as actually happened—that great droves of Paphlagonians, inspired by the news, would soon be coming on the run. When the city had become overcrowded with a mob of witless, senseless humans, not in the least resembling decent bread-eating men, but distinguished from sheep only by their looks, then Alexander took his seat on a couch in a small room. He was magnificently attired, worthily of the god. In his bosom he held our Asclepius of Pella —a very large and beautiful one [serpent], as I have said. He coiled its body around his neck, and let its long tail hang down across his lap and trail along the floor; the patient creature's head he kept hid under his arm, but showed the linen head on one side of his beard, just as if it belonged to the body you could see.

(16) Picture to yourself a little room, dimly lighted, with a crowd of people gathered from everywhere, excited, deliberately wrought up, all agog with expectation. When they came in, naturally they found a miracle: in a few days the tiny snake had become this huge, tame, human-looking serpent! But at once they were crowded toward the exit, and before they had got a good look were pushed along by those who were continually forcing their way in, for another door had been opened across from the first one. (That was what the Macedonians did, they say, when Alexander the Great [our Alexander's namesake!] was ill, in fact when he lay dying, and they surrounded the palace, eager to bid him farewell.) This exhibition our quack put on,

so it is said, not once but repeatedly, and especially whenever any of the well-to-do arrived.

[Naturally, the purpose of all this make-believe was to set up an oracle, and a lucrative one; the success of the scheme is recounted in the remaining chapters of the book.]

THE DEATH OF PEREGRINUS

Lucian The Death of Peregrinus *11–13. This story is based upon the self-immolation of a Cynic philosopher of the second century* A.D., *whose death Lucian had witnessed. For a time Peregrinus had been attached to Christianity, and it is at this point that the following passage begins. Lucian views him as an impostor, but many modern scholars think the man was sincere. His name was Peregrinus; Proteus was a later nickname.*

It was then that he learned the marvelous wisdom of the Christians, by associating with their priests and scribes in Palestine. And how? At once he made them look like children; for he was a prophet and a leader of the cult, and head of the synagogue and everything, all by himself. Some of their books he expounded and interpreted, but many of them he wrote; and they stood in awe of him as before a god, used him as their lawgiver, and inscribed him as their protector—next to that other one, of course, whom they still worship, the man who was crucified in Palestine because he introduced this new mystery initiation into the world.

Then Proteus was arrested for this and thrown into prison, which fact in itself provided him with no small reputation for his future career and for the wonder-working and the popularity-seeking that he longed for. When he had been imprisoned, accordingly, the Christians, viewing the fact as a misfortune, moved heaven and earth in their efforts to release him. Then, since this was impossible, every other kind of ministration was showered upon him, not incidentally, but with great zeal; from the break of dawn elderly widows and orphan children could be seen waiting outside the prison, while some of their more accomplished

leaders slept inside with him, after bribing the guards. Then
elaborate meals were brought in, and their sacred books were read
aloud, and the most excellent Peregrinus—for he was still called
by that name—was hailed by them as "the new Socrates."

Indeed, people came even from the cities in Asia, being sent
by the Christians at the common expense for the purpose of
supporting, defending, and encouraging the man. They manifest
an uncanny speed whenever any such public action is to be
taken; for they promptly spend all they possess. And so it was
with Peregrinus; he received a considerable amount of money
from them on account of his imprisonment, and it provided him
with a tidy income. For the poor devils have persuaded themselves that they are going to be entirely immortal and live forever
and ever, and for this reason they despise death and willingly
give themselves up when arrested—that is, most of them do.
Moreover, their original lawgiver persuaded them that they
should be like brothers to one another, after they have once
broken the law by denying the Greek gods and by worshiping
that crucified sophist of theirs and living according to his laws.
Therefore they despise all things equally, and view them as common property, accepting such doctrines by tradition and without
any precise belief. And so if any charlatan [goês] or clever trick-
ster, capable of taking advantage of every occasion, comes among
them, he at once gets rich by imposing upon simple-minded
people.

THE NEED TO SUSPEND JUDGMENT

Sextus Empiricus Outlines of Pyrrhonism *III. 218–238. Sextus
was a physician and polemical philosopher who rejected all
forms of dogmatic, i.e., positively formulated, philosophy, from
Thales on down. His criticisms of earlier thinkers are penetrat-
ing and give us almost a history of earlier thought in resumé.
See also his* Adversus Physicos *I. 13–194. He himself was a
Skeptic or Pyrrhonist, and lived from about 160 to 210 A.D. The
principles of his philosophy can be summed up in the phrase,
"suspense of judgment," i.e., we are in no position to render
positive verdicts, human knowledge being fragmentary and*

questionable. Having just said that on the subject of justice and injustice, and even on the virtue of courage or manliness, there is no agreed opinion, Sextus proceeds to say the same of religion.

And also on the subject of religion [i.e., piety] and the gods there is an enormous amount of disagreement. For although most men affirm that there are gods, still a few do deny their existence, like the followers of Diagoras of Melos, and Theodorus, and Critias the Athenian. And among those who affirm the existence of gods some believe in the gods of their ancestors, others in those which have been fashioned to fit the dogmatic systems of philosophy—like [that of] Aristotle, for example, who described God as bodiless [i.e., incorporeal] and the limit of heaven; or the Stoics, who said that he is a breath [*pneuma,* or spirit] which permeates [all things,] even that which is filthy; or Epicurus, who made him anthropomorphic; or Xenophanes, who described him as a sphere without feeling. (219) Some of them maintain that he cares about our affairs, others that he is not concerned over us; for Epicurus, for example, affirms that "the blessed and incorruptible [nature] is not troubled with concern for itself, nor does it provide trouble for others." Accordingly even the rank and file of people differ likewise, some insisting that there is one god, others that there are many, differing in shape, so that they even fall into the superstitions of the Egyptians, who think of the gods as long-faced, hawk-shaped, or cows and crocodiles and whatever else [strikes their fancy].

(220) Accordingly there is likewise great disagreement about sacrifices and the whole subject of the worship to be offered the gods. For what in some cults is considered holy in others is unholy, and this could never have been possible if the holy and the unholy were so by nature. For example, no one would think of sacrificing a pig to Sarapis, but they do sacrifice pigs to Heracles and Asclepius. It is unlawful to sacrifice a sheep to Isis, but to her who is called the Mother of the Gods, and to other gods as well, sheep are sacrificed with favorable omens. (221) The Carthaginians sacrifice a man to Kronos, which by most men is looked upon as impiety. In Alexandria they sacrifice a cat to Horus and a beetle to Thetis, which no one among us would

ever do. A horse is sacrificed to Poseidon; but to Apollo, especially to Apollo of Didyma, the animal is utterly detestable. It is a pious practice to offer goats to Artemis, but not to Asclepius. (222) And I might go on and add a whole list of similar examples, but I shall try to be brief. Certainly, if a sacrificial victim were either holy or unholy by nature, all men would have agreed on it.

The same sort of thing is to be seen in matters of human diet when viewed as religious observances. (223) A Jew or an Egyptian priest would sooner die than eat pork. A Libyan deems it the gravest impiety to taste the flesh of a sheep. Some Syrians look thus upon the eating of doves, and others upon the eating of [the flesh of] any sacrificial victims. In some cults it is lawful to eat fish; in others it is regarded as irreligious. Among the Egyptians, those looked upon as the wise men believe it to be a sin to eat the head of an animal, others the shoulders, others the feet, others some other part. (224) No one will bring an onion as an offering to Zeus Casius of Pelusium, just as no priest of Aphrodite in Libya will taste garlic. In some cults they abstain from mint, in others from sweet relish, in still others from parsley. And some assert that they would prefer to eat their fathers' heads rather than beans! But among others these are all matters of indifference. (225) To taste the flesh of dogs is thought by us to be sinful, but some of the Thracians are reported to eat dogs. This may perhaps have [once] been a custom among Greeks— Diocles accordingly, who learned medicine from the ancient guild of the Asclepiads, prescribes puppy meat for certain sufferers. Some [tribes] even eat human flesh, as I have observed above [§207], as a matter of indifference—which among us is looked upon as wicked. (226) And yet if the ritual rules and the food regulations were prescribed by nature, they would certainly have been recognized everywhere and by all men.

The same thing must be said of respect for the dead. Some wrap the dead completely and cover them over with earth, deeming it unholy to expose them to the sun. But the Egyptians remove the entrails, embalm the bodies, and keep them near and above ground. (227) Among the Ethiopians, the fish-eating tribes toss their dead into the lakes as food for the fish. The Hyrcanians expose them to be devoured by dogs; some of the Indians feed them to the vultures. And they say that the Troglodytes carry the dead body up a certain hill, and then, having tied its head to its feet, they toss stones upon it, laughing as they do so; and when they have piled up a heap of stones over it, they leave it there. (228) Some barbarians kill and eat those who are over sixty years of age, but those who die young they bury in the ground. Some burn the dead; and among these some gather up the bones and bury them, while others take no care of them but leave them scattered about. They say the Persians impale the dead and preserve them in niter, and afterward bind them up with bandages. And still others—what grief they suffer on account of the dead, we all recognize.

(229) And some think that death itself is something dreadful and to be avoided, while others do not. Euripides even says:

Who knows if life is really death,
And death is viewed as life, in the world below?
[Fragment 683 Nauck.]

And Epicurus declares: "Death is nothing to us; what is dissolved has no sensation, and what is without feeling means nothing to us." They also say that since we are put together as a combination of soul and body, and since death is the separation of soul and body, therefore as long as we exist death does not, for we are not being dissolved; but when death takes place we no longer exist, for when the combination of soul and body ceases we, too, cease to be. (230) But Heraclitus says that both life and death exist while we live as well as when we are dead; for while we are alive our souls are dead and buried inside us, and when we die our souls come to life again and live. And some even hold that death is preferable to life, as Euripides says:

For we ought instead to gather together and bewail
The babe newborn, who faces so many evils,
But the dead, for whom evils have ceased,
Let us bear off with joy and words of good omen.
[Fragment 449.]

(231) From the same point of view are the following words [of Theognis]:

Never to have been born at all would be the best thing for
    mortals,
Never to have seen the beams of the flaming sun;
Or, once born, to hasten quickly through the gates of Hades,
And lie down heaped over with earth.
                                        [Theognis 425–428.]

And we know what Herodotus tells about Cleobis and Biton in
the story of the Argive priestess [who asked the goddess for the
best gift for her sons and whose sons died in their sleep that
night]. (232) It is also related that some of the Thracians sit
around and sing dirges for the newly born. So then death should
not be thought to be one of the things that are dreadful by their
very nature, any more than life should be thought one of the
things that are by nature good. Nor do any of the things we have
mentioned have their attributes by nature, but all are matters of
custom and exist relatively to something or other.

(233) The same kind of treatment can be applied to each of
the other [customs], which we have not mentioned now because
of the brevity of the discussion. And even if we cannot at once
point out the disagreement in regard to them, it should be noted
that in certain nations unknown to us disagreement over them
is to be presupposed. (234) So, for example, if perchance we had
not been aware of the Egyptian custom of marrying one's sister,
we should have been quite mistaken in asserting that it is everywhere acknowledged to be wrong to marry a sister; likewise, in
the case of those practices in which we discover no disagreement,
it is appropriate to refrain from stating that none exists, since, as
I have said, there may quite possibly be disagreement over them
among certain races unknown to us.

(235) And so the Skeptic, observing all this variety of customs,
suspends his judgment about things that are either good or bad
by nature, or that are to be practiced or not to be practiced, and
in so doing he resists the dogmatic tendency and follows without
strong convictions either way the observances of everyday life.
And so he remains impassive on matters of received opinion,
while under conditions where no such evasion is possible he is
stirred up only moderately. (236) As a man, he of course suffers

through his senses; but since he does not add to his suffering the conviction that what he is suffering is evil by its very nature, he suffers only moderately. For the added burden of the belief that what is suffered is evil is really worse than the [original] suffering itself, just as sometimes the patient who undergoes an amputation or other surgical operation bears the pain well enough, while those watching the operation faint dead away because of their opinion that what is being done is bad. (237) In fact, anyone who assumes that anything is either good or bad by nature, or is unquestionably right to practice or not to practice, will be upset in a variety of ways. For when the things he thinks to be evil by their nature are present, he assumes that he is being punished for something [*poinelateisthai*]; but when good things happen to him he is seized with pride and the fear of losing them, and worried lest he find himself once more among those things which he accounts to be evil by nature, and so he falls into extraordinary perturbations. (238) As for the view [of the Cynics and of certain Stoics] that good things [*ta agatha*, the "goods" of life] cannot be lost, we shall refute this by merely citing the impossibility of settling the differences [noted above]. From this we conclude that if (a) whatever produces evil is evil and must be avoided, and if (b) the conviction that some things are good by nature, others evil, produces disturbance [of mind], then (c) the whole hypothesis and conviction that anything is either bad or good by its nature is an evil [view] and must be rejected.

And so, for the present, this is all we have to say about things that are good, bad, and indifferent.

III. CULTS

1. ORPHISM

Orphism is of especial interest as the first religious movement in the Greek world to have a personal founder and to set forth its doctrines in writing. Its origins go back to the sixth or seventh century B.C. But it enjoyed a wide revival and increased influence during the Hellenistic and Hellenistic-Roman age. New and ever profounder meanings were read into its rites and myths. (See M. P. Nilsson in *Oxford Classical Dictionary*, p. 627; Jane E. Harrison, *Prolegomena to the Study of Greek Religion*, p. xii.) Even its later literature is of uncertain date. We give here only passages which either certainly or at least probably belong to our period.

An earlier and classical expression of Orphism, describing retribution in the other world, is found in Pindar's *Olympian Ode* II. 53–83. See Ernest Maas, *Orpheus* (Munich, 1895); O. Kern, *Orphicorum Fragmenta* (1922); H. Diels, *Fragmente der Vorsokratiker*, sixth edition (1951), Vol. I, pp. 1–20; V. D. Macchioro, *From Orpheus to Paul* (1930); W. K. C. Guthrie, *Orpheus and Greek Religion* (1935; revised edition, 1952); Ivan M. Linforth, *The Arts of Orpheus* (1941). The old work of C. A. Lobeck, *Aglaophamus* (Königsberg, 1829) is still of great value.

THE ORPHIC COSMOGONY

Damascius De Principiis (On First Principles) *123 bis; Kern, Orphicorum Fragmenta, No. 54, p. 131; Nilsson, Lesebuch, p. 51. Damascius of Damascus was the last head of the Neoplatonic school, one of the seven philosophers who migrated to Persia after Justinian closed the schools of philosophy and law at Athens in 529 A.D. On the following passage, see T. Gomperz, Greek Thinkers, Vol. I, p. 92; E. Zeller, Philosophie der Griechen, fourth edition, Vol. I, pp. 85 ff. (English translation, I, pp. 100 ff.); I. M. Linforth, The Arts of Orpheus, pp. 154 f.; H. Diels, Fragmente der Vorsokratiker, sixth edition (1951), Vol. I, pp. 11 ff.; Kathleen Freeman, Companion to the Pre-Socratic Philosophers, pp. 1–18, and Ancilla to the Pre-Socratic Philosophers, p. 3.*

I assume that the teaching about the gods [*theologia*] contained in the rhapsodies [the *hieroi logoi*], which sets aside the two primal substances [or principles, *archai,* of the ordinary Orphic teaching, viz., water and earth] along with the one primal substance [*hyle,* matter] that preceded these two and was handed on by tradition without further explanation—I assume that this theology takes for granted as its basis a third primal substance, which is the first to offer something that can be described in words and understood by the human mind. For it is this primal substance that is so often praised in that teaching about the gods, as the "never-aging Kronos [Time], the Father of Ether and Chaos." At any rate, according to this teaching, Kronos is the serpent which brings forth from itself a triple birth—the moisture-bearing Ether, boundless Chaos, and cloudlike Erebus. According to the tradition, this second triad corresponds to the first, being dynamic as that is paternal. For this reason the third member in the triad, Erebus, is cloudlike, just as the [corresponding] paternal and superior member is not simply Ether but is the moisture-bearing, while the middle member, Chaos, is similarly [described as] boundless. However, among these three substances, it is said, Kronos begot an egg—for this tradition assumes Kronos' begetting—and it was within them that this egg was conceived, since from them goes forth the third intelligible triad.

What then is this triad? It is (1) the egg, containing within itself the twofold nature of male and female; (2) the mass, contained within it, of manifold and various seeds; and (3) an incorporeal god [some editors read "a dual-bodied god"] who bears on his shoulders golden wings, on his hips a growth of bulls' heads, and on his head an immense snake, which appears in various animal forms. This god must be looked upon as the thinking reason of the triad, the intermediate species (both the many and the two) as the power, but the egg itself as the paternal *prima materia* of the third triad, the third god. And this theology praises him as the First-begotten [*Protogonus*] and calls him Zeus, the ruler of all things and of the whole cosmos; and for this reason he is also called Pan [All]. So much and of this sort is [the teaching] concerning the genealogy of the intellectual principles [*archai*].

THE ORPHIC ANTHROPOGONY

Olympiodorus on Plato's Phaedo, *61C; Kern,* Orphicorum Fragmenta, *No. 220, p. 238; Nilsson,* Lesebuch, *pp. 51 f. Olympiodorus was a fifth-century Neoplatonic commentator on Plato and Aristotle. Apparently he lived in Alexandria.*

According to the tradition, Orpheus taught that there are four successive reigns, one after another. The first is that of Uranus, which made way for that of Kronos after he had mutilated his father. After Kronos, Zeus became king, when he had flung his father down to Tartarus. Then in Zeus's place came Dionysus; but after Hera's malicious trick the Titans standing around tore him to bits and devoured his flesh. At this Zeus was angry and smote them with his lightning, and out of the soot from the smoke that arose from them was formed a substance out of which have been fashioned men. We may not, therefore, take our own lives—not even if, as one well-known phrase seems to say, we live in our bodies as in prisons [*soma*=*sema*]. The saying is clear, and does not unfitly describe the situation. But we must not take our own lives, since our bodies have in them something of Dionysus; for we are particles of him, since at the least we consist of titanic soot and the Titans feasted on his flesh.

THE ORPHIC GOLD PLATES

Kern, Orphicorum Fragmenta, No. 32a and c; A. Olivieri, Lamellae aureae orphicae (Kleine Texte, No. 133, 1915). These gold plates, from Petelia and Thurii in Lower Italy, were found in graves dating from the fourth or third century B.C. Compare G. Murray, in Jane E. Harrison, Prolegomena to the Study of Greek Religion, pp. 659 ff. On the old Orphic doctrine of retribution in the other world, see Pindar Olympian II. 54–83. For other passages, see Kathleen Freeman, Ancilla to the Pre-Socratic Philosophers, pp. 5 ff.

[Plate from Petelia (32a)]

In the house of Hades, at the left hand, you will find a spring
And, just a few steps beyond it, a single white cypress.
But take care not to come near the spring;
Instead you will find other cooling waters, streaming forth
From Mnemosyne's lake—but here watchers are at hand.
Say to them: "I am a son of Earth and of starry Heaven,
[I am of heavenly descent;] this ye yourselves know.
I am languishing from thirst, and about to pass away; quickly
    then give me to drink
Cooling water from the spring, swelling from the lake of
    Mnemosyne [Memory]."
Gladly then will they give you to drink from the divine
    spring,
And thenceforth with other heroes you will reign.

[Plate from Thurii (32c)]

Pure I come hither from the pure, O divine mistress of Hades,
Eucles, Eubuleus, and ye other immortal gods.
For I claim for myself to be a sprout of your blessed stem.
But the Moira compelled me, and the other undying gods,
. . . and he hurled forth the lightning and thunder.

By good fortune I have escaped the circle of burdensome
  care,
And to the crown of yearning have I come with swift foot.
I bury myself in the lap of the Lady who rules in Hades,
Yea with swift foot have I attained the crown of desire.
"Fortunate art thou, and blessed, and wilt be no longer a man
  but a god."
Like a kid have I fallen into the milk!

ORPHIC HYMNS

E. Abel, Orphica, *pp. 68 f., 73 f. We possess a collection of
eighty-eight hymns, ostensibly composed by Orpheus, addressed
to various gods. Their date falls toward the close of antiquity,
but their religious content and style go back, in part, to far
earlier times. Eighty-six of these hymns were translated in
rhymed verse, with notes and a lengthy preface entitled "Preliminary Dissertation on the Life and Theology of Orpheus,"
by Thomas Taylor, in his* The Mystical Initiations; or Hymns
of Orpheus *(London, 1787). Compare Lehmann-Haas,* Text-
buch der Religionsgeschichte, *p. 203; von Christ,* Geschichte
der griechischen Literatur, *fifth edition, §791.*

XVIII. *To Pluto*

O thou who dwellest in the underearthly house, thou mighty
  of soul
Amid the deep-shadowed, never-lighted fields of Tartarus,
Thou scepter-bearing Zeus of the underworld,
Accept favorably this offering, O Pluto:
Thou who holdest the keys of the whole world,
Thou who vouchsafest all wealth to the generations of men
  year by year,
Thou who alone holdest all sway over the world's third part—
The world, dwelling place of the immortals, solid ground
  where mankind dwells—
Thou who hast set thy throne in the gloomy realm below,
In far-flung Hades, dismal, measureless, all-embracing, torn
  by tempestuous winds,
Where dark Acheron winds about the deep roots of earth;

Thou who rulest mortals by the power of death, and receivest
   all;
Great God, Wise Counselor [Eubuleus];
Thou who once didst marry the daughter of holy Demeter,
Snatching her away from the pleasant meadows
And carrying her through the sea in thy swift chariot
To the cave in Attica, in Eleusis' vale
Where stand the gates of Hades.
Thou alone art ruler of all things visible and invisible,
Inspired God, All-ruler [Pantocrator], most holy, most highly
   praised,
Who dost rejoice over the worthy mystes and his sacred
   ministrations.
I invoke thee and implore thee,
Graciously come, and show thyself favorable to thy initiates!

XXIX. To Persephone

O Persephone, daughter of great Zeus,
Come, only-begotten goddess, and receive the offering piously
   dedicated unto thee—
To thee, Pluto's honored bride,
The kindly [*kedne*], the lifegiver;
Thou who rulest the gates of Hades in the clefts of the earth,
Executrix of punishments, the lovely-tressed, pure offspring
   of Zeus;
Mother of the Eumenides, Queen of the nether world,
Whom Zeus by a secret union begat as his daughter;
Mother of the noisy, many-formed Eubuleus,
Leader of the dance of the Hours, Light-bringer, beautiful in
   form;
Exalted, all-ruling Kore, bounteous in fruits,
Clear-shining one, horned, the one and only desired of all
   mortals;
The bringer of springtime, when thou art pleased with the
   sweet-smelling meadows,
When thou dost let thy heavenly form be seen
In the green, fruit-bearing growth of the field,
And art set free for the gathering of the mighty harvest
   sheaves;
Thou who alone art life and death to mortals, greatly plagued,
Persephoneia! [well named]
For thou ever bringest forth [*phereis*] all things,

And slayest all [*phoneuseis*]!
Hear, O blessed goddess!
Let the fruits of the earth spring forth
And grant us peace alway, sound health, and a prosperous
   life;
Then at last, after a hale old age,
Lead us down to thy realm, O Queen,
And to Pluto, the Lord of all.

2. ORIENTAL CULTS

Our knowledge of the Oriental (i.e., Near Eastern) mysteries is very scanty and fragmentary. Their rites and their doctrines have to be reconstructed or inferred from scattered references in ancient authors, who are usually chary of speaking about them, and from archeological remains. Thus the doctrines, organization, and ritual of Mithraism have been reconstructed in the classic work of Franz Cumont, *Textes et Monuments figurés relatifs aux Mystères de Mithra* (1898–1899), and those of Asclepius in the recent work of E. J. and L. Edelstein, *Asclepius: A Collection and Interpretation of the Testimonies* (1945). See also Hugo Gressman, *Die orientalischen Religionen im hellenistisch-römischen Zeitalter* (1930); R. Reitzenstein, *Die hellenistischen Mysterienreligionen*, third edition (1927); P. Wendland, *Die hellenistisch-römische Kultur in ihren Beziehungen zum Judentum und Christentum*, second edition (1912); A. D. Nock, "The Development of Paganism in the Roman Empire," *Cambridge Ancient History*, Vol. XII (1939), Ch. 12; M. P. Nilsson, *Geschichte der griechischen Religion*, Vol. II (1950), pp. 555–672. The classic introduction is still Franz Cumont, *Les religions orientales dans le Paganisme romain*, fourth edition (1929). There is an English translation of the second edition by Grant Showerman (Chicago, 1911). See also H. R. Willoughby, *Pagan Regeneration* (1925).

THE RELIGION OF THE MAGI

From Dio Chrysostom (Dio of Prusa) Oratio XXXVI. 38–48. Dio lived in the first century A.D. *and was a Cynic philosopher —one of those banished from Italy by Domitian. He lived the life of a wandering exile among the barbarians west of the Black Sea but later returned to Greece and Asia Minor and became a successful orator. It is interesting to compare his account of Persian religion with that of Strabo (Bk. XV. 3. 13–17), written toward the end of the first century* B.C. *One suspects that both writers were hampered by inadequate sources of information; but so are we—and there were strange varieties of religion to be found in the ancient world. On the whole, foreign religions were very inadequately known by most ancient*

Greeks and Romans. Only the most sketchy information about the details of their beliefs and practices was available.

The Magi were members of the Persian priestly caste. In the Hellenistic age they were often met with in the Mediterranean world, communities of them being found throughout Asia Minor, and even in Egypt. Their principles were influential upon the changing theological views in the West; they held, for example, that sacrifices should be made only of inanimate objects. They also cultivated astrology. See J. Bidez and F. Cumont, Les Mages hellénisés, 2 vols. (Paris, 1938). Vol. II contains an invaluable collection of texts.

(38) This, then is the view of the philosophers, a theory which sets up a generous and kindly fellowship of gods [daemons] and men, and gives a share in law and citizenship, not indeed to all that happen to be alive, but to those who have a share in reason and understanding, thus introducing a far nobler and juster code than that of Laconia, according to which the Helots can never become Spartans and in consequence are always plotting against Sparta.

(39) Moreover, there is also an admirable myth which is sung in their secret rites by the Magi, who extol this god of ours as being the perfect and original driver of the most perfect chariot. For the chariot of Helios, they say, is relatively new when compared with that of Zeus, though it is visible to the many, since its course is run in full view of all. This is why, they say, the chariot of Helios has been acclaimed by all mankind; for the poets, almost from the earliest times it seems, are forever telling of its rising and its setting, and all in one and the same manner describe the yoking of the horses and how Helios himself mounts his car. [Cf. Hesiod, *Theogony*, 760 f.; *Hymn to Hermes*, 68 f.]

(40) But the powerful and perfect chariot of Zeus has never been worthily praised by any of our poets, neither by Homer nor by Hesiod; yet Zoroaster sings of it, and so do the sons of the Magi who learned the song from him. For the Persians say that Zoroaster, because of his love for wisdom and justice, left his neighbors and lived by himself on a certain mountain, and that soon thereafter the mountain caught fire from a great flame that descended from the sky above, and that it burned unceasingly.

When the king and the most distinguished of the Persians came near in order to pray to the god, Zoroaster came forth out of the fire unharmed; showing himself gracious toward them, he bade them be of good courage and offer certain sacrifices, as the god had come to that place. (41) Thereafter, they say, Zoroaster associated, not with them all, but only with those of the noblest nature with regard to truth [i.e., as shown by their telling the truth] and who were able to understand the god, that is, men whom the Persians have called Magi, since they know how to minister to the divinity—not like the Greeks, who ignorantly apply the term to magicians. And everything else the Magi do is in accordance with sacred words, and in patricular they rear for Zeus a team of Nisaean horses. These horses are the most beautiful and the largest to be found in Asia; but for Helios they keep only a single horse.

(42) The Magi expound their myth, not as our prophets of the Muses do, merely presenting each detail as persuasively as they can; instead, they insist upon its complete truthfulness. For they hold that the universe is steadily being drawn along a single road by a charioteer who is gifted with the greatest skill and power, and that this movement goes on forever in endless periods of time. But the courses of Helios and Selene [i.e., the sun and moon], as they say, are only movements of parts of the whole, and so are more readily observed by mankind. The movement and progress of the universe as a whole is not understood by the majority of mankind, who are ignorant of the magnitude of this contest [i.e., chariot race].

(43) What follows about the horses and how they are driven I am somewhat ashamed to tell in the way they explain it, since they are not concerned to be consistent on all points in the picture they draw. Indeed it is possible that I may seem absurd when, instead of our charming Hellenic songs, I sing one that is barbarian; and yet I must try.

[The Magi say] that of the two horses the one which stands highest in the heavens [i.e., the ether] is vastly superior in beauty, size, and swiftness, since running on the outside track it has the longest course; this horse is sacred to Zeus himself. Moreover, it is winged and has a shining brilliance like that of the purest flame; and in it Helios and Selene may be seen as conspicuous signs, just like, I suppose, the marks which horses bear here on earth, some crescent-shaped [like the new moon] and some with other devices. (44) And they say that these [marks] appear to us to be crowded together, like big sparks darting about in the midst of a bright fire; and yet each of them has its own proper motion. Moreover, the other stars also which appear through that horse of Zeus [i.e., are visible in the ether], and are all by nature parts of it, in some cases have their motion [i.e., revolve] along with it, and in others follow different tracks. Among men each of these stars [associated with the horse of Zeus] has a name of its own [i.e., the planets], but the rest are named collectively by groups, arranged so as to form certain figures or patterns [the constellations].

(45) The horse that is the most brilliant and the most bespangled and the dearest to Zeus himself, and is so praised in their hymns [i.e., fire], is quite properly the first to receive sacrifice and worship, since it is truly the first. The next in order after this one, touching it and in closest contact with it, is called Hera [air, according to Stoic exegesis], a horse gentle and responsive, but far inferior in strength and speed. The color of this horse is by nature black, but that part of it which receives the light of Helios [i.e., the sun] is always bright; only where it is shaded in its revolution does it have its own proper color. (46) The third [i.e., water] is the horse sacred to Poseidon, even slower than the second. About this horse the poets have told a myth, saying that its image appeared among men—the one they call Pegasus, I guess—and they say that he started a spring flowing at Corinth by pawing with his hoof. But the fourth seems the strangest of them all, a horse firm and immovable, and by no means winged, and named Hestia [i.e., earth]. However, the Magi do not hesitate so to describe it; they say that this horse also is harnessed to the chariot, but remains immovable, champing its steel bit. (47) From all sides the other horses press close to him with their various parts, and the pair that are nearest [i.e., air and water] swing toward him, simply falling upon him and crowding him; and yet

the horse that is farthest away [i.e., the ether] is always the first to round the stationary horse as they round the turning post in the hippodrome.

As a rule, the horses are peaceful and friendly and do not harm one another. But once upon a time, in the long course of ages and of many revolutions of the universe, a powerful snort from the first horse fell from above; and since it was a fiery-tempered steed, it inflamed the others, especially the last one [earth]. The fire set ablaze its mane, which was its chief glory, and also the whole universe [the Stoic *ekpurosis*]. (48) [The Magi] say that the Greeks, recalling this event as a single incident, attach it to the name of Phaëthon, not being willing to blame the driving of Zeus and equally loath to find fault with the course taken by Helios. And so they say it was a younger driver, a mortal son of Helios, eager for a sport that was difficult and dangerous for all mortals, who begged his father to let him mount his chariot and, racing along in reckless fashion, burned up everything with fire, all animals and plants, and at last was himself destroyed, being smitten by too powerful a flame.

THE CULT OF THE SYRIAN GODDESS

THE FESTIVAL OF THE SYRIAN GODDESS AT HIERAPOLIS

Lucian The Syrian Goddess *1 and 49–60. Lucian was born in Samosata, the capital of Commagene, and flourished in the reign of Marcus Aurelius, in the middle of the second century* A.D. *His account of the shrine of Atargatis is an exception to the usual brevity of ancient authors in describing Oriental cults. Although written as a literary performance (it is in Ionic Greek, in the style of Herodotus), it nevertheless contains a vast amount of factual detail. See the translation by H. A. Strong,* The Syrian Goddess, *with commentary by J. E. Garstang (London, 1913), and the brilliant translation by A. M. Harmon in the Loeb Classical Library (*The Works of Lucian, *Vol. IV, pp.* 339–411), *which is done in archaic English and is a good reflection of Lucian's archaic Greek. See also Carl Clemen,* Lukians Schrift über die syrische Göttin *(1938).*

The fascinating introductory paragraph, with which our selection opens, is composed with Herodotean touches and makes a bid for the reader's good will. Lucian then proceeds with a brief survey of the origin of temple building, which occurred in Egypt (2). Coming closer home, he mentions the shrines and cults in ancient Syria, at Tyre, Sidon, Byblus, Aphaca, and finally Hierapolis, where the greatest sanctuary of all was to be found (3–10). The various legends of its foundation are given in detail (11–29): "some of these legends are sacred [i.e., not to be divulged], others are common property; some are completely fabulous, others are the wild and implausible accounts of barbarians; still others tally precisely with sound Greek views of history." Lucian then turns to the description of the temple and its images and adornments, its officers and attendants (30–43), its sacrifices and its ritual (44–48). The concluding sections (49–60), which we give here, describe various customs and institutions connected with the cult. He has already described the sacrifices where three hundred priests were in attendance, and the multitude of corybantic worshipers who frequented the shrine: "holy men, pipers, flutists, Galli—and a crowd of frenzied, frantic women." (42)

(1) In Syria there is a city, not far from the river Euphrates, which is called the Sacred City; it is sacred to the Assyrian Hera. Yet it seems to me that this name was not given the city when it was first settled, but that originally it had another name. In the course of time the great sacrifices were held therein, and then this byname was given it. I am about to speak of this city and of what is in it. I will also tell of the laws that govern its holy rites, of its popular assemblies, and of the sacrifices offered there. I will also tell whatever traditions are recounted of the founders of this holy place and how the temple was founded. I write as a native Assyrian who has witnessed some things with his own eyes, while others he has learned from the priests; these occurred before my time, but I narrate them as they were told to me.

(49) The greatest of all the festivals I know is the one held in the early spring; some call this the [Feast of] Fire, others the Torch. At that time they offer sacrifice in the following way. They cut down great trees and set them up in the court; then they bring goats and sheep and other cattle, and hang them up alive on the trees; among them they hang birds and garments and ornaments of gold and silver. After all this is done, they carry their gods round the trees and set fire to them [the trees]; in an instant they are all afire. To this festival a great multitude gathers from Syria and all the regions roundabout, each of them bringing his own god and the images which each one has for this purpose.

(50) On certain days the multitude crowds into the temple, and the numerous Galli of whom I spoke, who are holy men, perform the ceremonies, gashing their arms and turning their backs to one another to be lashed. Many of the bystanders play flutes; many beat drums; others sing inspired and sacred songs. This performance takes place outside the temple, and those engaged in it do not enter the temple.

(51) During these days men become Galli. While the others play flutes and perform their orgies, the frenzy seizes many of them; and many who have come as spectators presently engage in the same activity. I will tell you what they do. The young man who is thus seized strips off his clothes, and with a loud shout pushes his way into the midst of the crowd [of flagellants] and picks up a sword—for many years, I suppose, these swords have been stacked there. He takes it and at once castrates himself and then runs through the city, carrying in his hands what he has cut off. He throws it into any house he chooses, and from this house he takes women's apparel and ornaments. This is what they do in their ceremonies of castration.

(52) When they die, the Galli are not buried like other men. When a Gallus dies, his companions carry him outside the city, leave him lying on the bier on which they had brought him and cover him over with stones, and then return home. They wait then for seven days before they enter the temple; to enter

earlier would be desecration. (53) The rules which they observe in this connection are as follows: If one of them has seen a corpse, he does not enter the temple the same day; on the next day, after he has purified himself, he enters. But those who belong to the family of the deceased wait for thirty days and then enter the temple, after shaving their heads; before they have done this it is not lawful to enter.

(54) They [the Syrians] sacrifice cattle, both bulls and cows, and goats and sheep; only pigs, which they view as unclean [literally, unholy], they neither sacrifice nor eat. Others look upon swine as not unclean, but sacred. Of birds they view the dove as most holy, and they do not think it right even to touch them; if anyone does so, unintentionally, he is unclean for that day. For this reason doves live right among them, and enter their homes and usually feed on the ground.

(55) I will also tell you what those who come to these festivals do. The first time a man sets out to visit the Sacred City [Hierapolis] he shaves his head and his eyebrows; then he sacrifices a sheep and cuts up its flesh and eats it. The fleece he lays on the ground and kneels on it, but the feet and head of the animal he places on his own head; as he does so, he prays that the present sacrifice may be accepted and promises a greater one next time. When this rite is completed, he crowns his head with a garland, and also the heads of all the others who have come with him on the same pilgrimage. Then, leaving his home, he sets out on the road, using only cold water for bathing and drinking, and always sleeping on the ground; for he is not permitted to sleep in a bed until his pilgrimage is over and he has come home again.

(56) Arrived at the city of Hierapolis, he is received by a public host, even though he is unknown to him; for there are public hosts appointed in each city who entertain guests according to their country. These men are called by the Assyrians "teachers," because they teach them everything [relating to the solemn rites].

(57) They sacrifice victims, but not in the temple itself. After the victim has been presented at the altar and a libation poured

there, the animal is brought home alive. Returning to his house, the owner slays the animal and offers prayers.

(58) There is also another method of sacrifice, like this: They adorn the live animals with garlands and throw them headlong down from the temple's entrance; naturally they die after such a fall. Some even throw their own children down, not as they do the cattle, but they first sew them into a sack and carry them in [and toss them down], jesting the while and saying that they are not children but oxen.

(59) They all tattoo [or brand?] themselves, some on the wrists and some on the neck; and so it is that all the Assyrians bear stigmata.

(60) They have another custom which they share with the Troezenians alone of the Greeks. I will tell you what they do. The Troezenians have made a law for their maidens and youths never to marry until they have shorn their locks in honor of Hippolytus, and that is what they do. It is the same thing at Hierapolis. The young men dedicate the first growth of their chin. And the locks of the children's hair, which have been sacred from their birth, they cut off when they bring them [the children] to the temple, and they place the locks in vessels, some of silver but many of gold; after fastening these to the temple [wall] and inscribing their names on them, they depart. I performed this rite myself when I was young, and my lock of hair and my name are still there in the temple.

A SYRIAN BAAL ARRIVES AT ROME

Dittenberger, OGIS, 594; R. Cagnat, Inscriptiones Graecae ad Res Romanas Pertinentes, Vol. I, p. 420.

In the consulship of Lucius Caese[nnius and Publius Calvisius] in the year 204 according to the Tyrian reckoning [79 A.D.], on the eleventh of Artemision, the god Helios Sareptenos came from Tyre by ship to Puteoli; Elim brought him by command [of the god].

MENDICANT PRIESTS OF THE SYRIAN GODDESS

Apuleius Metamorphoses *VIII 27–28. In the following account Lucius appears as an ass among the frenzied priests of the Syrian Goddess (cf. the description by Lucian above, pp. 116 ff.). The story of his transformation and eventual restoration to human shape, through the intercession of Isis, is also told by Apuleius. (See below, pp. 136 ff.)*

(27) The day following they arrayed themselves in robes of various colors, their faces hideously daubed with paint, and their eyes smeared with pigment, turbans on their heads, cloaks colored like saffron, and garments of silk and linen. Some wore white tunics dyed with purple stripes that pointed every way like spears and were girded with belts, and on their feet they wore yellow shoes. They attired the goddess in a silken robe and put her upon my back. [Lucius is now an ass.] Then they went forth with their arms naked to their shoulders, bearing with them huge swords and axes, shouting and dancing like madmen to the sound of the pipe. After we had passed many small farms, we happened to come to a certain rich man's country house, where as soon as we entered they began to howl discordantly and dashed about here and there, as if they were mad. They danced about fanatically with a sinuous motion of legs and necks; they bent down their heads and spun round so that their hair flew out in a circle; now and then they bit their own flesh; finally, everyone took his two-edged knife and slashed his arms in various places. Meanwhile there was one who raved more madly than the rest; deep pantings arose as from the bottom of his heart, as if some divine spirit filled him, and he feigned a wild injury, as if, forsooth, the presence of the gods did not as a rule make men better than before, but weak and sickly! (28) But note how by divine providence he received a just recompense: he began uttering violent prophecies, and invented and forged a great lie, incessantly upbraiding and accusing himself, saying that he had somehow sinned against the

laws of their holy religion; moreover he demanded that the penalty might be inflicted by his own hands upon himself. Thereupon he seized a whip, the kind these eunuch priests always carry with them, having many twisted knots and tassels of wool and strung with sheep's knucklebones, and with these knotted thongs he savagely scourged his own body. It was wonderful how he bore the pain of the blows. You could see that the ground was wet and discolored with the blood of these effeminates, as it spurted out from the gashes of the swords and the cutting blows of the scourge. Indeed it caused me a good deal of fear to see such wounds and effusion of blood, lest the same foreign goddess should likewise desire to fill her stomach with the blood of an ass [Lucius], as some men have a longing for ass' milk. But at last they were weary, or at least had had enough of this self-inflicted torture; they stopped their butchery, and began collecting their monetary reward into the bosoms [of their flowing robes]: bronze, yes, and silver too, which the crowd offered eagerly, along with jars of wine, milk, cheese, flour, and wheat; and among them were some who brought barley for the ass that carried the goddess. But the greedy beggars stuffed it all into their sacks, which they had brought along for the purpose, and then loaded them on my back, so that I had to serve two purposes: as a storehouse for the provender, and as a temple for the goddess carried on my back.

AN ALTAR IS DEDICATED TO THE SYRIAN GODDESS

Bulletin de Correspondance hellénique, 21 (1897), 60; Latte, Lesebuch, p. 43. This dedication from Syria was made under the Empire.

To the Syrian Goddess of Heliopolis, Lucius her slave has dedicated the altar, after twenty begging journeys during which he filled forty sacks.

THE DIVINE GUIDANCE OF ARKESILAOS

W. K. Prentice, Greek and Latin Inscriptions, No. 242, Pt. III of Publications of an American Archaeological Expedition to Syria in 1899–1900 (New York, 1908), pp. 205–214; Latte, Lesebuch, p. 42; CIG 4464, 9899. This inscription is from the tomb of Abedrapsas and is dated 324 A.D.

So speaks thankfully Abedrapsas: When I had come of age, the god of my fathers, Arkesilaos, clearly appeared [manifested himself] to me and showed me many favors. At the age of twenty-five I gave myself to learn a trade, and in a short while I had learned this trade; further, through his good providence I bought myself a piece of land, without anyone knowing about it, and so was set free from the necessity of going into the city; for I was a righteous person, and so was rightly guided.

3. EGYPTIAN CULTS

The various ways in which Egyptian religion entered into
Hellenistic culture have been indicated in the general intro-
duction. The subject is treated in T. A. Brady, *The Reception
of the Egyptian Cults by the Greeks* (330–30 B.C.), University
of Missouri Studies (1935). See also F. Cumont, *Les Religions
orientales,* Ch. IV; M. P. Nilsson, *Geschichte der griechischen
Religion,* II (1950), pp. 597–613; W. Schubart, *Aegypten von
Alexander dem Grossen bis auf Mohammed* (1922); A. Erman,
Die Religion der Aegypter (1934); F. Cumont, *L'Egypte des
Astrologues* (1937); S. A. B. Mercer, *The Religion of Ancient
Egypt* (1949); J. Cerny, *Ancient Egyptian Religion* (1952);
W. Otto, *Priester und Tempel im hellenistischen Aegypten,* two
vols. (1905, 1908).

THE TRANSLATION OF EGYPTIAN SACRED
LITERATURE INTO GREEK

*Oxyrhynchus Papyri XI. 1381. This is the verso of No. 1380
which follows, and is presumably somewhat later in date, but
still second century, probably under the Antonines. It is preceded by an account, preserved only in its last part, of the
Egyptian original of the Miracle of Asclepius-Imhotep. Imouthes (Imhotep) was a celebrated physician in the Third Dynasty,
and was worshiped after his death.*

Nectenibis on hearing this, being extremely vexed with the
deserters from the temple and wishing to ascertain their number
speedily by a list, ordered Nechautis, who then performed the
duties of *archidicastes,* to investigate the book within a month,
if possible. Nechautis conducted his researches with much strenu-
ousness, and brought the list to the king after spending only two
days instead of thirty upon the inquiry. On reading the book
the king was quite amazed at the divine power in the story, and
finding that there were twenty-six priests who conducted the god
from Heliopolis to Memphis, he assigned to each of their de-

scendants the due post of prophet. Not content with this, after completing the renewal of the book [?], he enriched Asclepius himself with three hundred and thirty arurae more of corn land, especially because he had heard through the book that the god had been worshiped with marks of great reverence by Mencheres.

Having often begun the translation of the said book in the Greek tongue, I learned at length how to proclaim it; but while I was in the full tide of composition my ardor was restrained by the greatness of the story, because I was about to make it public; for to gods alone—not to mortals—is it permitted to describe the mighty deeds of the gods. For if I failed, not only was I ashamed before men, but also hindered by the reproaches [?] that I should incur if the god were vexed and by the poverty of my description, in course of completion, of his undying virtue [?]. But if I did the god a service, my life would be happy and my fame undying; for the god is disposed to confer benefits, since even those whose pious ardor is only for the moment are repeatedly preserved by him after the healing art has failed against diseases which have overtaken them.

Therefore, avoiding rashness and putting off the fulfillment of my promise, I awaited a favorable occasion afforded by old age; for youth especially is wont to aim too high, since immaturity and enterprise too quickly extend our zeal. But when a period of three years had elapsed, in which I was no longer working, and for three years my mother was distracted by an ungodly quartan ague which had seized her, at length, having with difficulty comprehended, we came as suppliants before the god, entreating him to grant my mother recovery from the disease. He, having in dreams shown himself favorable, as he is to all, cured her by simple remedies; and we rendered due thanks to our preserver by sacrifices. When I too afterward was suddenly seized with a pain in my right side, I quickly hastened to the helper of the human race; and he, being again disposed to pity, listened to me, and displayed still more effectively his peculiar clemency, which, as I am intending to recount his terrible powers, I will substantiate.

It was night, when every living creature was asleep except those in pain, but divinity showed itself the more effectively; a violent fever burned me, and I was convulsed with loss of breath and coughing, owing to the pain proceeding from my side. Heavy in the head with my troubles, I was lapsing half-conscious into sleep, and my mother, as a mother would for her child (and she is by nature affectionate), being extremely grieved at my agonies, was sitting without enjoying even a short period of slumber, when suddenly she perceived—it was no dream or sleep, for her eyes were open immovably, though not seeing clearly—a divine and terrifying vision, easily preventing her from observing the god himself or his servants, whichever it was. In any case there was someone whose height was more than human, clothed in shining raiment and carrying in his left hand a book, who, after merely regarding me two or three times from head to foot, disappeared. When she had recovered herself she tried, still trembling, to wake me; and finding that the fever had left me and that much sweat was pouring off me, she did reverence to the manifestation of the god, and then wiped me and made me more calm. When I spoke with her she wished to declare the virtue of the god, but I, anticipating her, told her all myself; for everything that she saw in the vision had appeared to me in dreams.

After these pains in my side had ceased and the god had given me yet another assuaging cure, I proclaimed his benefits. But when we had again besought his favors by sacrifices, to the best of our ability, he demanded through the priest who serves him in the ceremonies the fulfillment of the promise long ago announced to him; and we, although knowing ourselves to be debtors in neither sacrifices nor votive offering, nevertheless supplicated him again with them. But when he said repeatedly that he cared not for these but for what had been previously promised, I was at a loss, and found it hard, since I disparaged it, to assume the divine obligation of the composition.

Now that thou hadst noticed, Master, that I was neglecting the divine book, invoking thy providence and filled with thy divinity, I hastened to the inspired task of the history. But I hope to extend by my proclamation the fame of thy inventiveness, for by a physical treatise in another book I unfolded truly the convincing account of the creation of the world. Throughout the composition I have filled up defects and struck out superfluities, and in telling a rather long tale I have spoken briefly and narrated once and for all a complicated story. Hence, Master, I conjecture that the book has been completed in accordance with thy favor, not with my aim; for it becomes thy divinity to have such a record in writing. And as the discoverer of this art, Asclepius, greatest of gods and my teacher, thou art distinguished by the thanks of all men.

For every gift of a votive offering or sacrifice lasts only for the immediate moment, and presently perishes, while a written record is an undying token of gratitude, from time to time renewing its youth in the memory. Every Greek tongue will tell thy story, and every Greek man will worship the son of Ptah, Imouthes. Assemble hither, ye kindly and good men; avaunt, ye malignant and impious! Assemble, all ye . . . who by serving the god have been cured of diseases, ye who practice the healing art, ye who will labor as zealous followers of virtue, ye who have been blessed by great abundance of benefits, ye who have been saved from the dangers of the sea! For every place has been penetrated by the saving power of the god.

I now purpose to recount his miraculous manifestations, the greatness of his power, the gifts of his benefits. The history is this: King Mencheres, by displaying his piety in the obsequies of three gods and being successful in winning fame through the book, has won eternal glory. He presented to the tombs of Asclepius, son of Hephaestus, Horus, son of Hermes, and also Caleoibis, son of Apollo, money in abundance, and received as recompense his fill of prosperity. For Egypt was then free from war for this reason, and flourished with abundant crops; since subject countries prosper by the piety of their ruler, and on the other hand, owing to his impiety, they are consumed by evils. The manner in which the god Asclepius bade Mencheres busy himself with his tomb. . . . [End of papyrus].

THE TITLES OF ISIS

Oxyrhynchus Papyri *XI. 1380. Dating from the early second century* A.D., *this papyrus was discovered in 1903 and edited by B. P. Grenfell and A. S. Hunt. The long list of titles used of Isis in various places all over the known world gives a good idea of the wide spread of her cult. The worship of Isis was a world religion in the days of Trajan.*

[I invoke thee, who at Aphrodito]polis [art called] One-. . . ; in the House of Hephaestus . . .chmeunis; who at . . .ophis art called Bubastis . . . ; at Letopolis Magna, one . . . ; at Aphrodito-polis in the Prosopite nome, fleet-commanding, many-shaped, Aphrodite; at Delta, giver of favors; at Calamisis, gentle; at Carene, affectionate; at Niciu, immortal, giver; at Hierasus . . . . athroichis; at Momemphis, ruler; at Psochemis, bringer to harbor; at Mylon, ruler . . . ; at Hermopolis, of beautiful form, sacred; at Naucratis, fatherless, joy, savior, almighty, most great; at Nithine in the Gynaecopolite nome, Aphrodite; at Pephremis, Isis, ruler, Hestia, lady of every country; . . . in Asia, worshiped at the three ways; at Petra, savior; at Hypsele, most great; at Rhino-colura, all-seeing; at Dora, friendship; at Stratonos Pyrgos Hellas, good; at Ascalon, mightiest; at Sinope, many-named; at Raphia, mistress; at Tripolis, supporter; at Gaza, abundant; at Delphi, best, fairest; at Bambyce, Atargatis; among the Thracians and in Delos, many-named; among the Amazons, warlike; among the Indians, Maia; among the Thessalians, moon; among the Persians, Latina; among the Magi, Kore, Thapseusis; at Susa, Nania; in Syrophoenicia, goddess; in Samothrace, bull-faced; at Pergamum, mistress; in Pontus, immaculate; in Italy, love of the gods; in Samos, sacred; at the Hellespont, mystic; at Myndus, divine; in Bithynia, Helen; in Tenedos, name of the sun; in Caria, Hecate; in the Troad and at Dindyma. . . , Palentra [?], unapproachable, Isis; at Berytus, Maia; at Sidon, Astarte; at Ptolemaïs, understanding; at Susa in the district by the Red Sea, Sarkounis; thou who expoundest by the fifteen commandments, first ruler of the world; guardian and guide of seas, and Lady of

the mouths and rivers; skilled in writing and calculation, understanding; who also bringest back the Nile over every country; the
beautiful animal [i.e., cow] of all the gods; the glad face in Lethe;
the leader of the muses; the many-eyed; the comely goddess in
Olympus; ornament of the female sex and affectionate; providing
sweetness in assemblies; the lock of hair [? or bunch of grapes]
in festivals; the prosperity of observers of lucky days; Har-
pocratis [i.e., the darling] of the gods; all-ruling in the processions of the gods, enmity-hating; true jewel of the wind and diadem of life; by whose command images and animals of all the
gods, having . . . of thy name, are worshiped; O Lady Isis,
greatest of the gods, first of names, Io Sothis; thou rulest over the
mid-air and the immeasurable; thou devisest the weaving of . . . ;
it is also thy will that women in health come to anchor with men;
all the elders at E . . . ctus sacrifice; all the maidens who . . . at
Heracleopolis turn [?] to thee and dedicated the country to thee;
thou art seen by those who invoke thee faithfully; from whom
. . . in virtue of the 365 combined days; gentle and placable is the
favor of thy two ordinances; thou bringest the sun from rising
unto setting, and all the gods are glad; at the risings of the stars
the people of the country worship thee unceasingly and the other
sacred animals in the sanctuary of Osiris; they become joyful
when they name thee; the . . . daemons become thy subjects; . . .
[the next few lines are very fragmentary] and thou bringest decay
on what thou wilt and to the destroyed bringest increase, and
thou purifiest all things; every day thou didst appoint for joy;
thou . . . having discovered all the . . . of wine providedst it first
in the festivals of the gods . . . ; thou becamest the discoverer
of all things wet and dry and cold [and hot], of which all things
are composed; thou broughtest back alone thy brother, piloting
him safely and burying him fittingly; . . . thou didst establish
shrines of Isis in all cities for all time; and didst deliver to all men
observances and a perfect year; . . . thou didst establish thy son
Horus Apollo everywhere, the youthful Lord of the whole world
and . . . for all time; thou didst make the power of women equal
to that of men; . . . thou hast dominion over winds and thunders
and lightnings and snows; thou, the Lady of war and rule, easily

destroyest tyrants by trusty counsels; thou madest great Osiris immortal, and deliveredst to every country . . . religious observances; likewise thou madest immortal Horus who showed himself a benefactor . . . and good; thou art the Lady of light and flames. . . .

INSCRIPTIONS ON THE TOMBS OF
ISIS AND OSIRIS

Diodorus of Sicily Bibliotheca Historica *I. 27. 3–6. Diodorus lived in the first century* B.C. *and wrote a universal history in forty books. It was very largely a compilation from earlier sources, not very critically sifted. Large parts of the work now exist only in fragments, but some of the material is invaluable, for lack of better. Note how each of the following aretalogies, or lists of divine claims, prerogatives, and titles (pp. 113 ff.), amplifies this one, which may however be an abridgment. The style is the sacral or hieratic style found elsewhere in ancient religious literature.*

(3) I am aware that certain writers say the tombs of these gods are at Nysa in Arabia, and so Dionysus is called Nysaeus; and that there is also a stele for each of these gods, inscribed in hieroglyphics. (4) On that of Isis is inscribed:

I am Isis, the Queen of every land, she who was taught by Hermes; and whatever laws I have ordained no one is able to annul. I am the eldest daughter of Kronos, the youngest of the gods; I am the wife and sister of King Osiris; I am the one who first found fruit for men; I am the mother of King Horus; I am she who rises in the constellation of the Dog; for me the city of Bubastis was founded. Rejoice, rejoice, O land of Egypt that nourished me!

(5) On the stele of Osiris they say it reads:

My Father is Kronos, the youngest of all the gods, and I am Osiris the King, who has fought wars in every land, as far as the uninhabited regions of India and the far borders of the North, even to the springs of the river Ister [the Danube], and again

to the other parts of the earth even as far as Oceanus. I am the
eldest son of Kronos, and I am the growth of a fair and noble
Egg, a seed by birth related to Day. There is no place in the inhabited world that I have not visited, freely granting to all men
the things of which I am the discoverer.

(6) This much of what is written on the steles, they say, can
be read, but the rest, which is the main part, is almost undecipherable from age.

As for the tombs of these gods, therefore, varying accounts will
be found in most authors, as a result of the fact that the priests,
who received accurate information about these matters, but as
an ineffable secret [tradition], are unwilling to divulge the truth
to the public, since threats of danger hang over the heads of
those who disclose these secrets about the gods to the multitude.

THE PRAISES OF ISIS

*Bulletin de Correspondance hellénique, LI (1927), 379 f. (Text
in W. Haussmann, editor, Pantheion, 1948, p. 37.) Werner
Peek, Der Isishymnus von Andros und verwandte Texte (Berlin
1930); cf. Karl Kundsin, Charakter und Ursprung der Johan-
neischen Reden (Riga, 1939), pp. 291–293. This is a second-
century recension, found in Cyme in Asia Minor, obviously a
copy of an Isis aretalogy, or series of claims on behalf of the
goddess, from Memphis and the most complete of the various
parallel versions. It is interesting to compare the various recen-
sions and study the spread of the cult of Isis.*

*[Demetrius, son of Artemidorus, and Thraseas, the Magnesian
from the Maeander, crave the blessing of Isis. The following
was copied from the stele which is in Memphis, where it stands
before the temple of Hephaestus:]*

I am Isis, the mistress of every land, and I was taught by
Hermes, and with Hermes I devised letters, both the sacred
[hieroglyphs] and the demotic, that all things might not be
written with the same [letters].

I gave and ordained laws for men, which no one is able to change.

I am eldest daughter of Kronos.

I am wife and sister of King Osiris.

I am she who findeth fruit for men.

I am mother of King Horus.

I am she that riseth in the Dog Star.

I am she that is called goddess by women.

For me was the city of Bubastis built.

I divided the earth from the heaven.

I showed the paths of the stars.

I ordered the course of the sun and the moon.

I devised business in the sea.

I made strong the right.

I brought together woman and man.

I appointed to women to bring their infants to birth in the tenth month.

I ordained that parents should be loved by children.

I laid punishment upon those disposed without natural affection toward their parents.

I made with my brother Osiris an end to the eating of men.

I revealed mysteries unto men.

I taught [men] to honor images of the gods.

I consecrated the precincts of the gods.

I broke down the governments of tyrants.

I made an end to murders.

I compelled women to be loved by men.

I made the right to be stronger than gold and silver.

I ordained that the true should be thought good.

I devised marriage contracts.

I assigned to Greeks and barbarians their languages.

I made the beautiful and the shameful to be distinguished by nature.

I ordained that nothing should be more feared than an oath.

I have delivered the plotter of evil against other men into the hands of the one he plotted against.

I established penalties for those who practice injustice.

I decreed mercy to suppliants.
I protect [or honor] righteous guards.
With me the right prevails.
I am the Queen of rivers and winds and sea.
No one is held in honor without my knowing it.
I am the Queen of war.
I am the Queen of the thunderbolt.
I stir up the sea and I calm it.
I am in the rays of the sun.
I inspect the courses of the sun.
Whatever I please, this too shall come to an end.
With me everything is reasonable.
I set free those in bonds.
I am the Queen of seamanship.
I make the navigable unnavigable when it pleases me.
I created walls of cities.
I am called the Lawgiver [Thesmophoros, a classical epithet of
   Demeter].
I brought up islands out of the depths into the light.
I am Lord [note masculine form] of rainstorms.
I overcome Fate.
Fate harkens to me.
Hail, O Egypt, that nourished me!

AN ARETALOGY OF KARPOKRATES

An inscription found in Chalcis, from about 250–300 A.D. *Published by Richard Harder in* Karpokrates von Chalkis und die memphitische Isis-propaganda *(Berlin, 1944) and translated by A. D. Nock in* Gnomon XXI *(1949), 221. The ends of the lines are lost, but the text was obiously an aretalogy, like the "Praises of Isis" and similar pieces, and represents an aspect of the cult of Isis. It has been reprinted here by kind permission of Dr. Nock and the editor, Dr. Walter Marg. See the whole review in* Gnomon, *pp. 221–228.*

   I am Karpokrates, son of Sarapis and Isis . . . of Demeter and Kore and Dionysus and Iacchus . . . brother of Sleep and Echo.

I am every season and take thought for all seasons, the inventor of. . . . I created. . . . I was the first to make *adyta* and sanctuaries for the gods; I devised measures and numbers. . . . I produced the sistrum for Isis; I devised the ways to hunt all kinds of animals. . . . I established rulers for cities at all times; I preside over the upbringing of children; I established hymns . . . and dances of men and women, the Muses aiding me; I invented the mixing of wine and water; . . . of flutes and pipes; I am always at the side of litigants in order that nothing unjust may be done; I always share the *thiasoi* of Bacchoi and Bacchae; I caused . . . to spring up; I cleansed the whole earth; mountain dwelling, sea-dwelling, river dwelling, divining by throne, divining by stars; . . . horn-shaped, Agyieus, Bassareus, of the heights, Indian-slaying, thyrsus-shaking, Assyrian hunter, wandering in dreams, giver of sleep . . . ; approving . . . vengeful against those who are unjust in love. I hate the accursed; . . . all the science of drugs for doctors for healing, Titanian, Epidaurian. Hail Chalcis, my mother and nurse. [There follows the name of the dedicant, Ligyris, who —the translator thinks—was probably the author.]

ISIS ADDRESSES HORUS

From the Kore Kosmou, *quoted by Stobaeus (fifth century?) in* Eclogae I. 41. 44 ad fin. (p. 297 Meineke). Compare E. Bevan, Sibyls and Seers, p. 82; W. Scott, Hermetica, I (1924), pp. 491 ff., with a greatly emended text. The Kore Kosmou is a Hermetic tract, containing a discourse of Isis to her son Horus. It is of special interest in that it gives the contents of an Isis aretalogy in narrative style. As in most Isiac literature, the social significance of that religion is clearly marked.*

Then Horus said, "O Mother that bare me, tell me how the earth came to be blessed with the divine efflux!"

And Isis replied, "Excuse me from describing birth; it is not right to describe the origin of your begetting, O mighty Horus, lest perchance later on there should enter into men a birth of the immortal gods—except to say that the God who alone rules, the Creator and Fashioner of the whole universe, bestowed on the earth for a little while your great father Osiris and the great goddess Isis, that they might be the helpers of the world in its universal need. It was they who filled human life with that which is [truly] life, and thereby put a stop to the savagery of mutual slaughter. It was they who consecrated temples and instituted sacrifices to the ancestral gods, and gave to mortal men the blessings of laws, and of food and shelter. It is they who will come to know, said Hermes, all the secrets of letters, and will distinguish between them; and some they will keep for themselves, others which are for the welfare of mankind they will publish by inscribing them on tablets and obelisks. [This last sentence may be out of place, or the text may be corrupt.] It was they who first, having approved courts of law, filled the universe with good order and righteousness. It was they who, as the founders of pledges and of good faith, introduced into [human] life that mighty god, the oath. It was they who taught men the right way to wrap the bodies of those who have ceased to live. It was they who sought the [cause] of death; and they found that the breath which enters from without into men's bodily frames, if it ever fails, cannot be restored, and the result is unconsciousness. It was they who, having learned from Hermes that the surrounding atmosphere is full of daemons, inscribed [this statement, or the names of the daemons?] on hidden tablets. It was they alone who, having learned from Hermes the hidden ordinances of God governing the arts and sciences, and all studies, became the ones who introduced [them] among men, and [their] lawgivers. It was they who, having learned from Hermes how by the command of the Creator the things here below are bound by sympathy to those above, established upon earth the sacred rites previously ordained in the mysteries in heaven. It was they who, recognizing the corruption of bodies, devised the initiation [cj., *teleten,* or the order] of prophets [i.e., Egyptian priests] everywhere, so that no prophet about to lift his hands to the gods [in prayer] should ever be ignorant of any of the things that really exist, and so that philosophy and magic might nourish the soul, and the art of medicine save the body when it suffers.

"When we had done all this, my son, Osiris and I, seeing that the world had been filled as fully as possible with blessings, were asked to come back from now on by the dwellers in the heavens. But we had no return before invoking the Sole Ruler [and praying] that the atmosphere might be filled with this vision [of the world full of blessings], and that we ourselves might fortunately find our journey upwards well received."

"God rejoices in hymns, O Mother," said Horus, "and so grant to me the knowledge of the hymn, lest I be uninstructed."

And Isis replied, "Listen, son." [Presumably a hymn must have followed here; if so, Stobaeus omitted it.]

ISIS RESTORES LUCIUS

Apuleius Metamorphoses *XI. 1–25. Apuleius of Madaura, in North Africa, lived in the second century* A.D. *He was a lawyer, a novelist, and an orator. His famous* Metamorphoses, *which used to be called* The Golden Ass, *is a thinly veiled apologetic and autobiographic work in eleven books, replete with charming tales (e.g., "Cupid and Psyche" in IV, 28—VI. 24). The hero, Lucius, being over-curious about magic, is accidentally turned into an ass. His restoration to human shape by the mercy of Isis and his initiation into her rites form the climax of the work and are regarded as being based on direct acquaintance with the Isis mysteries. See the fascinating translation by William Adlington (London, 1566) revised by S. Gaselee and reprinted in the* Loeb Classical Library. *A good modern translation is that of H. E. Butler in the* Oxford Library of Translations *(1910). See also Elizabeth H. Haight,* Apuleius and His Influence *(1927).*

Introduction

[Book XI opens with an auspicious note of mystery. Lucius is spending the night asleep on the warm sand of the seashore.]

About the first watch of the night, I awoke in sudden terror; the full moon had risen and was shining with unusual splendor as it emerged from the waves. All about me lay the mysterious silence of the night. I knew that this was the hour when the goddess [Isis] exercised her greatest power and governed all things by her providence—not only animals, wild and tame, but even inanimate things were renewed by her divine illumination and might; even the heavenly bodies, the whole earth, and the vast sea waxed or waned in accordance with her will.

The Epiphany of Isis

[Lucius decides to make his appeal to Isis for release from his asinine disguise, and the goddess responds. His prayer in §2 recounts her titles as Queen of Heaven, Ceres, Proserpina, celestial Venus.]

(3) So I poured out my prayers and supplications, adding to them much pitiful wailing, and once more fell sound asleep on that same bed of sand. Scarcely had I closed my eyes when lo! from the midst of the deep there arose that face divine to which even the gods must do reverence. Then a little at a time, slowly, her whole shining body emerged from the sea and came into full view. I would like to tell you all the wonder of this vision, if the poverty of human speech does not prevent, or if the divine power dwelling within that form supplies a rich enough store of eloquence.

First, the tresses of her hair were long and thick, and streamed down softly, flowing and curling about her divine neck. On her head she wore as a crown many garlands of flowers, and in the middle of her forehead shone white and glowing a round disc like a mirror, or rather like the moon; on its right and left it was bound about with the furrowed coils of rising vipers, and above it were stalks of grain. Her tunic was of many colors, woven of the finest linen, now gleaming with snowy whiteness, now yellow like the crocus, now rosy-red like a flame. But what dazzled my eyes more than anything else was her cloak, for it was a deep black, glistening with sable sheen; it was cast about her, passing under her right arm and brought together on her left shoulder. Part of it hung down like a shield and drooped in many a fold, the whole reaching to the lower edge of her garment with tasseled fringe. (4) Here and there along its embroidered border, and also on its surface, were scattered sequins of sparkling stars, and in their midst the full moon of midmonth shone forth like a flame of fire. And all along the border of that gorgeous robe there was an unbroken garland of all kinds of flowers and fruits.

In her hands she held emblems of various kinds. In her right hand she carried a bronze rattle [the sistrum] made of a thin piece of metal curved like a belt, through which were passed a few small rods; this gave out a tinkling sound whenever she shook it three times with a quivering pulsation. In her left hand was a golden cup, from the top of whose slender handle rose an asp, towering with head erect and its throat distended on both sides. Her perfumed feet were shod with sandals woven of the palm of victory.

Such was the vision, and of such majesty. Then, breathing forth all the blessed fragrance of happy Arabia, she deigned to address me with voice divine: (5) "Behold, Lucius, I have come, moved by thy prayers! I, nature's mother, mistress of all the elements, earliest offspring of the ages, mightiest of the divine powers, Queen of the dead, chief of them that dwell in the heavens, in whose features are combined those of all the gods and goddesses. By my nod I rule the shining heights of heaven, the wholesome winds of the sea, and the mournful silences of the underworld. The whole world honors my sole deity [*numen unicum*] under various forms, with varied rites, and by many names. There the Phrygians, firstborn of men, call me the Mother of the Gods, she who dwells at Pessinus; there the Athenians, sprung from their own soil, know me as Cecropian Minerva; there the sea-girt Cyprians call me Paphian Venus; the Cretans, who are archers, call me Diana Dictynna [of the hunter's net]; the Sicilians, with their three languages, call me Stygian Proserpina; the Eleusinians, the ancient goddess Ceres. Others call me Juno, others Bellona, others Hecate, while still others call me the Rhamnusian. But those on whom shine the first rays of the Sun-God as daily he springs to new birth, the Arii and the Ethiopians, and the Egyptians mighty in ancient lore, honoring me with my peculiar rites, call me by my true name, *Isis the Queen*.

"I have come in pity for thy woes. I have come, propitious and ready to aid. Cease from thy weeping and lamentation, and lay aside thy grief! For thee, by my providence, the day of salvation

is dawning! Therefore turn thy afflicted spirit, and give heed to
what I command. The day, even the very day that follows this
night, is dedicated to me by an everlasting dedication; for on this
day, after I have laid to rest the storms of winter and stilled the
tempestuous waves of the sea, my priests shall dedicate to the
deep, which is now navigable once more, a new boat, and offer
it in my honor as the first fruits of the year's seafaring. Thou
must await this festival with untroubled heart and with no profane thoughts."

*[The goddess tells Lucius that he must mingle with the crowd
at the Ploiaphesia and edge his way up to the priest, who will
be wearing a garland of roses. Having been forewarned by the
goddess in a vision, the priest will be prepared for what is to
happen, namely, that Lucius (still the ass) will seize the priest's
garland and eat it, whereupon he will be restored to human
form. And so it takes place. Transformed once more into
human shape, Lucius is exhorted by one of the priests, "whose
smiling face seemed more than mortal":]*

(15) "O Lucius, after enduring so many labors and escaping
so many tempests of Fortune, you have now at length reached
the port and haven of rest and mercy! Neither your noble lineage
nor your high rank nor your great learning did anything for you;
but because you turned to servile pleasures, by a little youthful
folly you won the grim reward of your hapless curiosity. And yet
while Fortune's blindness tormented you with various dangers,
by her very malice she has brought you to this present state of
religious blessedness. Let Fortune go elsewhere and rage with her
wild fury, and find someone else to torment! For Fortune has no
power over those who have devoted themselves to serve the
majesty of our goddess. For all your afflictions—robbers, wild
beasts, slavery, toilsome and futile journeys that ended where
they began, and the daily fear of death—all these brought no
advantage to wicked Fortune. Now you are safe, under the pro-
tection of that Fortune who is not blind but can see, who by her
clear light enlightens the other gods. Therefore rejoice and put
on a more cheerful countenance, appropriately matching your
white robe, and follow with joyful steps the procession of this
Savior Goddess. Let all such as are not devout followers of the

goddess see and acknowledge their error[, saying]: 'See, here is
Lucius, freed from his former miseries by the providence of the
great goddess Isis, and rejoicing in triumph over his Fortune!'
And in order that you may live even more safely and securely,
hand in your name to this sacred militia [i.e., join the Isiac order]
—for it is only a little while ago that you were asked to take the
oath—and dedicate yourself to obey our religion and take upon
yourself the voluntary yoke of ministry. For when you have
begun to serve the goddess, then will you realize more fully the
fruits of your liberty."

The Initiation of Lucius

*[And so the priest prophesied and made his appeal to Lucius,
and Lucius consented and joined the procession, amid the jeers
of the unbelievers. But his conversion, like that of many others,
was a slow process, and only gradually did he come to identify
himself with the Isiac priests; for, like many another, he believed the strict profession of religion was something too hard
for him: "The laws of chastity and abstinence are not easy to
obey" (19). And yet he continued to frequent the services of
worship (21), and eventually came to desire earnestly to be
admitted to the mysteries of Isis. This took place on "the night
that is sacred to the goddess."]*

(22) The priest finished speaking, and I did not mar my obedience by any impatience, but with a quiet and gentle and edify-
ing silence I rendered attentive service at the daily observance
of the sacred rites. Nor did the saving grace of the mighty goddess
in any way deceive me or torture me with long delays, but in the
dark of night, by commands that were not in the least dark, she
clearly signified to me that the day so long desired had come, in
which she would grant the fulfillment of my most earnest prayers.
She also stated what amount I must provide for the supplications,
and she appointed Mithras himself, her high priest, to administer
the rites to me; for his destiny, she said, was closely bound up
with mine by the divine conjunction of the stars.

These and other gracious admonitions of the supreme goddess
refreshed my spirit, so that even before it was clear day I shook
off sleep and hastened at once to the priest's lodging. I met him

just as he was coming out of his bedchamber, and saluted him.
I had decided to request with even more insistence that I should
be initiated, now that it was due me. But he at once, as soon as
he saw me, anticipated me, saying, "Lucius, you happy, you
greatly blessed man, whom the august deity deigns to favor with
such good will! But why," he asked, "do you stand here idle,
yourself delaying? The day you have so long asked for by your
unwearied prayers has come, when by the divine commands of
the goddess of many names you are to be admitted by my hands into
the most holy secrets of the mysteries." Then, taking my right hand
in his, the gentle old man led me to the very doors of the huge
temple; and after celebrating with solemn ritual the opening of
the gates and completing the morning sacrifice, he brought out
from a hidden place in the temple certain books whose titles were
written in undecipherable letters. Some of these [letters] were
shaped like all kinds of animals and seemed to be brief ways of
suggesting words; others had their extremities knotted or curved
like wheels, or intertwined like the tendrils of a vine, which was
enough to safeguard them from the curiosity of profane readers.
At the same time he told me about the various preparations it
was necessary to make in view of my initiation.

(23) I lost no time, but promptly and with a liberality even
beyond what was required I either bought these things myself or
had my friends buy them for me. And now, the time drawing
near and requiring it, as he said, the priest conducted me with
an escort of the religiously-minded to the nearest baths; and when
I entered the bath, where it is customary for the neophytes to
bathe, he first prayed to the gods to be gracious to me and then
sprinkled me with purest water and cleansed me. He then led me
back to the temple, and since the day was now more than half
over he placed me at the feet of the goddess herself; then, after
confiding certain secret orders to me, those which were too holy to
be spoken, he openly, before all who were present, bade me for
ten successive days to abstain from all pleasures of the table, to
eat no meat and drink no wine. All these requirements I observed
with scrupulous care. And at last came the day designated by the
divine guarantee. The sun was sloping downward and bringing

on the evening when lo! from everywhere came crowds of the
initiates, flocking around me, and each of them, following the
ancient rite, presented me with various gifts. Finally, all the
uninitiated having withdrawn, they put on me a new linen robe,
and the priest, seizing me by the hand, led me to the very inmost
recesses of the holy place.

It may be, my studious reader, that you would very much like
to know what was said there and what was done. I would tell
you if it were lawful for me to tell, and you would know all if
it were lawful for you to hear. But both tongue and ear would
be infected as the consequence of such rash curiosity! Yet it may
of course be a pious longing that torments you, and so I will
torture you no longer. Hear then and believe, for what I tell you
is true. I drew near to the confines of death, treading the very
threshold of Proserpine. I was borne through all the elements and
returned to earth again. At the dead of night, I saw the sun
shining brightly. I approached the gods above and the gods below,
and worshiped them face to face. See, I have told you things
which, though you have heard them, you still must know nothing about. I will therefore relate only as much as may, without
committing a sin, be imparted to the understanding of the
uninitiate.

(24) As soon as it was morning and the solemn rites had been
completed, I came forth clothed in the twelve gowns that are
worn by the initiate, apparel that is really most holy, but about
which no sacred ban forbids me to tell, since at that time there
were many who saw me wearing it. For in the very midst of the
holy shrine, before the image of the goddess, there was a wooden
platform on which I was directed to stand, arrayed in a robe
which, although it was only of linen, was so richly embroidered
that I was a sight to behold. The precious cape hung from my
shoulders down my back even to the ground, and it was adorned,
wherever you looked, with the figures of animals in various colors.
Here were Indian dragons, there griffins from the Hyperborean
regions, winged like birds, but out of another world. This cape the
initiates call the Olympian. In my right hand I carried a flaming
torch, and my head was decorated with a crown made of white

palm leaves, spread out to stand up like rays. After I had been thus adorned like the sun and set up like an image of a god, the curtains were suddenly withdrawn, and the people crowded around to gaze at me.

Thereafter I celebrated this most joyful birthday of my initiation, and there were feasts and gay parties. The third day was likewise celebrated with formal ceremonies, with a solemn breaking of my fast, and the due consummation of my initiation. I remained a few days longer, enjoying the ineffable delight of being near the image of the goddess, to whom I was now pledged by blessings which I could never repay. But at length being admonished by the goddess, I offered up my humble thanks—not indeed in the full measure of my debt to her, but to the best of my poor abilities—and made a tardy preparation for my homeward journey; but it was hard to break the bonds of burning desire that held me back. At last I entered into the presence of the goddess and prostrated myself before her; and after I had for a long time wiped her feet with my face, I spoke, though there were tears in my eyes and my voice was so broken with sobs that my words were swallowed up:

(25) "O holy and eternal guardian of the human race, who dost always cherish mortals and bless them, thou carest for the woes of miserable men with a sweet mother's love. Neither day nor night, nor any moment of time, ever passes by without thy blessings, but always on land and sea thou watchest over men; thou drivest away from them the tempests of life and stretchest out over them thy saving right hand, wherewith thou dost unweave even the inextricable skein of the Fates; the tempests of Fortune thou dost assuage and restrainest the baleful motions of the stars. Thee the gods above adore, thee the gods below worship. It is thou that whirlest the sphere of heaven, that givest light to the sun, that governest the universe and tramplest down Tartarus. To thee the stars respond, for thee the seasons return, in thee the gods rejoice, and the elements serve thee. At thy nod the winds blow, the clouds nourish [the earth], the seeds sprout, and the buds swell. Before thy majesty the birds tremble as they flit to and fro in the sky, and the beasts as they roam the moun-

tains, the serpents hiding in the ground, and the monsters swimming in the deep. But my skill is too slight to tell thy praise, my wealth too slender to make thee due offerings of sacrifice. Nor has my voice that rich eloquence to say what I feel would suffice for thy majesty—no, not even had I a thousand mouths, a thousand tongues, and could continue forever with unwearied speech! Therefore the only thing one can do, if one is devout but otherwise a pauper, that I will strive to do. Thy face divine and thy most holy deity—these I will hide away deep within my heart; thine image I shall treasure forever!"

Having thus pleaded with the mighty deity, I embraced Mithras the priest, now my spiritual father, and hanging upon his neck with many a kiss I begged his forgiveness, since I could make no proper return for all the great benefits that he had conferred upon me. (26) Then, after many words of thanks, long drawn out, I finally set out for home by the shortest route . . . a few days later, led on by the mighty goddess, I reached Rome on the eve of the Ides of December.

THE CULT OF SARAPIS

Papiri Greci e Latini, *Pubblicazioni della Società Italiana per la ricerca dei Papiri greci e latini in Egitto, IV. 435; Latte,* Lesebuch, *pp. 36 f. This papyrus is dated 258–257* B.C. *See also Otto Weinreich,* Neue Urkunden zur Sarapis-Religion (1919), *and the long passage from Aelius Aristides,* Oratio VIII, *given in Edwyn Bevan's* Later Greek Religion, *pp. 71–76.*

To Apollonios, greetings from Zoilos of Aspendos . . . which the king's cousins will deliver to you. As I was worshiping the god Sarapis and interceding for your health and your favor with King Ptolemy, Sarapis repeatedly, in dreams, laid upon me the duty of going to you and conveying to you the following directions: A Sarapieion and a sacred area must be built for him in the Greek quarter beside the harbor; a priest must be appointed and offer sacrifices there for us. When I begged him to release me from this duty, he let me fall into a severe illness, so that I was even in danger of my life. Then I prayed to him [and promised] that, if he would make me well, I should undertake the mission and carry out his command. Just when I had recovered, someone came from Cnidus and began building a Sarapieion at the place, and had ordered the stone brought there. Later on, the god forbade him to build, and he went away. When I came to Alexandria and hesitated to go to you with my message until you at last granted me the opportunity, I had a relapse that lasted for four months, and so I could not come to you immediately. Please, Apollonios, carry out the command of the god, so that Sarapis may be gracious to you and lead you to still greater influence with the king and [grant you] fame and physical health. You need not be alarmed over this commission and the large expenditure it entails; instead, it will be greatly to your advantage, for I will myself share in managing the whole undertaking. May all go well with you!

4. ATTIS AND MITHRAS

The cult of Attis arose in Asia Minor, where the god was associated with the Mother Goddess Cybele. The cult was probably a prehistoric vegetation rite, which reached its climax in the self-mutilation of the devotees. Greece never adopted the cult, but it was known in Rome and even attained official recognition under Claudius.

Mithras (originally Mithra) was an ancient Aryan deity adopted by the Persians, and was passed on by them to the West. He was identified with Helios, the Sun-God, whose importance increased steadily during the later Hellenistic-Roman age. Brought from Asia Minor to Italy by Pompey's soldiers, the cult spread wherever the Roman armies were stationed, even as far north as Germany and Britain. See F. Cumont, *Textes et Monuments figurés relatifs aux Mystères de Mithra*, 2 vols. (1896, 1899); *Les Mystères de Mithra*, third edition (1913; English translation, second edition 1910); *Les Religions orientales dans le Paganisme romain*, fourth edition (1929; English translation of the second edition, 1911).

THE MYSTERIES OF ATTIS

Firmicus Maternus, De Errore Profanarum Religionum 22.

On a specified night, the image of the god [Attis] is laid upon a portable bier, and is mourned in rhythmic, oft-repeated laments. When they have had their fill of this feigned grief, a light is brought in. Then the priest anoints the throats of all present, and afterward whispers softly to them:

Take courage, ye mystae, the god is saved;
So shall salvation be ours, sometime, from all need.

THE SACRIFICE OF THE TAUROBOLIUM

Corpus Inscriptionum Latinarum *VI. 510; H. Dessau,* Inscriptiones Latinae Selectae *II. 1 (1902), No. 4152. This inscription was found at Rome, dated August 13, 376* A.D.

To the Great Gods, to the Mother of the Gods, and to Attis, the honorable Sextilius Agesilaus Aedesius, the worthy Solicitor in the African court, Imperial Councilor, President of the Supreme Commission on Petitions and Investigations, Head of the Chancellery, Captain of the Prefects in Spain in all the most important matters, Father of Fathers of the Invincible Sun God Mithras, Hierophant of Hecate, Chief Shepherd of Dionysus, reborn unto eternity through the sacrifice of a bull and a ram—has dedicated the altar, on the Ides of August, while our Lords Valens, for the fifth time, and Valentinian the younger, the Augusti, were consuls.

INITIATION OF MITHRAIC MYSTAE

CIL *VI. 750, 751a; H. Dessau,* Inscriptiones Latinae Selectae, *4267 b–c. This inscription was found at Rome, dated 358* A.D.

(b) In the consulship of Datianus and Cerealis the honorable Nonius Victor Olympius, Father of Fathers, and the honorable Aurelius Victor Augentius, Father, undertook the initiation of the rank of Persian on the fourth of April. Hail! In the same year they undertook the initiation of the rank of the Sun on the sixteenth of [April]. Hail!

(c) In the consulship of Datianus and Cerealis the honorable Nonius Victor Olympius, Father of Fathers, and the honorable Aurelius Victor Augentius, Father, undertook the initiation of the rank of Father on the nineteenth of April. Hail! In the same year they were shown the hidden things [*cryfios*] on the twenty-fourth of April. Hail!

DESCRIPTION OF AN INITIATION

Plutarch On the Soul 2, *quoted in Stobaeus* Florilegium *120; G. N. Bernardakis, Plutarchi Moralia, VII (1896), p. 23. Stobaeus credits the fragment to Themistius, but Wyttenbach claimed it for Plutarch. Konrat Ziegler, in* Plutarchos von Chaironea *(1949), preprint of the forthcoming article in Pauly-Wissowa, Cols. 115 f. says: "Das Stück ist echtester Plutarch, auch nach Stil und Sprache, und hiatfrei." Compare A. O. Prickard, Selected Essays of Plutarch, Vol. II (Oxford, 1918), pp. 215–216.*

[Death is not destruction, but release—as even Homer implies; the dead are at rest, released from great distress, beyond the capacity of nature to endure. Death is an experience like that of initiation into the great mysteries:]

Thus death and initiation closely correspond; even the words [*teleutan* and *teleisthai*] correspond, and so do the things. At first there are wanderings, and toilsome running about in circles, and journeys through the dark over uncertain roads and *culs de sac;* then, just before the end, there are all kinds of terrors, with shivering, trembling, sweating, and utter amazement. After this, a strange and wonderful light meets the wanderer; he is admitted into clean and verdant meadows, where he discerns gentle voices, and choric dances, and the majesty of holy sounds and sacred visions. Here the now fully initiated is free, and walks at liberty like a crowned and dedicated victim, joining in the revelry; he is the companion of pure and holy men, and looks down upon the uninitiated and unpurified crowd here below in the mud and fog, trampling itself down and crowded together, through fear of death remaining still sunk in its evils, unable to believe in the blessings that lie beyond. That the wedding and close union of the soul with the body is a thing really contrary to nature may clearly be seen from all this.

THE PIETY OF INITIATES

F. Bücheler, Carmina Latina Epigraphica, *No. 111. This inscription is dated a little after 384* A.D. *See the introduction to this volume. The inscription begins with an account of the honors paid the deceased, and then continues:*

But these are nothing. Thou, O pious mystes,
Dost hide, within that secret inmost shrine
Of thy pure heart, what holy initiates know,
Honoring the manifold majesty of God.
Thy spouse thou takest for fellow in thy prayer
At every sacrifice; she truly shares
With thee all mysteries in heaven and earth.
Shall I recount thine honors, or thy power,
Or those rich joys that all men long to gain?
All these were ever fleeting, in thine eyes;
The holy priestly fillet was thy crown.
Belov'd, by virtue of the teaching thou
Hast set me free from this fell lot of death!
For pure and chaste was I when thou
Unto the temple leddest me, and to the gods
Devoted me their servant, guiding me,
A full initiate in the holy rite
As priestess of the Mother of the Gods
And Attis; so thou honoredst me as spouse
Through the red sacrament, the blood of bull,
And taught me that deep threefold mystery
Of Hecat, yea, and made me worthy e'en
To share Demeter's blessed age-old rites.

IV. RELIGIOUS IDEAS OF THE PHILOSOPHERS

There are many works dealing with Hellenistic philosophy. In addition to the great standard histories, such as Eduard Zeller's *Philosophie der Griechen* (incompletely translated into English), Karl Praechter's edition of Friedrich Ueberweg's *Grundriss der Geschichte der Philosophie des Altertums*, §§ 54a–87, W. Windelband's *Geschichte der Abendländischen Philosophie im Altertum*, E. Brehier's *Histoire de la Philosophie*, Vol. I, and W. Nestle's edition of Zeller's *Grundriss der Geschichte der griechischen Philosophie* (translated), see also M. P. Nilsson, *Geschichte der griechischen Religion*, Vol. II (1950), pp. 237–256, 376–447. See further the many illustrative passages given in Gordon H. Clark, *Selections from Hellenistic Philosophy* (1940); R. W. Livingstone, *The Mission of Greece* (1928); Edwyn Bevan, *Later Greek Religion* (1927).

CLEANTHES

Cleanthes of Assos (331–233 B.C.) was the disciple and successor of Zeno as head of the Stoic school. He was the real founder of Stoic theology. The surviving fragments of his works are given in H. von Arnim, *Stoicorum Veterum Fragmenta*, Vol. I, pp. 103 ff. Both the prayer and hymn given here reflect a deeply religious outlook. See J. Adam, *The Vitality of Platonism* (1911), pp. 104–189.

INVOCATION

H. von Arnim, Fragment 527. This beautiful prayer is often quoted. Cicero and Epictetus were among the first to use it.

Lead me, O Zeus, and thou, O Destiny, to the end that ye have ordained for me. I will follow without reluctance. Were I a fool, and refused, I should nevertheless have to follow!

HYMN TO ZEUS

Stobaeus Eclogae *I. 1. 12.*

Most glorious of immortals, Zeus
The many-named, almighty evermore,
Nature's great Sovereign, ruling all by law—
Hail to thee! On thee 'tis meet and right
That mortals everywhere should call.
From thee was our begetting; ours alone
Of all that live and move upon the earth
The lot to bear God's likeness.
Thee will I ever chant, thy power praise!

For thee this whole vast cosmos, wheeling round
The earth, obeys, and where thou leadest

It follows, ruled willingly by thee.
In thy unconquerable hands thou holdest fast,
Ready prepared, that two-tined flaming blast,
The ever-living thunderbolt:
Nature's own stroke brings all things to their end.
By it thou guidest aright the sense instinct
Which spreads through all things, mingled even
With stars in heaven, the great and small—
Thou who art King supreme for evermore!

Naught upon earth is wrought in thy despite, O God,
Nor in the ethereal sphere aloft which ever winds
About its pole, nor in the sea—save only what
The wicked work, in their strange madness.
Yet even so thou knowest to make the crooked straight,
Prune all excess, give order to the orderless;
For unto thee the unloved still is lovely—
And thus in one all things are harmonized,
The evil with the good, that so one Word
Should be in all things everlastingly.

One Word—which evermore the wicked flee!
Ill-fated, hungering to possess the good
They have no vision of God's universal law,
Nor will they hear; though if obedient in mind
They might obtain a noble life, true wealth.
Instead, they rush unthinking after ill:
Some with a shameless zeal for fame,
Others pursuing gain, disorderly;
Still others folly, or pleasures of the flesh.
[But evils are their lot,] and other times
Bring other harvests, all unsought—
For all their great desire, its opposite!

But, Zeus, thou giver of every gift,
Who dwellest within the dark clouds, wielding still
The flashing stroke of lightning, save, we pray,
Thy children from this boundless misery.

Scatter, O Father, the darkness from their souls,
Grant them to find true understanding—
On which relying thou justly rulest all—
While we, thus honored, in turn will honor thee,
Hymning thy works forever, as is meet
For mortals, while no greater right
Belongs even to the gods than evermore
Justly to praise the universal law!

EPICTETUS ON PROVIDENCE

Epictetus, *Discourses* I. 16. Epictetus, noblest of the Stoics, was the son of a slave woman, and was himself a slave for part of his life, and lame—a brutal master had broken his leg while he was still a child. Saint Chrysostom preserves his epitaph, which has been translated by H. Macnaghten:

Slave, poor as Irus, halting as I trod,
I, Epictetus, was the friend of God.

After being driven from Rome by the Emperor Domitian, Epictetus went across the Adriatic to Nicopolis (ca. 90 A.D.) and opened a school. His *Discourses* were compiled by his disciple, the historian Arrian. Only four of the eight books have survived.

Do not marvel that the other animals have their bodily needs all supplied—not only food and drink, but also a bed to lie on —and that they have no need for shoes or coverlets or clothing, while we are in need of all these things. For it would not have been expedient if these creatures, which were born, not for themselves but for service, had been created in need of various things. Consider what it would be for us to have to take thought not only for ourselves, but also for our sheep and asses—how they were to be clothed and how shod, how they were to eat and how to drink! But just as soldiers when they appear before their general are already shod, fully clothed, and fully armed—and it would be a strange thing indeed if the tribune had to go around and shoe or clothe his regiment—so also nature has made the animals that are born for service ready and equipped and in need of no further attention. So one small child with a stick can drive a flock of sheep.

And yet we forbear to give thanks that we do not have to pay the same attention to them as to ourselves, and proceed to complain against God on our own account. I declare, by Zeus and all the gods, one single fact of nature would be enough to make any reverent and grateful person realize the providence of God. Don't tell me about great matters; take the mere fact that milk is produced from grass, and cheese from milk, and wool from skin. Who is it that has created or planned these things?

"No one," says somebody. Oh, what dreadful stupidity and shamelessness! Come now, let us leave the products of nature, and look at her by-products. Is anything more useless than the hairs on the chin? So, then, what are they for? Has she not used even these in the most suitable way possible? Does she not use them to distinguish between male and female? Does not the nature of each of us cry out at once, even from a distance, "I am a man. On that basis approach me and talk with me. Do not ask further evidence; see the signs [that show I am a man]." Again, in the case of women, just as nature mingled in their voices a certain softness, so she left off hair from their chins. "Oh no," you say—the human creature ought to have been left without any distinguishing marks, so that each of us would have to proclaim, "I am a man!" But see how fair and becoming and dignified the mark is—how much handsomer than the cock's comb, how much more magnificent than the lion's mane! Therefore we ought to preserve the marks God has given us; we ought not to give them up, nor, as far as we can prevent it, confuse the sexes which have been thus distinguished.

But are these the only works of Providence in us? [Not at all!] What words are adequate to praise them or to bring them home to us? Why, if we had good sense, ought we to do anything else, either in public or in private, than praise God and bless him and recount his benefits? Should we not, while we dig and plough and eat, sing the hymn that belongs to God?

> Great is God, for he has given us these instruments with which to till the earth.
> Great is God, for he has given us hands, and ability to swallow, and a belly, and the power to grow without knowing it, and to breathe even while we are asleep.

This is what we ought to be singing all the time, and above all the greatest and divinest hymn of praise, that God has given us the ability to understand these gifts and to follow the road of knowing how to use them.

And then what else? Since most of you have grown blind, should there not be someone to officiate for you and on behalf of all sing the hymn that belongs to God? What else can I do, a lame old man, except sing hymns to God? If, somehow, I were a nightingale, I should be singing like a nightingale; if I were a swan, like a swan. But since I am a rational being, I must be singing hymns to God. This is my task and I do it, and I will not desert my post as long as it is given me. And I invite you all to join me in the same song.

EPICURUS ON HUMAN HAPPINESS AND THE GODS

Epicurus *Letter to Menoeceus*, 122–127, 132–135. Epicurus (342?–270 B.C.) was the founder and head of the philosophical school which bears his name. He was born in the island of Samos and taught at Athens from 306 B.C. onward. In studying his philosophy, we are reminded that Epicurus suffered for many years from a most excruciating ailment, a kidney stone; his philosophy marked his personal triumph over this painful handicap. The remaining fragments of his work may be found in Cyril Bailey, *Epicurus, the Extant Remains* (1926), pp. 83 ff., 327 ff.; or in Hermann Usener, *Epicurea* (1887), pp. 59 ff. See also A. J. Festugière, *Epicure et ses Dieux* (1946).

(122) Let no one when he is young postpone the study of philosophy; nor let him when he is old grow weary of its study. For neither can one start too early nor continue too late in attending to his soul's health. And anyone who says either that the time for philosophy has not come yet, or has already gone by, is like one who says that the time for happiness has not yet come [for him], or is no longer present. Accordingly, a man ought to study philosophy both when he is young and when he is old, in order that as he grows old he may remain young in [enjoying] good things through his gratitude for what has taken place [in his life], and so that equally in youth and in age he may know no fear of things to come. We ought to take care, then, for those things that make for happiness, seeing that when happiness is present we have everything, but when it is absent we do everything to possess it.

(123) The things I used constantly to urge upon you, these practice and care for, recognizing that they are the first principles of the good life. First of all believe that God is a being incorruptible [i.e., immortal and unchangeable] and blessed, just as in the common idea of God which is engraved on the mind, and do not assign to him anything contrary to his incorruption or unsuited to his blessedness, and believe about him whatever safeguards his blessedness and incorruption. For gods there certainly are, since the knowledge of them is a matter of immediate perception. But they are not what the majority of men believe them to be; in fact, they do not take care to represent them as they really believe them to be. And the irreligious man is not the one who denies the gods of the majority, but the one who applies to the gods the opinions of the majority. (124) For what the majority say about the gods are not conceptions derived from sensation [prolepseis], but false suppositions [hypolepseis], according to which the greatest injuries overtake the wicked and the greatest blessings come to [the good] from the gods. For since men are always accustomed to their own virtues, they welcome those who are like themselves; but whatever is not of this sort they regard as alien.

Get accustomed to the idea that death means nothing to us. For all good and evil consist in sensation, and death is only the deprivation of sensation. Hence a real understanding that death means nothing to us makes the mortality of [our] life enjoyable, not by adding to it an unlimited length of time, but by taking away the desire for immortality. (125) For there is nothing dreadful in life for the man who has really grasped the idea that there is nothing dreadful in *not* living. So that anyone is foolish who says that he is afraid of death, not because it will be painful when it comes, but because it is painful in prospect. For what gives [us] no trouble when it comes is only an empty pain as we look forward to it. So death, the most terrifying of evils, is nothing to us; for as long as we exist death is not present with us, and when death comes then we no longer exist. It is no concern, therefore, either of the living or the dead; for the former it does not exist, while the latter themselves no longer exist.

But the majority at one time flee from death as the greatest of all evils, but at another time [they yearn for it] as a rest from the [evils] in life. (126) [But the wise man neither seeks to escape from life] nor fears to cease living; for neither does life annoy him nor does nonliving seem to be anything evil. Just as in the case of food he does not by any means choose the larger share, but rather the most delicious, so he seeks to enjoy [literally, plucks as fruit], not the longest period of time, but the most pleasant.

And whoever counsels the young man to live well but the old man to make a good end is silly, not merely because life is desirable, but also because it is the same discipline which teaches [us] to live well and to die well. Yet far worse is the man [Theognis, it is supposed] who says it is good not to be born, "but once being born, make haste to pass through the gates of death." For if he says this from conviction, why does he not depart out of life? For it is open to him to do so, if he has firmly made up his mind to it. But if he is only jesting, his words sound idle to men who cannot receive them.

We must bear in mind, then, that the future is neither ours

not yet altogether not ours, so that we may not look forward to
it as absolutely sure to come nor give up hope of it as if it will
certainly not come.

[*Having dealt with the nature of the gods and the fact of
death, Epicurus goes on to the moral principles which he has
taught Menoeceus: Some desires are good, others are not; one
must choose his course with reference to (a) health of the
body and (b) repose of the soul* (ataraxia); *in both, pleasure—
or rather happiness—is the standard and test, the beginning and
the end of the life of blessedness* (128). *Pleasure is always
good, but not all pleasures are free from pain; we must judge, and
choose the relatively better* (129 f.). *We must be content with
little; then the luxuries will be sweeter if they come. Health, for
example, is fostered by a simple diet* (130 f.). *Pleasure is not the
enjoyment of the physical senses, but health of body and the
occupation of the mind with philosophy* (131 f.). *The greatest
thing of all is prudence* [phronesis], *which teaches us the other
virtues, and the virtues are inseparable from a life of happiness*
(132 f.).]

The beginning of all these [achievements of philosophy] and
the greatest good [of all] is prudence. Therefore prudence is
something even more precious than philosophy itself. From it
the other virtues are born, since it teaches [us] that it is impossible to live happily unless we live prudently, honestly, and
justly; or to live prudently, honorably, and justly without living
happily. For the virtues are one in origin with the life of happiness, and the life of happiness is inseparable from the virtues.
(133) For who do you imagine is better than the man who
thinks reverently of the gods, and is entirely fearless of death,
and has thought through the purpose of nature? He realizes
that the limit of [attainable] good things is easy to fulfill and
easy to reach, while the limit of [possible] evils is short and
slight as regards either their duration in time or the intensity of
the suffering involved; and he simply laughs at [Destiny], whom
some have introduced as the supreme goddess ruling over all
things. . . . [A lacuna in the text occurs here.] [Some things
happen by necessity,] others by chance, and some are entirely

within our control. Since necessity cannot be called to account and since chance is obviously inconstant, what is committed to us is free from [external] control, and accordingly praise or blame must be attached to what we do. (134) For it would be much better to follow some myth about the gods than to be a slave to the Destiny pictured by the natural philosophers; for the myth [at least] sketches out a hope of winning over the gods by worship, whereas the latter represents Necessity [Anagke] as inexorable. Nor does he suppose Chance [Tyche] to be a god, as the majority assume (for there is nothing disorderly in what a god does), nor that it is the unstable cause [of all things]; for he does not think that good or evil have been given men by chance for [the making of] the blessed life, but that the starting points of great good and great evil are thus provided. (135) He deems it better to be unlucky but reasonable than to be unreasonable but favored by fortune. For it is better in practice to choose the right and fail than to choose the wrong and succeed by luck.

Cherish these things and those like them day and night, by yourself and with someone [a companion] like yourself, and you will never be upset, but will live like a god among men. For the man who lives among the eternal values has lost all likeness to the beasts that perish.

DIOGENES: A PHILOSOPHICAL TESTAMENT

J. William, *Diogenis Oenoandensis Fragmenta*, II (Leipzig, 1907), Col. 2.7, p. 5. This inscription on a portico beside the road near Oenoanda, in Lycia, is the philosophical legacy of an Epicurean named Diogenes, who lived ca. 200 A.D. In a world of superstition, in which the after-life was usually thought of with uneasy forebodings, the following brief summary of the teachings of philosophy with its account of the views of various schools must have brought peace of mind to many a weary traveler. See also Gilbert Murray, *Five Stages of Greek Religion*, second edition (1925), pp. 204 f.; Karl Praechter, *Fr. Ueberwegs Grundriss der Geschichte der Philosophie des Altertums*, eleventh edition (1920), pp. 605 f.

Having arrived by our years at the sunset of life, and expecting at any time now to depart out of the world with a glad song and a heart filled with happiness, we have decided, lest we be snatched away too soon, to offer some help to the rightly disposed.

For if even one person, or perhaps two or three or four or five or six, or any larger number you choose—but not everyone— were in trouble, O fellow mortal, and I were called upon to help them one after another, I would do everything I could to give them good advice. But now, as I have said, the majority of mankind are everywhere sick as with a pestilence, by reason of their false beliefs about things. And the number of the diseased grows steadily; for they imitate one another, and catch the illness from each other like an epidemic in a flock of sheep.

Furthermore, it is only right to help those who are to come after us, since they too belong to us, though not yet born. And finally, love for mankind bids us render aid to strangers passing by.

Since, therefore, the help provided in writing [or from *the* writings, i.e., of Epicurus] is more certain, I have decided to use this wall [literally, stoa] to set forth the medicine needed for the healing [of mankind].

[Then follows a doxographical account of previous philosophies, with criticisms of Empedocles, Democritus, and the Stoics. It is a good example of the popularization of philosophy in the Hellenistic-Roman age. The beautiful fugitive "tetractys" which Gilbert Murray quotes (p. 205) is not among the fragments of Diogenes, though Fragment XXIX col. 2 (p. 38) and Fragment XLIII (p. 51) approximate it. It sounds very much like a summary of Epicurus' letter to Menoecceus, § 133 ff., given above.]

> Nothing to fear in God;
> Nothing to feel in Death;
> Good can be attained;
> Evil can be endured.

DIO CHRYSOSTOM'S OLYMPIC ORATION

Dio Chrysostom is one of the most interesting figures in the world of popular philosophy and oratory at the beginning of the second century. His "Olympic" oration (Oration XII), which follows, was delivered at the assembly gathered for the Olympic games in 105 A.D. It is, as Sir Richard Livingstone remarks, "a Greek sermon." (See R. W. Livingstone, *The Mission of Greece*, Ch. VI, p. 130.) The temple at Olympia was still standing, and the famous statue of Zeus by Phidias, "the truly blessed statue," of which he says (51):

"Even a man whose soul is utterly burdened, who in the course of his life has drained the cup of misfortune and grief, and has not closed his eyes in sleep, will I believe forget, when he stands face to face with this statue, all the terrors and hardships that come in human life. Such is the vision that you, O Phidias, have created and brought to pass."

Dio himself had been just such a man, an exile and a refugee, and the experience he is describing was no doubt his own. This sublime passage introduces the problem of anthropomorphism, which was no invention of the sculptor, but the tradition of all Greek literature from Homer down. Poets, of course, may describe the divine in other terms, but the sculptor is limited to portrayal in human form. Dio pictures Phidias making a defense of his use of anthropomorphism (55), since he himself was not tongue-tied and belonged to a city not given to taciturnity.

Gentlemen, my fellow Hellenes, this contest is the greatest that has ever arisen! It has nothing to do with empire or the military ascendancy of a single state, or with the big navy program or the infantry, [or] whether the affairs of state have been properly administered or not. What I am called to answer for is my representation of the god who rules the whole universe: whether it has been made with due reverence and as a fitting likeness of him, in no way falling short of the best portrayal of the divine that a human being can make, or [whether it] is altogether unworthy and improper.

(56) Remember that I am not the first to be your expounder and teacher of the truth; for I had not yet been born when Hellas came into existence and still lacked firmly fixed ideas on this subject, but when it was more or less old and already had strong convictions and beliefs about the gods. I omit to mention the works of sculptors or painters before my time which were in agreement with my art, except for technical achievement in execution. (57) But your views I found to be so ingrained, so unchangeable, so irresistible that I turned to others who have portrayed divine beings, i.e., to those much older than I and considered to be much wiser—I mean the poets, who are able by means of poetry to lead people to any conception they choose, whereas the works of our art have only one standard of comparison.

(58) For those divine manifestations—i.e., of the sun and the moon, the whole heavens and the stars—are utterly marvelous, viewed simply by themselves. But if one wishes to portray the figure of the moon or the orb of the sun, this is a simple matter and requires no artistic skill. Furthermore, although these divinities have profound moral character and purpose of their own, nothing of this is revealed by a mere representation of them, and this perhaps explains why the Greeks did not at first regard them as deities. (59) For no sculptor or painter can portray reason and intelligence as they are in themselves; they are completely invisible and can by no means be depicted. But as for that in which intelligence manifests itself, this is knowledge and not guesswork; people eagerly fly to it for refuge and ascribe to God a human body, because that is the form in which intelligence and reason are found. For lack of a better exemplar we try to reveal the invisible and the unportrayable in a shape that can be seen and portrayed; we use symbolic means, in a somewhat better way than some of the barbarians [foreign nations] are said to do when they give to the deity the likeness of animals—a stupid and improper method. But he who is the supreme master, surpassing all others in beauty, magnificence, and majesty, he [i.e., Homer] has been by far the greatest creator of images of the divine beings.

(60) Certainly no one will say that it would have been better if no statue or image of the gods had been exhibited among men, for the reason that we should look only at the heavenly bodies. It is true that all intelligent men do reverence them and view them from afar as the blessed gods. But owing to our attraction toward the divine all men have a strong desire to honor and worship God close at hand, approaching and laying hold of him and appealing to him, offering him sacrifices and garlands. (61) Just as little children, when torn from their father or mother, feel a terrible longing and homesickness for them, and while dreaming often hold out their hands to their absent parents, so also do men to the gods. For they rightly love them for their beneficence and kinship, and are eager in every way to be with them and to converse with them. So also many savage peoples, in their poverty and their lack of artistic resources, give the name of God to mountains, unhewn logs, and shapeless stones—utterly inappropriate in form. . . .

(73) But you, Homer, wisest of poets and far the first in power as in time, you will say that you were the first to reveal to the Hellenes many beautiful likenesses, not only of all the gods in general, but espcially of the greatest among them, some of your images being gentle, others terrible and awe-inspiring. (74) But my Zeus is peaceful and completely gentle, as befits the one who presides over a Hellas free from faction and of one mind. I have set him here after consulting my own art and after taking counsel with the wise and good city of the Eleans— a gentle, majestic, untroubled figure, the giver of life and of livelihood, and of all good things, the father, the savior, the guardian of all mankind. I did all that a mortal could conceive to represent the divine and inconceivable nature.

(75) And consider whether you do not find my statue in keeping with all the titles by which the God is known. For Zeus is the only one of the gods who is called Father [*Pater*] and King [*Basileus*], God of the City [*Polieus*]. (76) God of Friendship [*Philios*], God of Comradeship [*Hetaireios*], and also Protector of Suppliants [*Hikesios*], and God of Hospitality [*Xenios*], Giver of Increase [*Epicarpios*]; and he has numberless other

titles, all expressing his goodness. He is called King for his sovereignty and power; Father, I believe, for his gentleness and care; God of the City, for upholding law and the commonweal; God of the Race, for his kinship which unites gods and men; God of Friendship and Comradeship, because he brings all mankind together and wills that they should be friends of one another, and that none should ever be the private enemy or public foe of another; Protector of Suppliants, since he hears and is gracious when men pray; God of Refuge [*Phuxios*], because he provides refuge from the evils of life; God of Hospitality, because we must neither neglect the stranger nor regard any man as a foreigner; Giver of Wealth [*Ktesios*] and Giver of Increase, because he is the cause of the [growth of] crops and the giver of wealth and power.

(77) As far, then, as one can portray these qualities without using words, has not my art achieved its end? The strength and magnificence of my Zeus are designed to reveal the ruler and king; the gentleness and friendliness portray the father and his loving care; his majesty and severity show the god of the city and the protector of its laws. The kinship of god and man is expressed by his human form itself, as a kind of symbol. His benevolence, his look of goodness and of gentleness, express his attributes as god of friendship, protector of suppliants, god of hospitality, and god of refuge, and all such attributes. His simplicity and magnanimity represent the giver of wealth and giver of increase, for he looks just like one who gives and bestows good things in abundance.

(78) I have represented all these qualities as well as I could, since I was unable to express them in words. But the god who lets fly the lightning flash, bringing wars and destruction to multitudes, or floods of rain or violent hail or snow; or who stretches the dark-blue rainbow across the sky, the sign of war; or who sends the shooting star with its stream of sparks, dread portent to sailors and soldiers; or who sends dread strife to Greeks and barbarians, inspiring an undying passion for war and battle in weary and despairing men; or who weighs in the balance the fates of men noble as the gods themselves, or of

whole armies, and lets the decision be determined by its auto-
matic tilt—that god, I tell you, it was impossible for my art to
portray. And even if it had been possible, I should never have
wished to do it.

. . . (84) If Phidias had made such a speech as this in his
own defense, I am sure the assembled Hellenes would quite
properly have voted him a crown.

ALEXANDER ON TOPICS IN PRAISE OF GOD

Rhetores Graeci III. 4–6. Alexander, son of Numenius, was
a rhetorician in the reign of Hadrian. The following fragment
of his writings is printed in *Rhetores Graeci,* edited by Spengel.
On Alexander himself, see Brzoska, in Pauly-Wissowa, *Real-
Encyclopädie,* Vol. I, cols. 1456–1459. On topics for addresses to
the gods, see J. Amann, *Die Zeusrede des Ailios Aristeides*
(Stuttgart, 1931), pp. 1–14.

You should say, then, that the philosophical account of God
tells us that God is unbegotten and always indestructible, but
that Plato also set forth some such account as that gods came
into being from the first God, so that it is possible for us to accept
the ordinary account, since from that statement of his the way
leads on to the generated gods. It is up to you to use both of the
established accounts, saying with Plato that it is for God to know
all things, but that in human explanations one is the more wise
and the other the more ordinary. First you should mention the
more learned because it is concerned in general with the nature
of God, second the view of the many—whether there is one god
or more than one. For concerning God most men have the same
opinion, but the gods have various origins and characters and
names; and since different statements are made by each race,
Greeks and barbarians, one must speak of the genealogy of the
god, and hence of his antiquity or novelty—that is, of his age.
For some of the gods are older, while some are younger. Concerning some of them questions arise, e.g., in the case of Heracles,

who is regarded differently by Egyptians and Greeks. In other cases the god seems to be the same, and attracts the power of many gods to himself; thus people say that Helios and Apollo are the same, and that Selene and Artemis and Hecate are the same.

Then one must consider whether the god is worshiped by all nations or only by some, for not all gods are considered gods by all men. Instead, some gods are so regarded by some people. If, then, the god is worshiped by all, this is the greatest praise; for it is seldom that you can say he is worshiped by all. But if he is worshiped only by some, you must praise the nations which regard him highly, and prove that they are the most famous or the strongest or the oldest or the most kingly or the best-ordered nations—or whatever good there is in the nation which considered this god a god and established him. Then he can be praised by a contrast with the nations which do not worship him. If he is worshiped by Greeks and not by barbarians, you should say that the god wished to avoid having the Greeks considered barbarians. Then, from the circumstances, it is necessary for the barbarians to avoid him, since they are defiled with blood; similarly other grievances may be used. But if he is worshiped among barbarians, as is Apollo among the Lydians, you will say that even the barbarians were not ignorant of the god.

Next you should consider those who have made statues of him; then his power, what it is and what works prove it; then the sovereignty of the god and the subjects of his rule, heavenly, marine, and earthly. The town and the district should be praised. Then his relation to art should be mentioned, whether to one or to all or to many, as Athena is over all the arts, and Zeus and Apollo over divination. Then what things have been rectified through the art which he practices and leads. Then what discoveries the god has made or is said to have made. Then whatever works he has done among the gods or for the gods, as Zeus has primacy of power and Hermes heraldry. Then how he appeared to men, and his philanthropy. Then what animals are sacred to him, what trees, what lands, and whatever dwelling places and abodes are given for his visitation; and with what gods he is associated, as Apollo is with the Muses.

MAXIMUS ON THE USE OF IMAGES

Maximus of Tyre *Oration VIII*. 10 (or XXXVIII Stephanus, or II Hobein). Maximus (ca. 125–185 A.D.) was a Sophist and eclectic philosopher in the reign of Commodus who traveled widely and lectured both at Athens and at Rome. The best edition of his *Orations* is that edited by H. Hobein, in the Teubner series (1910). An older edition, with Latin translation, is the one by F. Dübner (Paris, 1877) in the volume beginning with Theophrastus' *Characters*. There is an interesting French translation by J. J. Combes-Dounous (Paris, 1802). See also Guy Soury, *Aperçus de Philosophie religieuse chez Maxime de Tyr* (1942).

For the God who is the Father and Creator of all that is, older than the sun, older than the sky, greater than time and eternity and the whole continual flow of nature, is not to be named by any lawgiver, is not to be uttered by any voice, is not to be seen by any eye. But we, being unable to grasp his essence, make use of sounds and names and pictures, of beaten gold and ivory and silver, of plants and rivers, of mountain peaks and torrents, yearning for the knowledge of him, and in our weakness naming all that is beautiful in this world after his nature. The same thing happens to those who love others; to them the sweetest sight will be the actual figures of their children, but sweet also will be their memory—they will be happy at [the sight of] a lyre, a little spear, or a chair, perhaps, or a running ground, or anything whatever that wakens the memory of the beloved. Why should I go any further in examining and passing judgment about images? Let all men know what is divine; let them know, that is all. If Greeks are stirred to the remembrance of God by the art of Phidias, or the Eygptians by paying worship to animals, or others by a river, or others by fire, I will not quarrel with their differences. Only let them know, let them love, let them remember.

PLOTINUS

Plotinus (205–270 A.D.) was the real founder of Neoplatonism, although he had forerunners. His life was written by his disciple Porphyry, as the introduction to the *Works of Plotinus,* which he edited in six enneads, or groups of nine, and published about 300 A.D. For the text of Porphyry's *Life of Plotinus,* see *Plotin: Ennéades,* edited and translated by E. Bréhier, Vol. I (Paris, 1924); also the new edition by Paul Henry and H. R. Schwyzer, Vol. I (Museum Lessianum, 1951). For his philosophy, see W. R. Inge, *The Philosophy of Plotinus,* third edition (1929); E. Bréhier, *La Philosophie de Plotin,* second edition (1938); R. Arnou, *Le Désir de Dieu dans la Philosophie de Plotin* (1921).

PORPHYRY'S DESCRIPTION OF PLOTINUS AS A MYSTIC

Porphyry, Life of Plotinus 23.

We have explained [in a long oracle in verse, quoted in the preceding chapter] that he was "good and gentle, and above all mild and merciful"; we who lived with him could feel it. It was said that he was sleeplessly vigilant and pure of soul, and always striving toward the divine, which with all his soul he loved; that he did everything he could to liberate [himself], and to "calm the troubled seas incarnadine." And so it happened to this extraordinary man, constantly lifting himself up toward the first and transcendent God by the power of thought and along the ways explained by Plato in the *Symposium,* that there actually appeared to him in vision that God, who is without shape or form, established above the understanding and all the intelligible world. I, Porphyry, confess that I too once drew near to this God and was made one with him, in my sixty-eighth year. But Plotinus "had a vision of the goal close at hand." For his whole aim and goal was to be made one with and draw near to the supreme God. And this goal he attained four times, I believe, while I was living with him—not potentially but actually, though by an actuality which it is beyond the power of language to describe. "Often," so said the oracle, "the gods will correct the oblique direction of your march, to let you see the splendor of their light." His writings are the record of these researches and revelations given him by the gods.

CAUSES, INNER AND OUTER

Ennead III. 1.10.

To sum up the argument, all things are foreshown and all events are brought into being by causes, which are of two kinds: there are some things which are caused by the soul and others which result from other causes, those of the surrounding environment. The actions of the souls may result from their own motion and in accordance with sound reason; that is when they do their own proper work. But when they are hindered from their own proper action, they do not act but rather suffer. So that the causes which prevent the soul from thinking lie outside the soul, and perhaps one ought to say that this takes place in accordance with Fate [or Destiny], that is, if one holds that destiny is a cause external to ourselves. But the best actions are those which spring from within ourselves. We are our real selves when we are alone. The wise and the good perform wise and good acts by themselves; the others, when they can catch their breath [or when the passions are in abeyance], do good deeds, but not because they draw these wise thoughts from outside themselves, whenever they do think wisely, but simply because they are for the moment unhindered by obstacles.

HYMNS OF PROCLUS

From the Neoplatonist Proclus (410–485 A.D.) we have a late collection of seven syncretistic, theosophical hymns addressed to Helios, Aphrodite, the Muses, all the gods, the goddess of Proclus' home, Lycian Aphrodite, Hecate and Janus, and Athena. They are found at the end of the collection of the

Orphic hymns. See the edition of these hymns by Eugene Abel, in his *Orphica* (Leipzig, 1885), pp. 276 ff.; see also W. Nestle, *Griechische Religiosität*, Vol. III (1934), pp. 172 ff.

IV. A HYMN TO ALL THE GODS

Hear me, ye Gods, who hold firmly the tiller of sacred wisdom,
Ye who kindle within men's souls a fire that flames upward
And draws them toward heavenly things, when they have abandoned
Their dark caves, and have cleansed themselves by your holy mysteries.
Hear me, ye Saviors, ye great ones! and from holy scriptures
May the sacred light shine forth upon me and scatter the shadows,
So that I may rightly understand both the eternal God and mortal men;
So that no daemon may harm me, and drag my soul downward
Beneath the stream of forgetfulness, and thus ever hold me back, remote from the blessed ones—
My soul, tossed about by the vast horrifying waves of Becoming,
Threatening ever to sweep it down to unplumbed depths of destruction—
And let no torturing pain entangle me in the deceitful snares of life.
Hear me then, ye Gods, who are leaders of enlightened wisdom,
And while I toil up the path that leads on high
Reveal to me the hidden truth contained in the sacred words.

I. HYMN TO HELIOS

This hymn is a prayer that the suppliant may be cleansed from sin (33 f.).

Arise, shine, thou greatest of the gods, thou blessed one, crowned with flame,
Image of God, the begetter of all, thou guiding star of souls!
Hear me, and cleanse me from all the defilements of sin!
Accept my bitter tears and pleading! The horrid stain

Remove from me, and keep far from me the penalty I deserve,
And make mild the stern eye of all-seeing Dike!

VI. HYMN TO HECATE AND JANUS

*In this hymn Proclus prays that Hecate, who here represents
the Mother of the Gods, and also Janus, here identified with
Zeus, may favor his career with their blessing (4 ff.).*

Hail, Mother of the Gods, the many-named, the nobly born!
Hail, Hecate, guardian of the gates, the Mighty one! And
    thou too,
Hail, O Janus, the Forefather, Zeus the Immortal! Hail, Zeus
    supreme!
Be it mine to enjoy a life radiant on its journey, weighed
    down with good things!
Keep far from my body the sickness that destroys,
And upward lead my soul, from wandering in error here
    below,
After it has cleansed itself in soul-awakening mysteries!
Reach out to me your hands, I pray you, and show to my
    yearning heart
The path divine, that I may behold [its] glorious light
And find an escape from the bane of gloomy Becoming!
Reach out to me your hands, I pray, and with favoring winds
Bring me at last, and weary, to safe anchor in the harbor of
    devotion!
Hail, Mother of the Gods, the many-named, the nobly born!
Hail, Hecate, guardian of the gates, the Mighty one! And thou
    too,
Hail, O Janus, the Forefather, Zeus the Immortal! Hail, Zeus
    supreme!

III. HYMN TO THE MUSES

*Proclus closes his "Hymn to the Muses" with the following
prayer (8 f.).*

From the confusing tumult of Becoming, do thou lead me
Steadily upward and onward, a wandering soul, to the holy
    light.

RELIGIOUS IDEAS OF THE PHILOSOPHERS

IAMBLICHUS

Iamblichus, the Neoplatonist philosopher, was born in Syria and lived from ca. 250 to 325 A.D. His book *On the Mysteries,* edited by Thomas Gale (1678), G. Parthey (1857), and Th. Hopfner (1922), is in the form of a reply by a certain Abammon to a letter by Porphyry addressed "To Anebo" and is a defense of ritualistic magic or theurgy. Iamblichus' presentation of Neoplatonism fell far below the high teaching of Plotinus and incorporated much popular superstition. Theurgy is a kind of magic designed to induce the presence of the gods. The following passages illustrate the range of Iamblichus' teaching, which moves from deep, sincere piety to frivolous superstition.

THE ARTS AND EFFECTS OF ECSTASY

On the Mysteries *III* 4–6.

(4) Among the signs by which those who are truly possessed by the gods may be known, the greatest is the fact that many [of those who experience ecstasy] are not burned, though fire is applied to them, since the deity breathing within them does not permit the fire to touch them; many, though burned, are unaware of it, since at that moment they are not dwelling in the body [literally, not living an animal life]. Many have daggers thrust through their bodies without feeling it; others have their backs cut [open] with hatchets, or cut their arms with knives, without taking any notice. The activities in which they are engaged are not of a human kind, and since they are borne by God they can reach places which are inaccessible to men: they pass through fire unharmed; they tread upon fire and cross over streams, like the priestess in Castabala [who walked barefoot on snow and hot coals]. This proves that in their enthusiasm [i.e., their state of inspiration] they are not aware of what they are doing and are

not living a human or bodily existence as far as sensation and volition are concerned, but live instead another and diviner kind, which fills them and takes complete possession of them.

(5) There are many different kinds of divine possession, and there are different ways of awakening the divine spirit; consequently there are many different indications of this state. For one thing, there are different gods from whom we receive the spirit [i.e., are inspired], and this results in a variety of forms in which the inspiration manifest itself; further, the kinds of influence exerted are different, and so there are various ways in which the divine seizure takes place. For either the god takes possession of us, or else we are entirely absorbed in him, or else [thirdly] we co-operate with him. At times we partake of the lowest power of God, at others of the middle [power], at still others of the highest [i.e., first]. Sometimes it is a mere participation, again it is a communion [fellowship or sharing], or again it becomes a union of these [two] kinds. Now the soul enjoys complete separation; again it is still involved in the body, or [else] the whole nature is laid hold of [and controlled].

Hence the signs of possession are manifold: either movement of the body and its parts, or complete relaxation; [either] singing choirs, round dances, and harmonious voices, or the opposite of these. [The] bodies have been seen to rise up, grow, or move freely in the air, and the opposite has also been observed. They have been heard to utter [different] voices of equal strength, or with great diversity and inequality, in tones that alternated with silence; and again in other cases harmonious crescendo or diminuendo of tone, and in still other cases other kinds of utterance.

(6) But the greatest thing [about this experience] is that the one who thus draws down a deity beholds the greatness and the nature of the invading spirit; and he is secretly guided and directed by him. So too he who receives a god sees also a fire before he takes it into himself. Now and then the god manifests himself to all who are present, either as he comes or as he goes. From this it is made known, to those who have the knowledge, wherein his truth and his power chiefly consist and his place

[in the divine hierarchy], and what qualifies him by his nature to make known the truth; and also what power he is able to grant or to maintain. Those, however, who without this beatifying view invoke the spirits are merely reaching out and touching things in the dark, and do not know what they are doing, save for certain minor signs in the body of the possessed person and other indubitable, visible symptoms; but the full understanding of divine possession is denied them, being hid in the invisible.

THE ARTS AND EFFECTS OF PRAYER

On the Mysteries V. 26.

Since prayers are by no means the least part of sacrifice, but instead contribute something that is essential to its completion and thus supply to the whole rite its power and its effect, [and] since, moreover, they serve to enhance the general reverence for God and create a sacred, indissoluble bond of fellowship with the gods, it seems not inappropriate to say a few words upon the subject. Moreover, it is a subject that is worth knowing about in and for itself; further, it completes our knowledge of the gods. I therefore affirm that the first kind of prayer is that which brings [God and man] together, since it brings about the association with the divine and gives us the knowledge thereof. The second establishes a bond of fellowship founded upon like-mindedness and calls down gifts sent by the gods, which arrive before we can ask for them and perfect our efforts even without our knowledge. The third and most perfect form finally seals the secret union, which hands over every decision privately to the gods and leaves our souls completely at rest in them.

In these three stages, which embrace all that is divine, prayers gain for us harmonious friendship of the gods and also a threefold advantage from the gods: the first has to do with illumination, the second with fellowship in a common task, the third with the state of being filled with the [divine] fire. Sometimes this precedes the sacrifice; sometimes it interrupts the sacred rite; sometimes it comes as its conclusion.

No sacral act can be effective without the supplication of prayer. Steady continuance in prayer nourishes our mind, enlarges the soul for the reception of the gods, opens up to men the realm of the gods, accustoms us to the splendor of the divine light, and gradually perfects in us [our] union with the gods, until at last it leads us back to the supreme heights. Our mode of thinking is drawn gently aloft and implants in us the spirit of the gods; it awakens confidence, fellowship, and undying friendship [with them]; it increases the longing for God; it inflames in us whatever is divine within the soul; it banishes all opposition from the soul, and strips away from the radiant, light-formed spirit everything that leads to generation; it creates good hope and trust in the light. In brief, it gives to those who engage in it intercourse with the gods.

THE PHILOSOPHICAL FOUNDATION FOR MAGICAL PRACTICES

On the Mysteries *IV. 2.*

What we are now about to consider is something that we occasionally experience. Now and then it happens that commands are addressed to spirits which do not possess reason or judgment. But this is no irrational procedure. Our mind naturally possesses the power of reasoning and judging affairs, and combines in itself many living powers, and is used to managing the most irrational creatures and such as are complete with the possession of one sole energy. Hence it calls upon them [viz., the spirits] as if they were superior beings, since it tries to draw from the whole surrounding cosmos that which will benefit particular things and be useful to the whole. It commands them as inferiors, although it is often true that some particular things are purer and more perfect than those which pervade the whole world. For example, if something [e.g., the human mind] is wholly intellectual and another is entirely inanimate and physical, then the one which is the more limited certainly has a greater authority than the one which is the more extended, even though the latter may exceed it greatly in magnitude and force.

And for this there is likewise an explanation. In all theurgic practice [the priest possesses] a twofold character, on the one hand as a man, thus maintaining our place within the universe; on the other, as is corroborated by divine signs, he is allied to the Mighty Ones and rises upward, and is introduced into their beautiful order and may indeed share their form. Corresponding to this distinction, [the theurgist] invokes the powers of the universe as superior [i.e., to himself], since he who invokes them is a man; again, he commands them, since by [the utterance of] secret formulas he has, so to speak, assumed the sacred form of the gods.

EPIPHANIES OF THE GODS

On the Mysteries *II. 4.*

Along with this goes magnitude of the epiphanies. In the case of gods, this is such that they sometimes obscure the whole sky and the sun and the moon, and the earth itself can no longer endure while they are coming down. When archangels appear, certain portions of the world are agitated; and at their coming a light goes before them, but divided. And the archangels themselves differ in greatness of splendor according to the size of the provinces over which they rule. Angels are distinguished by being smaller in size and by being divided numerically. In the case of daemons, the division goes even farther, and their magnitudes change and are not always the same. Heroes present a still smaller appearance than daemons, but have a greater majesty of bearing. Of the archons, those who belong to the outer regions of the cosmos are large and puffed up; those, on the other hand, who are scattered about in the region of matter are apt to employ boasting and delusion. The appearances of souls are not all equal in size, and at any rate they seem to be smaller than heroes. In brief, the size of the epiphanies is such as belongs to the various orders of beings and is proportionate to the magnitude of their power and authority.

Next, let us note the differences in the images presented by the beings who make themselves manifest. In the case of self-manifestation by gods, the things we see are clearer than truth itself; every detail shines out exactly and appears in brilliant light. The epiphanies of archangels are likewise true and full. Those of angels maintain the same character, but they have declined from the full clearness of presentation. Those of daemons are blurred, and still more so those of heroes. Of archons, those who are cosmic powers are clearly discerned; those who are involved in matter are blurred. Yet both give by their appearance an impression of power, whereas the appearance of souls is only shadowy.

SALLUSTIUS CONCERNING THE GODS AND THE UNIVERSE

Sallustius (Greek *Saloustios*) was a philosopher who lived, presumably, in the later fourth century. He was probably a friend of the Emperor Julian. Sallustius is best known for his treatise *Concerning the Gods and the Universe,* which he wrote as an introduction to religious studies—perhaps, as Franz Cumont has suggested, as a kind of "official catechism for the Roman Empire," in which case it was probably never authorized. In this work Sallustius sums up the doctrinal views of that group of philosophically educated, spiritually-minded pagans who were still hoping, at the end of the fourth century, to see the old religion restored. The book was probably written between 363 and 394 A.D. The *editio princeps* was prepared by Leo Allatius (Rome, 1638), and it was he who gave the work its title. The text, with Latin translation, may be found in F. W. A. Mullach, *Fragmenta Philosophorum Graecorum,* Vol. III (1881), pp. 30 ff.; but the best edition of the text, accompanied by the translation which we give herewith and by a full Introduction and Commentary, is that of Professor A. D. Nock (Cambridge University Press, 1926). The student is urged to consult both the Introduction and Commentary in Nock's edition.

§1. *Prerequisites for the study: what the disciple must be like; and concerning universal opinions*

Those who would learn about the gods need to have been well educated from childhood and must not be bred up among foolish ideas; they must also be good and intelligent by nature, in order that they may have something in common with the subject. Further, they must be acquainted with universal opinions, by which I mean those in which all men, if rightly questioned, would concur; such opinions are that every god is good and impassive and unchangeable (since whatever changes, changes for better or for worse: if for worse, it becomes bad; if for the better, it proves to have been bad in the first place.)

§2. *The nature of the First Cause*

Such must be the learner, and his instruction should be as follows. The essences of the gods never came into being, for whatever always exists never comes into being, and all things that have first power and are by nature impassive do exist always; they are not formed of bodies, for even of bodies the powers are bodiless; they are not limited by space, for that certainly is an attribute of bodies; and they are never separated from the First Cause or from one another, any more than are thoughts from the mind, sciences from the soul, or the senses from a living creature.

§3. *The nature and value of myths*

It is worth our while to inquire why the ancients left the statement of these truths and employed myths, and so to obtain this first benefit from the myths, that we inquire and do not keep our intellects in idleness. Consideration of those who have employed myths justifies us in saying that myths are divine; for indeed the inspired among poets, and the best of philosophers, and the founders of solemn rites, and the gods themselves in oracles, have employed myths. Why myths are divine is a question belonging to philosophy. Since all things in existence rejoice in likeness and turn from unlikeness, it follows that our statements about the gods ought to be like the gods, in order that being worthy of their true nature they may find favor for their narrators (and such favor can by myths alone be won). So the myths represent the gods in respect of that which is speakable and that which is unspeakable, of that which is obscure and that which is manifest, of that which is clear and that which is hidden, and represent the goodness of the gods; just as the gods have given to all alike the benefits to be drawn from objects perceptible to the senses while restricting to the wise the enjoyment of those received from objects perceptible to the intellect, so the myths proclaim to all that the gods exist, telling who they are and of what sort to those able to know it. Again, myths represent the active operations of the gods. The universe itself can be called a myth, since bodies and material objects are apparent in it, while souls and intellects are concealed. Furthermore, to wish to teach all men the truth about the gods causes the foolish to despise, because they cannot learn, and the good to be slothful; whereas to conceal the truth by myths prevents the former from despising philosophy and compels the latter to study it. Why, however, have the ancients told in their myths of adulteries and thefts and binding of fathers and other strange things? Is this also admirable, meant to teach the soul by the seeming strangeness at once to think the words a veil and the truth a mystery?

§4. *The various types of myth*

Of myths some are theological, some physical; there are also psychical myths and material myths and myths blended from these elements. Theological myths are those which do not attach themselves to any material objects, but regard the actual natures of the gods. Such is the tale that Kronos swallowed his children; since the god is intellectual, and all intellect is directed toward itself, the myth hints at the god's essential nature. Again, it is possible to regard myths in a physical way when one describes the activities of the gods in the universe; so some before now have thought Kronos to be Chronos or Time, and calling the parts of Time children of the whole say that the father swallows his children. The psychical interpretation lies in considering the activities of the soul itself: the thoughts of our souls, even if they go forth to others, still remain in their creators. The worst explanation, the material, is that which the Egyptians because of their ignorance used most; they regarded and described material things as gods: earth as Isis, moisture as Osiris, heat as Typhon, or water as Kronos; the fruits of the soil as Adonis, wine as Dionysos. To say that these things, as also plants and stones and animals, are sacred to the gods, is the part of reasonable men; to call them gods is the part of madmen, unless by a common figure of speech, as we call the sphere of the sun and the ray coming from that sphere the sun. The blended kind of myths can be seen in numerous examples; one is the tale they tell that at the banquet of the gods Strife threw a golden apple and the goddesses, vying with one another for its possession, were sent by Zeus to Paris to be judged; Paris thought Aphrodite beautiful, and gave her the apple. Here the banquet signifies the supramundane powers of the gods, and that is why they are together; the golden apple signifies the universe, which, as it is made of opposites, is rightly said to be thrown by Strife; and as the various gods give various gifts to the universe they are thought to vie with one another for the possession of the apple; further, the soul that lives in accordance with sense-perception (for that is Paris), seeing beauty alone and not the other powers in the universe, says that the apple is Aphrodite's.

Theological myths suit philosophers, physical and psychical myths poets; blended myths suit solemn rites, since every rite seeks to give us union with the universe and with the gods. If I must relate another myth, it is said that the Mother of the Gods saw Attis lying by the river Gallos and became enamored of him, and took and set on his head the starry cap, and kept him thereafter with her, and he, becoming enamored of a nymph, left the Mother of the Gods and consorted with the nymph. Wherefore the Mother of the Gods caused Attis to go mad and to cut off his genitals and leave them with the nymph and to return and dwell with her again. Well, the Mother of the Gods is a life-giving goddess, and therefore she is called mother, while Attis is creator of things that come into being and perish, and therefore is he said to have been found by the river Gallos: for Gallos suggests the Galaxias Kyklos or Milky Way, which is the upper boundary of matter liable to change. So, as the first gods perfect the second, the Mother loves Attis and gives him heavenly powers (signified by the cap). Attis, however, loves the nymph, and the nymphs preside over coming into being, since whatever comes into being is in flux. But since it was necessary that the process of coming into being should stop and that what was worse should not sink to the worst, the creator who was making these things cast away generative powers into the world of becoming and was again united with the gods. All this did not happen at any one time but always is so: the mind sees the whole process at once; words tell of part first, part second. Since the myth is so intimately related to the universe we imitate the latter in its order (for in what way could we better order ourselves?) and keep a festival therefore. First, as having like Attis fallen from heaven and consorting with the nymph, we are dejected and abstain from bread and all other rich and coarse food (for both are unsuited to the soul). Then come the cutting of the tree and the fast, as though we also were cutting off the further progress of generation; after this we are fed on milk as though being reborn; that is followed by rejoicings and garlands and as it were a new ascent to the gods. This interpretation is supported also by the season at which the ceremonies are performed, for it is about the time of spring and the equinox, when things coming into being cease so to do, and day becomes longer than night, which suits souls rising to life. Certainly the rape of Kore is said in the myth to have happened near the other equinox, and this signifies the descent of souls. To us who have spoken thus concerning myths may the gods themselves and the spirits of those who wrote the myths be kind.

§5. *Summary: the nature of the First Cause*

Next, the learner should know the First Cause and the classes of the gods subordinated to it and the nature of the universe, the essential characters of mind and soul, Providence too and Fate and Chance, virtue and vice, and should see the good and evil constitutions arising from them, and whence it was that evils came into the universe. Each of these topics requires many long discussions, but there is perhaps no reason why we should not treat them here in a summary way, to prevent readers from being completely ignorant of them.

The First Cause must be one, since the unit is superior to all other numbers, and surpasses all things in power and goodness, for which reason all things must partake of it; because of its power nothing else will bar it, and by reason of its goodness it will not keep itself aloof. Now if the First Cause was soul, everything would be animated by soul; if intelligence, everything would be intellectual; if being, everything would share in being. Some in fact, seeing that all things possess being, have thought that the First Cause was being. This would be correct if things that were in being were in being only and were not good. If, however, things that are, are by reason of their goodness and share in the good, then what is first must be higher than being and in fact good. A very clear indication of this is that fine souls for the sake of the good despise being, when they are willing to face danger for country or friends or virtue. After this unspeakable power come the orders of the gods.

§6. *The divine hierarchy of mundane and supramundane gods*

Of the gods some are mundane, some supramundane. By mundane I mean the gods who make the universe. Of the supramundane some make the essences of the gods, some the intelligence, some the souls: they are therefore divided into three orders, all of which may be found in treatises on these matters. Of the mundane some cause the universe to exist, others animate it, others harmonize it out of its varied components, others guard it when so harmonized. These are four operations, and each has a beginning, a middle, and an end; their superintendents, therefore, must be twelve in number. The creators of the universe are Zeus, Poseidon, and Hephaestos; the animators Demeter, Hera, and Artemis; the harmonizers Apollo, Aphrodite, and Hermes; and the guardians Hestia, Athena, and Ares. Hints of these functions may be seen in their images: Apollo strings a lyre, Athena is armed, and Aphrodite is naked because harmony causes beauty . . . and beauty in things seen is not concealed. While these gods possess the universe in a primary way, the other gods must be supposed to be contained in them, as for instance Dionysos in Zeus, Asklepios in Apollo, and the Graces in Aphrodite. Further, we can see their spheres, earth as Hestia's, water as Poseidon's, air as Hera's, fire as that of Hephaestos, and six spheres, those higher, belonging to the gods to whom they are usually assigned; for we must regard Apollo and Artemis as Sun and Moon. We must give the sphere of Kronos to Demeter, the ether again to Athena, while the firmament is common to them all. So in this manner have the orders and powers and spheres of the twelve gods been set forth and hymned.

§7. *The universe itself is uncreated and imperishable*

The universe itself must be imperishable and uncreated, imperishable because if it perishes God must necessarily make either a better or a worse or the same or disorder: if He made a worse, then He is bad in that He makes what is worse from what is better; if He made a better, He must have been deficient in power not to have made the better thing in the first place; if the same, that will be a purposeless creation; if disorder, why, that will not bear hearing. That it is uncreated even what I have said suffices to show, because if it does not perish, neither did it come into being, since whatever comes into being perishes; coupled with the fact that, since the universe exists because of God's goodness, it follows that God is ever good and the universe ever exists, as light accompanies the existence of sun and fire, and shadow that of body.

Of the bodies in the universe some imitate mind and have a circular motion, while others imitate soul and have a rectilinear motion. Of the latter, fire and air move upwards, earth and water downwards; of the former the sphere of the fixed stars moves from East to West, and the seven planetary spheres move from West to East: among the many reasons for this is the need of preventing the process of creation from being imperfect if the rotation of the spheres is rapid. This difference of motion implies a difference in the nature of the bodies; the heavenly body cannot scorch or chill or perform any other function of the four elements. Since the universe is a sphere (as is shown by the zodiac), and the lowest part of a sphere, being furthest distant from all points on its circumference, is its centre, and heavy bodies move downwards and move toward the earth, it follows that the earth is the centre of the universe. All these things are made by the gods, ordered by mind, and set in motion by soul. Concerning the gods I have spoken earlier.

§8. *Concerning mind and soul*

Mind is a power inferior to being and superior to soul, deriving existence from being and perfecting soul (as the sun perfects sight). Of souls some are rational and immortal, others irrational and mortal: the former are derived from the primary gods, the latter from the secondary. We must first investigate the nature of soul. It is that whereby animate differs from inanimate, and the difference lies in motion, perception, imagination, and intelligence. Irrational soul is life with perception and imagination; rational is life controlling perception and imagination and employing reason. Irrational soul is subject to the feelings of the body; it desires and is angered unreasonably. Rational soul despises the body reasonably and fights against the irrational; if it is successful, it produces virtue; if it is worsted, vice. Immortal it must be, because it knows the gods (and nothing mortal knows what is immortal), and despises human affairs as not affecting itself, and, not being of the nature of body, has an experience which is the opposite of the body's;

when the body is beautiful and young, the soul errs; when the body is aging, the soul is at its prime. Again, every good soul has employed mind, and mind is created by no body; how indeed could things lacking in mind create mind? The soul uses the body as an instrument, but is not within it, just as the engineer is not within the engine, and in fact many engines move without any one touching them. If the soul is often caused by the body to err, we must not be surprised: even so the arts cannot do their work if their instruments are spoiled.

§9. *On Providence, Fate, and Fortune*

The providence of the gods can be seen even from these facts which have been stated. Whence comes the order of the universe if there is nothing that sets it in order? Why is it that everything comes into being for a purpose, as, for instance, irrational soul that there may be perception, rational soul that the earth may be adorned? Providence can be seen again from its application to our bodies. The eyes were made transparent that we might see, the nose put over the mouth that we might distinguish evil-smelling food; of the teeth those in front are sharp, to cut the food, those within flat, to grind it. In this way we see that every detail in every part is in accordance with reason. But it is impossible that there should be providence to such an extent in mean details, and not at all in first things. The oracles and healings which happen in the universe also belong to the good providence of the gods. We must consider that the gods bestow all this attention on the universe without any deliberation or toil: just as bodies with a function do what they do merely by existing, as the sun lights and warms merely by existing, in this way and much more so does the providence of the gods benefit its objects without involving toil for itself. Hence the questions of the Epicureans are answered: their contention is that what is divine neither is itself troubled nor troubles others. Such is the incorporeal providence of the gods for bodies and souls. Their providence exercised from bodies upon bodies is different from this and is called Heimarmene, because the

Heirmos or chain appears more clearly in bodies. It is with reference to this Heimarmene that the art of astrology has been invented. It is reasonable and correct to believe that not only the gods but also the divine heavenly bodies govern human affairs, and in particular our bodily nature. Hence reason discovers that health and disease and good and evil fortune come as deserved from this cause. On the other hand, to suppose that acts of injustice and wantonness come thence is to make us good and the gods bad, unless what is meant thereby is that everything happens for the good of the universe as a whole and of all things in a natural condition, but that evil education or weakness of nature changes the blessings of Heimarmene to evil, as the sun, good as it is for all, is found to be harmful to those suffering from inflammation of the eyes or from fever. Otherwise, why do the Massagetae eat their fathers and the Jews circumcise themselves and the Persians preserve their nobility by begetting children on their mothers? How, when astrologers call Saturn and Mars maleficent, do they again make them beneficent, ascribing philosophy and kingship, commands in war and finding of treasures to them? If they talk of trines and squares, it is strange that human virtue should remain the same everywhere, but the gods change their natures with their positions. The mentioning in horoscopes of good birth or evil birth of ancestors shows that the stars do not cause all things, but do no more than indicate some. How indeed could events before the moment of birth be produced by the conjunction of heavenly bodies at that moment?

So then, as Providence and Heimarmene exist for tribes and cities and exist also for each individual, in like manner does Fortune, about which I must next speak. The power of the gods that orders for the good diverse and unexpected happenings is considered to be Fortune: and for this reason in particular cities ought to pay corporate worship to this goddess, since every city is composed of diverse components. Fortune's power rests in the moon, since above the moon nothing whatsoever could happen because of her. If the bad prosper and the good suffer poverty, we must not be surprised. The former do anything to obtain wealth, the latter nothing: from the bad prosperity cannot take their badness, while the good will be content with virtue alone.

§10. *Parts of the soul; virtue and vice*

This discussion of virtue and vice requires again a discussion of the soul. When the irrational soul enters bodies and at once produces spirit and desire, the rational soul, presiding over these, causes the entire soul to consist of three parts, reason, spirit, and desire. The excellence of reason is wisdom, of spirit courage, of desire temperance, of the whole soul justice. Reason must make a right judgment, spirit must, in obedience to reason, despise seeming dangers, and desire must pursue not seeming pleasure but reasonable pleasure. When these conditions are fulfilled life becomes just (justice in money matters is but a small part of virtue). For this reason in the educated all virtues may be seen, while among the uneducated one is brave and unjust, one temperate and imprudent, one prudent and intemperate, and indeed it is not right to call these qualities virtues when shorn of reason and imperfect and occurring in certain unreasoning creatures. Vice must be considered by examining the opposites; the vice of reason is folly, of spirit cowardice, of desire intemperance, and of the whole soul injustice. Virtues are the products of a rightly constituted state and of good upbringing and education, vices of their opposites.

§11. *Corresponding political constitutions*

Constitutions also correspond to the triple division of the soul: the rulers resemble reason, the soldiers spirit, and the commoners desire. Where everything is done in accordance with reason, and the best man of all rules, monarchy results; where everything is done in accordance with reason and spirit, and more than one rule, the product is aristocracy; where men regulate their political life by desire, and honours go by wealth, the constitution is called timocracy. The opposite of monarchy is tyranny, since monarchy acts always in accordance with reason, tyranny never; of aristocracy, oligarchy, since not the best but a few and the basest rule; of timocracy, democracy, since not men of property but the commons control the state.

§12. *The origin of evil, which has no objective reality*

But how is it, if the gods are good and make everything, that there are evils in the universe? Perhaps we must first say that, since the gods are good and make everything, evil has no objective existence, and comes into being through the absence of good, just as darkness has no absolute existence, and comes into being through the absence of light. If evils exist, they must be in gods or in minds or in souls or in bodies. But in gods they cannot be, since every god is good, and if anyone says that mind is evil, he represents it as the negation of itself; if soul, he will make it worse than the body, since every body in itself is free from evil; if he asserts that evil arises from the soul and the body, it is unreasonable that they should not be evil when separate but should, when combined, create evil. If again spirits are called evil, they, if they owe their existence to the gods, cannot be evil; if they owe it to some other source, it follows that the gods do not make everything, and if they do not make everything, either they wish to do so but cannot, or they can but will not; neither supposition is suitable to a god. From these considerations it can be perceived that there is nothing naturally evil in the universe; evils appear in connection with the activities of men, and not of all men or at all times. Now, if men caused these evils for the evil's sake, Nature itself would be evil; but if the adulterer thinks adultery evil, but pleasure good; or the murderer, murder bad, but money good; or he who harms an enemy, harm bad, but vengeance good; and all the soul's sins happen in this way, evil arises because of goodness. In fact, the soul sins because, though desiring good, it errs in respect of what is good through not being of First Being. That it may not err, and that if it errs it may be cured, is the object of many things which the gods have created and we can see; arts and sciences and virtuous deeds, prayers and sacrifices and solemn rites, laws and constitutions, trials and punishments came into being to prevent souls from sinning, and when souls have left the body they are purged of their sins by gods and spirits of purification.

§13. *Creation does not mean creation in time*

Of the gods and of the universe and of human affairs this account will suffice for those who neither can be steeped in philosophy nor are incurably diseased in soul. It remains that we should discuss the fact that all these things never came into existence nor are separated from one another, since I have spoken earlier of second things proceeding from first things.

Everything that comes into being is created by technical skill or by natural process or in virtue of a function. Creators by skill or by a natural process must be prior to their creations; creators in virtue of a function bring their products into existence with themselves, since their function, like the sun's light, fire's heat, snow's cold, cannot be separated from them. If then the gods make the universe by skill, they make its character but not its existence, since form is what technical skill always makes. Whence in that case does the universe derive its existence? If the gods create by nature, we know that what creates by nature must give of itself to its creation. So, as the gods are incorporeal, the universe ought to be incorporeal; and if it is maintained that the gods are corporeal, whence comes the power of things incorporeal? If we accepted this view, the destruction of the universe involves also the destruction of its creator, if he created by natural process. If, however, the gods make the universe neither by technical skill nor by nature, the remaining view is that they make it by a function. Everything made in virtue of a function comes into being with the possessor of the function, and things so made cannot ever perish, unless their maker is deprived of the functional power. Accordingly, those who suppose that the universe perishes deny the existence of gods, or, if they assert that existence, make the Creator powerless. Therefore, as He makes everything in virtue of a functional power, He makes all things coexistent with Himself. So, as He had the greatest power, it was necessary that He should make not only men and animals, but also gods and angels (?) and spirits, and the wider the gap is between our nature and the first god, the more powers must there be between us and Him, since all things furthest removed have many intermediate points.

§14. *The gods are without passions*

If any man thinks it a reasonable and correct view that the gods are not subject to change, and then is unable to see how they take pleasure in the good and turn their faces away from the bad, are angry with sinners and propitiated by service, it must be replied that a god does not take pleasure (for that which does is also subject to pain) or feel anger (for anger also is an emotion), nor is he appeased by gifts (that would put him under the dominion of pleasure), nor is it right that the divine nature should be affected for good or for evil by human affairs. Rather, the gods are always good and do nothing but benefit us, nor do they ever harm us: they are always in the same state. We, when we are good, have union with the gods because we are like them; if we become bad, we are separated from them because we are unlike them. If we live in the exercise of virtue, we cling to them; if we become bad, we make them our enemies, not because they are angry but because our sins do not allow the gods to shed their light upon us and instead subject us to spirits of punishment. If by prayers and sacrifices we obtain release from our sins, we do not serve the gods nor change them, but by the acts we perform and by our turning to the divine we heal our vice and again enjoy the goodness of the gods. Accordingly, to say that the gods turn their faces away from the bad is like saying that the sun hides himself from those bereft of sight.

§15. *Why we worship the gods*

These considerations settle also the question concerning sacrifices and the other honors which are paid to the gods. The divine nature itself is free from needs; the honours done to it are for our good. The providence of the gods stretches everywhere and needs only fitness for its enjoyment. Now all fitness is produced by imitation and likeness. That is why temples are a copy of heaven, altars of earth, images of life (and that is why they are made in the likeness of living creatures), prayers of the intellectual element, letters of the unspeakable powers on high, plants and stones of matter, and the animals that are sacrificed of the unreasonable life in us. From all these things the gods gain nothing (what is there for a god to gain?), but we gain union with them.

§16. *Why we offer sacrifice*

I think it worth while to add a few words about sacrifices. In the first place, since everything we have comes from the gods, and it is just to offer to the givers first fruits of what is given, we offer first fruits of our possessions in the form of votive offerings, of our bodies in the form of hair, of our life in the form of sacrifices. Secondly, prayers divorced from sacrifices are only words, prayers with sacrifices are animated words, the word giving power to the life and the life animation to the word. Furthermore, the happiness of anything lies in its appropriate perfection, and the appropriate perfection of each object is union with its cause. For this reason also we pray that we may have union with the gods. So, since though the highest life is that of the gods, yet man's life also is life of some sort, and since this life wishes to have union with that, it needs an intermediary (for objects most widely separated are never united without a middle term), and the intermediary ought to be like the objects being united. Accordingly, the intermediary between life and life should be life, and for this reason living animals are sacrificed by the blessed among men today and were sacrificed by all the men of old, not in a uniform manner, but to every god the fitting victims, with much other reverence. Concerning this subject I have said enough.

§17. *The universe is by nature immortal*

That the gods will not destroy the universe has been stated; that its nature is immortal must now be set forth. Whatever is destroyed is destroyed either by itself or by something else. If the universe its destroyed by itself, fire ought to burn itself and water dry itself. If the universe is destroyed by something else, that something must be either corporeal or incorporeal. Incorporeal it cannot be, since things incorporeal, as nature and soul, preserve things corporeal, and nothing is destroyed by what naturally preserves it. If corporeal, it must be one of existents or of nonexistents; if the first then bodies moving in circles must destroy bodies moving in straight lines or bodies moving in straight lines must destroy bodies moving in circles. But bodies moving in circles do not possess a destructive nature; otherwise, why do we see nothing perishing thence? Nor can bodies moving in straight lines touch bodies moving in circles; otherwise, why have they hitherto been unable to do so? Nor, again, can bodies moving in straight lines be destroyed by one another, since the destruction of one is the creation of another, and this is not destruction but change.

If the universe is destroyed by other bodies, whence they come or where they now are cannot be said. Further, whatever perishes, perishes either in form or in matter, form being the shape, matter the body. If the form perishes and the matter remains we see other things being produced; if matter perishes, why has it not failed in all these years? If matter perishes, and other matter takes its place, the latter must come either from existents or from nonexistents; if from existents, so long as they remain for ever, matter is for ever, and if existents perish, this means the destruction not merely of the universe but of everything; if from non-existents, firstly, it is impossible that anything should come from nonexistents, and secondly, if this should happen and it should be possible for matter to come from non-existents, so long as non-existents are, matter also will be: for surely non-existents do not also perish. But if they say that matter remains without form, firstly, why does this happen to the whole universe and not to parts? Secondly, they deprive bodies of beauty alone, not of being.

Further, whatever perishes either is resolved into its components or disappears into nothingness. If it is resolved into its elements, other things are again produced; if this were not so, why were the components made in the first place? If, however, existents will disappear into nothingness, what prevents this from

194   HELLENISTIC RELIGIONS

happening to God too? But if His functional power prevents it, such power does not belong to one able only to preserve himself. It is equally impossible for existents to be produced out of non-existents and for existents to vanish into nothingness.

Then too, the universe, if it perishes, must perish either in accordance with nature or contrary to nature. [If it perishes in accordance with nature, then the making and continuance till now of the universe prove to be unnatural, and yet nothing is made contrary to nature], nor does what is contrary to nature take precedence over nature. If it perishes contrary to nature, there must be another nature changing the nature of the universe, and this we do not see. Further, whatever perishes naturally we too can destroy: but the circular body of the universe no one has ever destroyed or changed, while the elements can be changed, but not destroyed. Moreover, whatever perishes is changed by time and grows old, but the universe remains unchanged by all the lapse of time. Having said so much in answer to those who require stronger proofs, I pray that the universe may itself be propitious to me.

§18. *The problem of godlessness*

Again, the fact that unbelief has arisen in certain parts of the earth and will often occur hereafter should not disturb men of sense. Such neglect does not affect the gods, just as we saw that honours do not benefit them: further, the soul, being of a middle nature, cannot always judge aright, and the entire universe cannot equally enjoy the providence of the gods: some sections can always participate therein, some at times, some in the first degree, some in the second degree, just as the head possesses all the senses; the body as a whole, one only. For this reason, it seems, the founders of festivals established also banned days, on which some temples were idle, some shut, some even stripped of their ornaments: this perfunctory service was done in view of the weakness of human nature. It is, moreover, not unlikely that unbelief is a kind of punishment: it is reasonable that those who have known the gods and despised them should in another life be deprived of this knowledge, and that Justice should cause those who honoured kings of their own as gods to be banished from the true gods.

§19. *Why sins are not punished at once*

But if neither for these sins nor for others the punishment follows directly on the offence, we must not be surprised, because not only are there spirits that punish souls, but also the soul brings itself to judgment, and because, since souls survive through eternity, they ought not in a short time to bear all their chastisement, and because there must be human virtue; for if punishments followed directly on offences, men would do right from fear and would not have virtue. Souls are punished after leaving the body, some wandering here, others to hot or cold places in the earth, others being tormented by spirits; all these things they endure together with the unreasonable soul, in whose company they sinned: because of this the shadowy form seen about tombs, especially of evil livers, comes into being.

§20. *The transmigration of souls*

If transmigration of a soul happens into a rational creature, the soul becomes precisely that body's soul; if into an unreasoning creature, the soul accompanies it from outside as our guardian spirits accompany us; for a rational soul could never become the soul of an irrational creature. The reality of transmigration can be seen from the existence of congenital complaints (else why are some born blind, some born paralyzed, some born diseased in soul?) and from the fact that souls which are naturally qualified to act in the body must not, once they have left it, remain inactive throughout time. Indeed, if souls do not return into bodies, they must either be unlimited in number or God must continually be making others. But there is nothing unlimited in the universe, since in what is ordered by limit there cannot be anything unlimited. Nor is it possible that other souls should come into being, for everything in which something new is produced must be imperfect, and the universe, as proceeding from what is perfect, should be perfect.

§21. *The reward of virtue both here and hereafter*

Souls that have lived in accordance with virtue have as the crown of their happiness that free from the unreasonable element and purified from all body they are in union with the gods and share with them the government of the whole universe. Yet, even if they attained none of these things, virtue itself and the pleasure and honour of virtue, and the life free from pain and from all other tyrants, would suffice to make happy those who had chosen to live in accordance with virtue and had proved able.